A LEVEL AND AS LEVEL LAW

AUSTRALIA
Law Book Co. Sydney

CANADA and USA
Carswell
Toronto

HONG KONG
Sweet & Maxwell Asia

NEW ZEALAND
Brooker's
Wellington

SINGAPORE and MALAYSIA
Sweet & Maxwell (Asia)
Singapore and Kuala Lumpur

A LEVEL AND AS LEVEL LAW

Second edition

by

Martin Hunt

THOMSON

SWEET & MAXWELL

2003

Published in 2003 by
Sweet & Maxwell Limited of
100 Avenue Road
London NW3 3PF
http://www.sweetandmaxwell.co.uk

Typeset by LBJ Typesetting Ltd, Kingsclere
Printed in Great Britain by
Ashford Colour Print, Hants

No natural forests were destroyed
to make this product; only farmed
timber was used and replanted

ISBN 0 421 798 300

A CIP catalogue record for this book
is available from the British Library

For Bill Whiteman
1922–1998

Preface

This book has been written specifically to cover the specifications for AS and A Level Law from both the AQA and OCR examination boards. It covers all the topics and modules for these specifications and includes all the essential information students will require. Each chapter begins with a list of key points, setting out clear learning objectives for the student. This is reinforced with a series of revision questions at the end of each chapter. Each chapter also has guidance on structuring revision notes with examples and suggested headings. Furthermore, the Study Skills section at the end of the book provides more detailed guidance on essay writing, problem solving, revision, keeping up-to-date, and exams. The How to Use this Book section details the contents of both the AQA and OCR specifications and matches this to the chapters in the book.

The internet is becoming an increasingly useful source of up-to-date information on many aspects of the law and legal system, and I have included a list of useful websites at the end of many chapters. I hope that lecturers and students alike will find these helpful in negotiating the mass of information available on the web. There are also PowerPoint™ presentations to complement each chapter, which are, available to view or download on the Sweet & Maxwell website at **www.sweetandmaxwell.co.uk/academic/hunt/**.

For this Second Edition, a number of chapters, such as those on police powers, have been significantly expanded in response to the experience of Curriculum 2000 and the new demands of the examiners in practice. Other new material includes an increase in the level of discussion, evaluation and analysis in the substantive law sections. I would like to thank my 2002–3 AS and A2 Law students at Yeovil College for their help and feedback in "classroom testing" this new material.

The text also includes many developments since the last edition—the Police Reform Act 2000, the new PACE Codes of Practice, the Sale and Supply of Goods to Consumers Regulations 2002, the report of the Leggatt Review of Administrative Justice, the Law Commission Report on Fraud (2002), and the decisions of the House of Lords on strict liability (*B v DPP* [2000] and *R. v K* [2001]), theft (*R. v Hinks* [2000]), vicarious liability (*Lister v Hesley Hall Ltd* [2001]), causation in negligence (*Fairchild v Glenhaven Funeral Services Ltd* [2002]) and liability for animals (*Mirvahedy v Henley* [2003]), to list but a few. The text also includes the main proposals contained in the Criminal Justice Bill currently before Parliament. Once the Bill receives Royal Assent, we will place an update on the Sweet and Maxwell website. I have endeavoured to state the law correctly as at April 30, 2003.

Finally, I would like to take this opportunity to thank all my colleagues, past and present, and friends (especially Rob Whiteman and Ariane Sherine), whose encouragement and support made this book possible. I would also like to thank my editors at Sweet & Maxwell for their unfailing support and efficiency in its preparation and publication.

Martin Hunt
Yeovil, April 30, 2003

Contents

Table of Cases

Table of European Cases

Table of Statutes

Statutory Instruments

Table of European Treaties

How to Use this Book

To help you find the information you need for your AS and A Level studies, below are tables listing the contents of both the AQA and OCR specifications (current as at date of publication) and identifying in which chapter you will find the relevant information for that topic:

AQA AS Modules:

Module 1: Law Making	Chapter
European Legislative Process and Institutions: Treaties, regulations, directives and decisions. The way in which European Law takes effect. The functions of the Council, Commission, Parliament and the European Court of Justice. Art.234 references.	3
Domestic Legislative Process and Institutions: Formal processes of statute creation; roles of House of Commons in formulating and introducing Bills, the House of Lords in acting as a check on the Government's power, the constitutional position of the Crown acting as "The Queen in Parliament". The doctrine of parliamentary supremacy, having the power to make or unmake any law, and limitations on it, such as the European Treaties, European Convention on Human Rights and Human Rights Act 1998.	1
Delegated legislation: Statutory instruments (Orders in Council and Ministerial Regulations), bye-laws (Local Authority, professional and public bodies/services/utilities). Control of delegated legislation: judicial, such as ultra vires and reasonableness, and parliamentary, such as the role of the Scrutiny Committee, positive and negative processes, Ministerial approval. Advantages and disadvantages of delegated legislation.	2
Influences upon Parliament: The role of the Law Commission in initiating research and proposing reform. The work of Royal Commissions investigating and proposing changes in specific areas. Political considerations and power through the manifesto and electoral mandate. The media and the pressure of events. Pressure groups, including, for example, lobbying by Trade Unions and agricultural, scientific, industrial, and commercial concerns.	1
Statutory Interpretation: Approaches to interpretation: literal, golden and mischief 'rules', purposive approach, integrated approach. Intrinsic and extrinsic aids.	4

The Doctrine of Judicial Precedent: The hierarchy of the courts, ratio decidendi and obiter dicta, law reporting. The obligations and powers of the courts in following, overruling, distinguishing and disapproving precedents, supported by examples drawn from any area of law and illustrating the differing approaches adopted by judges.	5
Module 2: Dispute Solving	
The Court structure: Original and appellate jurisdiction of civil and criminal courts: outline knowledge of civil process: promotion of pre-trial settlement, allocation of claims to tracks/courts, relative informality of small claims track and routes and grounds of appeal. Outline knowledge of criminal process: distinction between bail and remand, classification of offences (summary, indictable and 'either way'), mode of trial, committal, administrative hearing, routes and grounds of appeal.	7 8
Alternatives to courts: Tribunals, arbitration, mediation, conciliation, negotiation. Comparison of these alternatives with each other and with civil courts: issues of cost, time, privacy, appeals, formality, representation, accessibility and appropriateness for particular issues.	9
The legal profession: The work of barristers, solicitors and legal executives. Training and regulation.	10
Finance of advice and representation: Private finance, insurance, conditional fees, *pro bono* work. Statutory provision of Legal Help and Legal Representation in civil and criminal matters. Alternative sources of advice, *e.g.* CAB, media.	13
The judges: Selection and appointment, training, role, independence and immunity, dismissal.	11
Lay people: Magistrates: selection and appointment, training, role, powers. Jurors: qualification and selection, role.	12
Module 3: The Concept of Liability	
Introduction to criminal liability: *Actus reus*: voluntary acts and omissions, causation. *Mens rea*: intention and subjective recklessness, transferred malice. Coincidence of *actus reus* and *mens rea*. The principle of strict liability. Concepts of *actus reus* and *mens rea* should be explored in the context of assault, battery, actual bodily harm, wounding and grievous bodily harm.	14 17
Introduction to tort: Liability in negligence for physical injury to people and damage to property: duty, breach and damage.	30

Sanctions and remedies: Outline of aims of sentencing. Outline of sentences available to criminal courts for adult offenders: custodial, community sentences, fines and discharges. Basic knowledge of aggravating and mitigating factors in sentencing. Outline of damages: personal injury and property: general and special, pecuniary, non-pecuniary and associated heads of damage. Lump sum and structured payment.	20 30

AQA A2 Modules:

Module 2: Criminal Law (Offences Against the Person) *OR* Contract	Chapter
Murder: *Actus reus*, malice aforethought.	16
Voluntary manslaughter: Defences of provocation, diminished responsibility and suicide pact.	16
Involuntary manslaughter: Gross negligence manslaughter. Unlawful act manslaughter.	16
Non-fatal offences against the person: Assault, battery, actual bodily harm, wounding, grievous bodily harm.	17
Defences: Insanity, automatism, consent, intoxication, self-defence/prevention of crime. The effect of mistake.	15
OR	
Contract Formation: Offer, acceptance, consideration (including an outline of the privity rule), intention to create legal relations.	21
Contract terms: Conditions and warranties. Express and implied terms. An outline of common law and statutory approaches to exclusion clauses.	23 27
Vitiating factors: Effect of void and voidable contracts. Mistake and misrepresentation.	22
Discharge of contract: Performance, agreement, frustration, breach.	24
Remedies: Damages and equitable remedies.	25
Module 5: Criminal Law (Offences Against Property) *OR* Tort *OR* Human Rights *OR* Consumer Protection	
Theft: *Actus reus* (appropriation, property, belonging to another). *Mens rea* (dishonesty, intention permanently to deprive).	18
Robbery: Theft with use or threat of use of force.	18
Burglary: Elements of s.9(1)(a) and s.9(1)(b) Theft Act 1968, burglary in dwellings and other buildings.	18

Deception Offences and making off without payment: Obtaining property (s.15 Theft Act 1968), obtaining services (s.1 Theft Act 1978), evasion of liability (s.2 Theft Act 1978), Making off without payment (s.3 Theft Act 1978)	18
Criminal Damage: Basic (s.1(1), Criminal Damage Act 1971) and aggravated (s.1(2), Criminal Damage Act 1971) and by fire (arson s.1(3), Criminal Damage Act 1971).	18
Defences: Intoxication, duress, duress of circumstances, self-defence/prevention of crime. The effect of mistake.	15
OR	
Negligence: Issues of duty, breach and damage with respect to pure economic loss, negligent misstatement, psychiatric harm.	30
Occupiers' Liability: Liability in respect of visitors and trespassers, specific defences.	31
Nuisance: Elements of public and private nuisance, specific defences.	32
Strict and vicarious liability: *Rylands v Fletcher*, specific defences. Vicarious liability.	34
Defences: Contributory negligence, consent.	30
Remedies: Outline of damages. Injunctions.	30 32
OR	
Rights: The range of rights protected by the European Convention on Human Rights, with particular emphasis on a knowledge of Arts 8, 10 and 11 (the right to respect for private and family life, home and correspondence; the right to freedom of expression; the right to freedom of assembly and association). Mechanism for recognition in English Law. Human Rights Act 1998.	36
Restrictions: Restrictions permitted by the Convention and their relationship with UK statutes and English common law, for example: public order offences and preventative powers, police powers of stop and search and arrest, interception of communications, duty of confidentiality, obscenity, torts of defamation and trespass, harassment (criminal law and tort).	37
Enforcement: Role of domestic courts; process of judicial review; role of European Court of Human Rights.	38
Underlying concepts: Basic human rights, rule of law, due process.	40
OR	
Consumer contracts: Offer, acceptance, consideration, intention, privity. Standard form contracts.	21
Consumer legislation: Statutory provisions relating to the sale and supply of goods and services.	26

Exclusion clauses: Common-law rules and UK and European legislation.	27
Criminal law and tort: Trade descriptions, tort of negligence and liability for dangerous products in civil law.	28
Enforcement, sanctions and Remedies: Role of local authorities, advice to traders and prosecutions; civil actions by the consumer; ombudsmen, sources of advice, small claims. Sanctions and remedies.	29
Module 6: Concepts of Law	
Law and morals: The distinction between law and morals; the diversity of moral views in a pluralist society; the relationship between law and morals and the legal enforcement of moral values.	39
Law and justice: The meaning of "justice", theories of justice. The extent to which substantive legal rules, legal institutions and processes achieve justice.	40
Fault: The meaning and importance of fault in civil and/or criminal law.	42
Judicial creativity: The extent to which the judges are able to display creativity in the operation of the system of judicial precedent and in statutory interpretation. Consideration of the balance between the roles of Parliament and the judiciary.	41

OCR AS Modules:

Module 2568: Machinery of Justice	Chapter
Civil courts: county court and High Court; jurisdiction at first instance: small claims; fast track; multi-track. Appeals and appellate courts. Problems of using the courts.	8
Alternatives to the courts: Arbitration; conciliation; mediation. Role and composition of administrative tribunals in outline.	9
European Court of Justice: Art.234 (formerly Art.177) referrals; relationship to English courts.	3
Police powers: Powers to stop and search; powers of arrest; powers of detention and the treatment of suspects at the police station. Balance of individual rights and the need for investigative powers.	6
Criminal courts: Pre-trial matters: bail, mode of trial, committal proceedings. Jurisdiction of Magistrates' Courts, Youth Courts and Crown Courts at first instance. Appeals. Role of the Criminal Cases Review Commission.	7

Principles of sentencing: Aims of sentencing; purpose and effect of sentences; reoffending rates.	20
Powers of the courts: An understanding of different types of sentences, *e.g.* custodial, community, fines and discharges; compensation and other powers.	20
Module 2569: Legal Personnel	
Judiciary: Appointment; tenure; independence; role, including role in judicial review and enforcement of human rights in outline; role of the Lord Chancellor. The theory of the separation of powers.	11
Barristers and solicitors: Training; work; supervisory role of Bar Council and Law Society. Role of paralegals in outline. Legal Services Ombudsman.	10
Crown Prosecution Service: Role; personnel; Director of Public Prosecutions.	10
Lay magistrates: Appointment; social background; training; role; evaluation and criticism. Role of the magistrates' clerk in outline.	12
Juries: Qualifications of jurors; selection of jury panels; role in criminal and civil cases; evaluation and criticism. Alternatives to jury.	12
Government funding: Legal Aid Board / Legal Services Commission; Community Legal Service; Criminal Defence Service; funding of civil and criminal cases; advice schemes in civil and criminal cases. Access to justice.	13
Advice agencies: Purpose and role of Citizens' Advice Bureaux; law centres; other advice agencies in outline only.	13
Role of legal profession: Private funding of cases; conditional fees.	13
Module 2570: Sources of Law:	
Mechanics of precedent: Precedent as operated in the English Legal System; *stare decisis; obiter dicta, ratio decidendi*; hierarchy of the courts; binding and persuasive precedent; overruling; reversing; distinguishing.	5
Law-making potential: Original precedent; the Practice Statement 1966; distinguishing; the role of the judges.	5 41
Acts of Parliament: Green papers, White Papers, legislative stages in Parliament.	1
Delegated legislation: Orders in Council; statutory instruments; bylaws; control of delegated legislation including Parliamentary Scrutiny Committees and Judicial Review; reasons for delegating legislative powers.	2
Statutory interpretation: Literal rule, Golden rule, Mischief rule, purposive approach; rules of language; presumptions; intrinsic and extrinsic aids; effects of membership of the European Union on interpretation.	4
European Institutions: The law-making functions of the Council, Commission, Parliament; the role and composition of the European Court of Justice.	3

Primary and secondary sources of EU Law: Treaties, regulations, directives and decisions; their implementation by the courts; the impact of European Union law on domestic legal institutions and law.	3
Impetus for law reform: The role of Parliament; the role of the judges; effect of public opinion and pressure groups.	1
Law reform agencies: The role of the Law Commission; Royal Commissions and other agencies in outline.	1

OCR A2 Modules:

Module 2571: Criminal Law 1	Chapter
Actus reus: General principles of proof of positive acts before liability may be incurred; omissions as *actus reus* in certain duty situations; principles of causation; *"sine qua non"*; factors affecting the chain of causation.	14
Mens rea: General principles of intention; direct intent; oblique intent; foresight of consequences; specific intent; basic intent; recklessness; gross negligence; knowledge; transferred malice.	14
Strict liability: Principles of strict / absolute liability; statutory nature; interpretation by courts; policy issues; social utility; no negligence—due diligence defences.	14
Participation: *Actus reus* and *mens rea* required for accessorial liability; the meaning of aid, abet, counsel and procure.	19
Incitement: Common law rules in outline only.	19
Conspiracy: Statutory conspiracy in outline only.	19
Attempts: Statutory definition; *mens rea* and *actus reus*; meaning of "more than merely preparator"; attempts to do the impossible.	19
Murder: The *actus reus* and *mens rea* required; defences of diminished responsibility, provocation and suicide pact.	16
Manslaughter: Involuntary manslaughter; constructive (unlawful act) manslaughter; gross negligence manslaughter; corporate killing; recklessness.	16
Module 2572: Criminal Law 2	
Insanity: *M'Naghten* rules; effects of insanity as a defence.	15
Automatism: Definition of automatism; self-induced automatism; distinctions between insane and non-insane automatism.	15
Duress, necessity: Scope and nature of these as defences; self-induced duress; duress of circumstances; limits to their availability.	15

Module 2578: Law of Torts 2	
Trespass to land: Unlawful entry; intention; defences of lawful authority including licence, right of entry.	33
Nuisance: Public nuisance: class of persons; role of Attorney-General; when individual can sue. Private nuisance: unlawful interference/ physical damage; interference with health and comfort; unreasonable user; relevance of locality and utility; abnormal sensitivity; duration; effect of malice. Specific defences - prescription, statutory authority.	32
Rylands v Fletcher: Dangerous things; accumulation; escape; non-natural user; damage. Specific defences of consent, act of stranger, statutory authority, Act of God; default of claimant.	34
Liability for Animals at common law: Negligence (in outline); assault and battery.	35
Animals Act 1971: Distinction between dangerous and non-dangerous species; identity of "keeper"; defences of default of claimant; straying livestock; liability for injury to livestock by dogs.	35
Trespass to the person — Assault and battery: Elements of each; defences of consent, lawful authority, including outline knowledge of police powers of arrest; self-defence.	33
Trespass to the person — False imprisonment: Elements; defence of lawful detention.	33
Remedies: Damages: purpose; categories (in outline only). Injunctions: nature; when available.	30 32
The nature of the law of tort: Function of tortious liability; Distinctions between strict liability and fault-based liability.	42

SECTION ONE: LAW MAKING

1 | Primary Legislation

Key Points

What you need to know:

- The pre-parliamentary stages of the enactment process: proposal, consultation, and drafting.
- The parliamentary stages of enactment in the House of Commons, House of Lords and Royal Assent.

What you need to discuss:

- The advantages and disadvantages of pressure groups and the law reform agencies.
- The differences between Public Bills and Private Members' Bills.
- The effectiveness of the consultation process.
- The effectiveness of the drafting process.
- The relationship between the House of Commons and the House of Lords.

The Law-Making Process

English law is made up of a number of different sources or types of law:

- **legislative sources**: primary legislation (Acts of Parliament); delegated (or secondary/subordinate) legislation; and European legislation
- **judicial sources**: Common Law (legal principles developed by the courts) and Equity.

There are also a number of minor sources, such as custom and the writings of legal academics. In addition to considering these major sources, any examination of the law-making process must also include discussion of statutory interpretation (the way in which the courts interpret and apply legislation).

NOTES

Before examining these major sources in detail, it is useful to consider the reasons for this variety of laws. The law is required to perform a wide range of functions and the legal system has to use a number of different techniques to achieve this. No single form of law-making is able to cope with this variety of demands. As we shall see, each has particular advantages and is suited to particular tasks. It may help to imagine English law as a large wall protecting society—the bricks being made of Acts of Parliament, European Regulations, etc., with the Common Law as the mortar, binding the whole system together. It is also important to remember that these various sources complement, rather than compete with each other, ensuring that English law develops in response to changing social and economic demands.

The Importance of Acts of Parliament

Acts of Parliament are the highest form of law in England. All other sources either derive their validity from or are subordinate to Acts of Parliament: powers to make delegated legislation are granted in enabling Acts; European Union law is incorporated into English law by the **European Communities Act 1972**; Common Law and Equity are both subordinate to legislation—where there is conflict, legislation prevails.

The reason for this is constitutional. Under England's unwritten constitution, Parliament is **sovereign**. Therefore, its enacted will, in the form of Acts of Parliament, cannot be challenged in the courts. There are, of course, practical political limitations on this sovereignty. Membership of the European Union (see **Chapter 3**) and the incorporation of the European Convention on Human Rights into English law by the **Human Rights Act 1998** (see **Section 6**) have also imposed limits on Parliament's theoretically absolute sovereignty. Nevertheless, given their sovereign status, together with the fact that they deal with fundamental questions of social and economic policy, it is essential that the process by which new Acts of Parliament are made is:

- **efficient** (producing new legislation promptly when required);
- **effective** (producing legislation of sufficient technical quality);
- **democratic** (ensuring all interested and affected parties have an opportunity to participate).

Sources of Legislative Proposals
Proposals for new legislation come from a number of sources, the most important being:

- the Government;

NOTES

- advisory agencies;
- pressure groups;
- individual Members of Parliament.

New legislation may also result from an initiative by the European Union, to give effect to international treaty obligations, or in response to prompting by the courts.

The Government

The Government introduces most new legislation as Public Bills. Some of these may be a result of election manifesto pledges. Others (for example, Finance Acts), must be passed whichever party is in power. Some legislation may be passed in response to an unexpected emergency. For example, following the Omagh bombing on August 15, 1998, the Government published a Terrorism Bill on September 2, 1998. The Bill passed through all its parliamentary stages on September 3, and received Royal Assent, becoming the **Criminal Justice (Terrorism and Conspiracy) Act 1998** on September 4. However, most government legislation results from discussions in Cabinet, whereby general manifesto and policy commitments are translated into concrete proposals for new legislation. As the Government is democratically elected, well informed, and served by a large number of highly qualified and experienced advisors in the Civil Service, this complies with the requirements of an efficient, effective and democratic process.

Advisory Agencies

A large number of proposals come from the various advisory committees and commissions established to advise the Government. These agencies are either standing (permanent) bodies or *ad hoc* (temporary) bodies. The most important standing agency is the **Law Commission**. Established in 1965, its brief is to keep all areas of law under review and produce a systematic programme of reform. In addition to achieving a number of significant reforms such as the **Children Act 1989**, the Commission plays an important role in stimulating debate on the state of the law. However, the Commission has expressed concern that, due to insufficient parliamentary consideration of its reports, much of its work is wasted. *Ad hoc* agencies (for example, **Royal Commissions**) investigate a particular issue and disband once they have reported. For example, the **Royal Commission on Criminal Procedure** was established following concerns over miscarriages of justice and the conduct of police investigations, and its 1981 report resulted in the enactment of the **Police and Criminal Evidence Act 1984** (see **Chapter 6**). The recent Auld Review of the Criminal Courts, the Halliday Review of

NOTES

Sentencing, and the Leggatt Review of Tribunals would also fall into this category. The use of these agencies, with their high degree of expertise, enhances the efficiency and effectiveness of the legislative process. Furthermore, the extensive consultation they undertake makes an important contribution to its democratic nature.

Pressure Groups

A pressure group is any group that seeks to influence the legislative process by organised lobbying. This includes not only "cause" groups (for example, CND, Greenpeace) but also "sectional" or "interest" groups (for example, CBI, TUC). The role of these groups has increased dramatically in recent years, as more people become involved in these organisations rather than the traditional political parties.

Pressure group activity brings a number of **benefits** to the legislative process:

- It informs and assists the legislature on the need for new legislation and the form it should take, enhancing the efficiency and effectiveness of the process.
- It also informs and stimulates public debate by ensuring that alternative views and voices are heard. For example, a report on mobile phone safety by the Consumers Association challenged the findings of the Government's own research.
- By bringing people together collectively and involving them in the process, it empowers the naturally weaker groups in society.

This all contributes to the democratic nature of the process.

However, there are also **potential disadvantages**. A well-organised and resourced group may be able to achieve a degree of influence out of all proportion to its size and the level of support it enjoys in society at large. This danger has increased with the growth of professional lobbying agencies and the number of MPs acting as consultants to these organisations. There is, therefore, a risk that pressure group activity may distort, rather than enhance, the democratic nature of the process.

Nevertheless, pressure group activity is inevitable and, in many respects, beneficial. Therefore, a system of regulation is required in order to prevent abuse of influence. Measures have been introduced to achieve this following the report of the **Nolan Committee on Standards in Public Life (1996)**.

Furthermore, it is important to note that the impact of the various advisory agencies and pressure groups can be cumulative and cooperative. For example, in 2003 the Government

NOTES

announced it was considering a new criminal offence of joint homicide to apply in situations where a child must have been killed by one of its parents, but both deny responsibility. This was in response to two reports, one from the Law Commission and the other from the NSPCC.

Individual MPs

Some parliamentary time is reserved for discussing proposals put forward by individual MPs, known as **Private Members' Bills**. These are often based upon suggestions by pressure groups or advisory agencies. MPs' views and voting are also influenced by their constituency party, communications from individual constituents, and media coverage. Most successful Private Members' Bills are uncontroversial, minor and technical. This is largely because the Government can use its control of the parliamentary timetable to block any Bill to which it is opposed. Nevertheless, some major and controversial legislation has come about in this way (for example, the **Murder (Abolition of the Death Penalty) Act 1965** and the **Abortion Act 1967**). The most important feature of Private Members' Bills is ensuring the legislative process is not dominated entirely by the Government.

Consultation

Once the Government has adopted a proposal for new legislation, a consultation period follows. This involves issuing a discussion document—either a **Green Paper** or **White Paper**. A Green Paper announces tentative proposals for discussion, where the Government is not yet firmly committed to any particular course of action. By contrast, a White Paper announces firm government policy for implementation and will be followed by the preparation of a Bill to be presented to Parliament. Consultation is essential to the efficient, effective and democratic nature of the process, as it allows interested parties to comment on the desirability of the proposals and to point out any technical defects or contradictions.

Drafting

Following consultation, the proposal must be translated into draft legislation (a **Bill**). All government Bills are drafted by expert civil servants in the **Office of Parliamentary Counsel**. While perfection in drafting is inevitably unobtainable, concerns have been expressed that growth in the volume of legislation, together with its increasing complexity, has led to a decline in its technical quality. This results in problems for the courts when interpreting legislation. Suggestions for improvement (for example, Dale's for the establishment of a Law

Council to review the technical quality of draft legislation) have not been implemented. Nevertheless, it appears that some reform is required in order to ensure efficiency and effectiveness.

Enactment

For a Bill to become an Act of Parliament, it must pass through the process of enactment in both Houses of Parliament and receive Royal Assent. The enactment process is, therefore, a law-making partnership between the House of Commons, the House of Lords, and the Crown (or "Queen-in-Parliament"). The various stages in this process are:

- **First Reading**—the title of the Bill is announced to the House (a purely formal stage with no debate or vote).

- **Second Reading**—a general debate on the main principles and purpose of the Bill.

- **Committee Stage**—arguably the most important stage, where the Bill is debated in detail, clause by clause. This is done normally by a Standing Committee, though it may also be done by the appropriate Select Committee or, in the case of constitutional Bills, by the full House sitting as a Committee. The Bill may be amended at this stage. This sharing out of Bills allows them to proceed more quickly, thereby enhancing efficiency.

- **Report Stage**—where the Committee reports its proceedings to the full House. Amendments made in the Committee are either accepted or reversed. Further amendments may also be made.

- **Third Reading**—another general debate on the Bill in its final, amended form. Only minor, technical amendments are allowed.

- **Other House**—the Bill then proceeds to the other House, where this process is repeated. Any further amendments are referred back to the originating House. On the rare occasions where the Commons and Lords cannot reach agreement or compromise, the Commons can use its powers under the **Parliament Acts 1911 and 1949** to by-pass the Lords and send the Bill directly for Royal Assent (see, for example, the **Sexual Offences (Amendment) Act 2000**). This has occurred on only four occasions since 1945. The role of the House of Lords is, therefore, to act as a **revising chamber**, requesting that the Commons reconsider its proposals where appropriate. Hence, the Lords can only delay, and not block, legislation passed by the Commons.

- **Royal Assent**—once the Bill has passed through both Houses, it proceeds for **Royal Assent** by the Monarch (again, a purely formal stage—the last time Royal Assent was refused was by Queen Anne in 1707).

NOTES

Following Royal Assent, the Bill becomes an Act of Parliament and its provisions come into force either immediately, upon a date specified in the Act, or upon the issuing of a Commencement Order by the appropriate minister.

This may appear a rather slow and cumbersome procedure. However, it is important that Bills dealing with major questions of social and economic policy receive adequate scrutiny and debate before becoming law. Furthermore, emergency legislation can be processed very quickly if necessary (as we saw earlier with **Criminal Justice (Terrorism and Conspiracy) Act 1998**). Nevertheless, a government with a secure majority is able to ensure its proposals are enacted without significant amendment, sometimes regardless of doubts as to its effectiveness (for example, the **Dangerous Dogs Act 1991**).

Conclusion

The process by which tentative proposals for new legislation finally emerge as Acts of Parliament is a complex and lengthy one. It involves not only legal but also various social, political and economic considerations. While it appears that most aspects of this process operate efficiently, effectively and democratically, some reform is necessary, particularly to improve the technical quality of draft legislation.

Revision Notes

You should now write your revision notes for this topic. Here is an example for you and some suggested headings:

PL④—Consultation

- proposal adopted—consultation follows
- Green Paper (tentative proposals for discussion)
- White Paper (firm proposals for implementation)
- consultation essential to EED

NOTES

PL①—Introduction (status, etc.)
PL②—Proposals (Govt, Advisory Agencies)
PL③—Proposals (Pressure Groups, MPs)
PL④—Consultation
PL⑤—Drafting
PL⑥—Enactment
PL⑦—Conclusion

Using your cards, you should now be able to write a short paragraph in response to each of the following questions:

1. Describe the status and importance of Acts of Parliament.

2. Describe and evaluate the sources of legislative proposals.

3. Describe and evaluate the consultation and drafting process.

4. Describe and evaluate the formal enactment of a Bill.

Useful Websites

- For information about UK legislation and access to legislative texts—see **www.hmso.gov.uk/legislation/lexhome.htm**

- An Introduction to Parliament—**www.parliament.uk/works/index.cfm** and **http://news.bbc.co.uk/hi/english/uk_politics/a-z_of_parliament/default.stm**

- Making new law—**www.parliament.uk/works/newlaw.cfm**

- Parliamentary stages of a Government Bill—**www.parliament.uk/commons/lib/fs01.pdf**

- Private Members' Bills—**www.parliament.uk/commons/lib/fs04.pdf** and **www.parliament.uk/commons/lib/fs67.pdf**

- The Law Commission—**www.lawcom.gov.uk/**

- The Committee on Standards in Public Life—**www.public-standards.gov.uk**

- The Office of Parliamentary Counsel—**www.parliamentary-counsel.gov.uk**

- Current Green and White Papers are available on the relevant Government Department websites—accessed via the UK-Online site—**www.ukonline.gov.uk**

NOTES

2 | Delegated Legislation

Key Points

What you need to know:

- The main types of delegated legislation.
- How delegated powers are controlled.

What you need to discuss:

- The advantages and disadvantages of delegated legislation.
- The effectiveness of the various forms of control.

Introduction

Delegated legislation is law made by certain individuals and institutions acting under a grant of legislative power from Parliament. These powers are generally granted in an **enabling Act** that establishes a framework of general principles and grants powers to others to fill in the details (for example, the **Health & Safety at Work Act 1974**). It should therefore be possible, by examining the delegated legislation, to work out the underlying principles contained in the enabling Act. For example, the **Undersized Spider Crabs Order 2000 (SI 2000/1502)** prohibits the landing of male spider crabs less than 130 millimetres in length. This is intended to protect immature individuals until they have been able to breed, thereby ensuring that stocks are maintained. It is therefore not surprising to discover that the order was issued under powers granted in the **Sea Fish (Conservation) Act 1967**.

Therefore, there are two important distinctions between primary and delegated legislation:

- While Parliament's legislative power is unlimited, the powers of the delegated legislator are limited and defined by the enabling Act.
- While primary legislation cannot be annulled by the courts (as there are no grounds on which to declare it unconstitutional), delegated legislation is subject to judicial review.

Types of Delegated Legislation

- **Statutory Instruments**—these are rules, regulations and orders issued by ministers and which are national in effect.

- **Byelaws**—these are issued by local authorities and are local in effect, being limited to the jurisdiction of the council concerned. Some state corporations (for example, London Underground Ltd) also have the power to issue byelaws to regulate conduct on their premises.

- **Orders in Council**—these are issued by the Privy Council and generally only used in emergencies, such as in time of war, or when urgent action is required and Parliament is not sitting.

The Reasons for Delegated Legislation

- **To save parliamentary time**—because of the limited time available, Parliament could not enact all the detailed rules and regulations required in a modern society. The use of delegated legislation to deal with the details leaves Parliament free to concentrate on debating and deciding major policy issues.

- **To deal with complex and technical issues**—much modern legislation is complex and technical (for example, health and safety regulations). The use of delegated legislation allows experts in the relevant field to become involved, thereby enhancing the effectiveness of the regulations.

- **To enable prompt amendments to the law**—in order to keep up with social and technological change, laws must be frequently amended and updated. Amending an Act of Parliament is often too long and complex to meet this challenge. By contrast, it is much easier and quicker to amend delegated legislation. This also means that delegated legislation can be used to respond quickly in **emergencies**.

- **To allow for local variation**—the power of local authorities and some corporations to issue byelaws allows for necessary variations to meet specific local or institutional needs.

Thus, the use of delegated legislation is both inevitable and beneficial in any modern state. However, delegated legislation results from the transfer of important legislative powers from Parliament (**the legislature**) to national and local government (**the executive**). This means there must be effective checks and controls to ensure that delegated powers are used properly and accountably. Otherwise there is a danger that important laws do not receive adequate

NOTES

scrutiny and debate. This is particularly important where the enabling Act grants the exceptional power to amend primary legislation through delegated legislation (a so-called "Henry VIII" clause). When such a power was included by the Government in the **Human Rights Bill**, Parliament insisted that the use of such a power must be subject to positive affirmation (see below).

Checks and Controls over the Use of Delegated Powers

- **Consultation**—the enabling Act commonly requires the person granted powers to consult before exercising them. The Act may specify who must be consulted or may merely require reasonable consultation. Even where consultation is not mandatory, it generally takes place as a matter of routine. This acts as a check in two ways:

  - ➤ **directly**—by requiring public exercise of the power;
  - ➤ **indirectly**—by forming the basis for a possible judicial challenge.

- **Parliamentary oversight**—this may seem to conflict with the need to save parliamentary time. However, a responsible Parliament must use some of the time it has saved by delegating powers to monitor their use, otherwise delegation becomes abdication. This is achieved in two ways:

  - ➤ **the affirmation process** most statutory instruments must be affirmed (approved) before coming into force. This may involve positive affirmation, where the instrument does not come into force unless approved by a positive resolution in Parliament. The more common (and less time-consuming) procedure is negative affirmation, where the instrument comes into force unless annulled by a negative resolution in Parliament. However, this reliance on negative affirmation raises the danger that new instruments receive inadequate policy review. The **Hansard Society** has recommended that this be improved by referring draft instruments to the appropriate departmental select committee for policy review prior to affirmation. This would act as a policy filter, complementing the role of the Scrutiny Committee as a technical filter (see below).
  - ➤ **the Joint Select Committee on Statutory Instruments (the "Scrutiny Committee")**—this is a parliamentary committee with the task of reviewing the technical merits of draft instruments and referring to Parliament any that give cause for concern. Grounds for referral include where there is some doubt as to whether it is *intra vires* (within the power) or where it makes some unusual or unexpected use of the power. Therefore, the committee acts as a filter so that Parliament need only take time to consider the small proportion of instruments referred to it.

Notes

Parliament may also amend or revoke the grant of power if this proves necessary. It cannot, however, amend individual instruments as this would defeat the object of delegating the power in the first place.

- **Judicial review**—the courts' authority to review the validity of delegated legislation lies in the limited nature of delegated powers. The courts can annul delegated legislation where it is *ultra vires* (outside or beyond the power). There are two forms of *ultra vires*:

  - ➤ **substantive** *ultra vires*—this is where the subject matter lies outside the scope of the enabling power (*Attorney General v Fulham Corporation* [1921]).
  - ➤ **procedural** *ultra vires*—this is where the subject matter of the legislation lies within the scope of the enabling power but there was a serious failure to comply with a mandatory procedural requirement (for example, a failure to consult— *Agricultural Training Board v Aylesbury Mushrooms Ltd* [1972]).

We should also note that the courts may also annul delegated legislation where it is found to be incompatible with a convention right under the **Human Rights Act 1998** (see **Section 6**). However, we should also note that judicial review, as with all civil proceedings, can be expensive and time-consuming. Furthermore, such proceedings may only be brought by someone with sufficient *locus standi* (*i.e.* someone who is directly affected by the act or decision in question). This clearly reduces the practical effectiveness of judicial review as a form of control over the use of delegated powers.

Conclusion

The use of delegated legislation in a modern state is, therefore, both inevitable and beneficial. Nevertheless, it does represent the granting of significant legislative powers to the executive arm of the State. Therefore, it must be subject to effective checks and controls. The existing arrangements for control are largely satisfactory, though steps could be taken to improve parliamentary scrutiny of the policy merits of draft delegated legislation, perhaps along the lines suggested by the Hansard Society.

Revision Notes

You should now write your revision notes for this topic. Here is an example for you and some suggested headings:

NOTES

DL②—Types of

- Statutory Instruments—rules/regs/orders made by ministers, national in effect
- Byelaws—made by local authorities, some state corps, local in effect
- Orders in Council—made by Privy Council, mostly used in emergencies/when urgent response needed

---

DL①—Introduction (definition, enabling Acts, etc.)

DL②—Types of

DL③—Reasons for

DL④—Need for controls

DL⑤—Consultation

DL⑥—Parliamentary oversight

DL⑦—Judicial review

DL⑧—Conclusion

Using your cards, you should now be able to write a short paragraph in response to each of the following questions:

1. Define what is meant by delegated legislation and how delegated powers are granted.
2. Describe the main forms of delegated legislation.
3. Identify the main reasons for and advantages of delegated legislation.
4. Explain why checks and controls are needed over the use of delegated powers.
5. Describe the existing check and control mechanisms.
6. Evaluate the effectiveness of these mechanisms.

Useful Websites

⊕ For more information on Statutory Instruments and Orders in Council there is a House of Commons Factsheet (No.14) available at **www.parliament.uk/commons/lib/fs14.pdf**

NOTES

3 | European Legislation

Key Points

What You Need to Know:

- The main institutions of the European Union.
- The main types of European Union legislation (regulations, directives, and decisions).
- The concepts of direct applicability, direct effect, and indirect effect.

What You Need to Discuss:

- The impact of European Union membership on the national sovereignty of the Member States.
- The relationship between the English courts and the Court of Justice of the European Union.

Introduction

Following World War II, there was a strong desire among Western European nations for political and economic co-operation. It was hoped this would not only assist with post-war physical and economic reconstruction, but also that the resulting inter-dependency of nations would prevent future conflicts. This led to the establishment of the European Coal and Steel Community in 1952, followed by the European Economic Community and European Atomic Energy Community in 1958. These Communities merged in 1965, and are now known as the **European Union**. Britain became a member of the Communities on January 1, 1973.

The original aims of the Union were to promote the economic development of the Member States and improve the living standards of their citizens. These have since expanded to include environmental policy, social policy, and monetary and political union. In order to achieve these aims, the Union has had to establish its own legal institutions and laws—a **European Legal Order**.

The Institutions of the European Union

The European Council—this was established in 1974 and consists of the heads of government and foreign ministers of the Member States. It is the body that takes major decisions on the future of the Union at "Euro-Summits".

The Council of Ministers—this is the main decision-making and legislative body of the Union. It consists of ministers from the governments of the Member States, and is advised by the Committee of Permanent Representatives (civil servants from the Member States). It is this body that adopts (enacts) most Union legislation following proposals put to it by the Commission.

The Commission—this is the main executive body of the Union. It is headed by the President of the Commission and is divided into Directorates-General (similar to UK ministries). Each Directorate is headed by a Commissioner. The President and the Commissioners are nominated by the Member States but act independently, their role being to represent the collective interest of the Union. The Commission is responsible for the administration of the Union. It also proposes most Union legislation to the Council of Ministers and has minor legislative powers of its own.

The Parliament—this is mainly a consultative and advisory body and, therefore, should not be thought of as being similar to the UK Parliament. Its members are directly elected from each Member State and sit in political, rather than national groupings.

The Court of Justice—the jurisdiction of the Court is essentially twofold:

> ➢ As an administrative court, it deals with actions against Member States and Union institutions. It also reviews the validity of Union legislation and can annul that legislation on four grounds:
>   - lack of competence (similar to substantive *ultra vires*);
>   - infringement of an essential procedural requirement (similar to procedural *ultra vires*);
>   - infringement of the Treaty (*i.e.* as unconstitutional);
>   - misuse of power.
> ➢ As a constitutional court, it provides definitive interpretations of Union law, including the Treaties. In doing this, it uses a purposive approach, seeking to advance the purpose behind the law.

The relationship between the Court of Justice and the national courts of the Member States will be discussed below. Since 1989, the Court has been assisted by a **Court of First Instance**

NOTES

that deals with many of the routine administrative cases, leaving the Court of Justice to concentrate on its constitutional role. Under the **Treaty of Nice (2003)**, the Court of First Instance was given the power to hear applications for preliminary rulings, further relieving the burden on the Court of Justice and hopefully reducing delays.

The Court consists of judges nominated by the Member States. In addition to hearing arguments from the parties, the Court also receives an advisory opinion from an Advocate-General. The Court then delivers a single judgment. While not strictly bound to follow its own previous decisions, in practice the Court will only depart from them in exceptional circumstances.

Direct Applicability and Direct Effect

Before considering the different forms of Union law, we must understand two central concepts of the European legal order:

- **direct applicability**—a provision of Union law is directly applicable where it **automatically** forms part of the national law of each member state. There is no need for the Member States to enact national legislation to incorporate it.

- **direct effect**—a provision of Union law is directly effective where it creates individual rights enforceable in national courts. There are two forms of direct effect:
    - ➤ **vertical direct effect**—this creates individual rights against the State;
    - ➤ **horizontal direct effect**—this creates individual rights against other individuals.

These notions have important consequences for the sovereignty of the UK Parliament, which we will discuss below.

The Sources of Union Law

The Treaties—these are the primary source of Union law. They establish the aims and principles of the Union, establish and empower its institutions, and provide for the introduction of Union legislation. Therefore, they may be regarded as the **constitution** of the Union. Provisions of the Treaties are not directly applicable. The Court of Justice has held that they may have both vertical and horizontal direct effect where they are clear, precise and unconditional (*Van Gend en Loos v Nederlandse Administratie der Belastingen* [1963]).

Union legislation—legislation under **Art.249** of the **Treaty of Rome** is the secondary source of Union law. There are three forms of Union legislation:

NOTES

➤ **Regulations**—these are directly applicable. They are binding in their entirety and, therefore, cannot be varied or amended by national legislation. Consequently, they create legislative **uniformity** throughout the Union. Regulations can have both vertical and horizontal direct effect where the *Van Gend* requirements are met (*Leonesio v Italian Ministry of Agriculture* [1973]).

➤ **Directives**—these are not directly applicable. They are binding as to the result to be achieved, but leave the choice of form and method of implementation to each Member State—*i.e.* binding as to ends but not as to means. In the United Kingdom this is usually done through delegated legislation acting under powers in the **European Communities Act 1972**, though primary legislation may be used. Therefore, they create legislative **harmony** throughout the Union. Directives may have vertical direct effect **only**, provided the *Van Gend* requirements are met (*Van Duyn v Home Office* [1974]) and the time limit specified for national implementation has expired (*Marshall v South-ampton and South-West Hampshire Area Health Authority* [1986]; *Faccini Dori v Recreb* [1994]). Thus, while an individual may be able to rely on a Directive against the State (broadly defined to include local government, the police, state agencies and nationalised industries), they cannot do so against another individual. This can, however, have unfair consequences. For example, Mrs Marshall was able to rely on her directive rights as she was employed by the State, but someone in a similar position with a private employer would have been left without a remedy. Consequently, various means have been found to mitigate this restriction:

   ■ **Indirect effect**—national courts are required to interpret national legislation, wherever possible, to ensure compliance with directive rights, even where the legislation is unrelated to implementation of the Directive (*Von Colson v Land Nordrhein-Westfahlen* [1984]; *Marleasing SA v La Comercial Internacional de Alimentacion SA* [1990]).

   ■ **State liability in damages**—the individual may have a remedy against the State where three conditions are met: the purpose of the Directive was to create individual rights; those rights are specified precisely in the Directive; there is a causal link between the failure of the Member State to implement the Directive and the damage suffered by the individual (*Francovitch and others v Italy* [1993]).

   ■ **Incidental horizontal direct effect**—this is where in order to resolve a dispute involving purely national law, the court has to refer to the provisions of a Directive. Hence, the individual is able to rely incidentally on their directive rights in the context of an action against another individual in national law. For example, in *Unilever v Central Foods* [2000], the court had to refer to an EU directive on product labelling in order to resolve a dispute in Italian contract law.

➤ **Decisions**—these are not directly applicable. They are binding in their entirety upon those to whom they are addressed. They may be addressed to Member States, companies and, exceptionally, individuals. A Decision may have vertical direct effect **only**, provided the *Van Gend* requirements are met and it is addressed to a Member State (*Grad v Finanzamt Traunstein* [1970]).

Union Membership and the Sovereignty of Parliament

The Union has, because of the potential for direct applicability and direct effect of its legislation, the power to make laws that automatically form part of English law and which create individual rights that the English courts must enforce. This raises the question of **sovereignty**, as it is necessary to decide which law, European or English, will prevail where they conflict. In order to resolve this question, both European and UK views must be considered:

- **The European view**—this is quite clear. The Court of Justice has stated if the objectives of the Union are to be achieved, European law must prevail over inconsistent national law. Member States have, therefore, by joining the Union, permanently transferred part of their sovereignty to the Union (*Costa v ENEL* [1964]). National courts must, in cases of conflict, give priority to European law and set aside inconsistent national law (*Minister of Finance v Simmenthal* [1978]).

- **The UK view**—this is less straightforward. **S.2(1)** of the **European Communities Act 1972** incorporates European law into English law and provides, where appropriate, for the direct applicability and direct effect of that law. There is, therefore, by virtue of **s.2(1)**, a potential conflict between the UK's Union obligations under the **1972 Act** and the traditional sovereignty of Parliament. **S.2(4)** of the **1972 Act** enacts a modified version of the *Costa* position, by stating (in effect) that all UK legislation takes effect subject to European law **with the exception** of the **1972 Act** itself. This seems to allow Parliament to restore the primacy of UK legislation by amending or repealing **s.2**—it is an "escape clause" from the permanency of the *Costa* position. This, together with subsequent case law, indicates the following position:

  ➢ English courts will attempt to resolve inconsistency between European and English law through interpretation—*i.e.* will interpret the English law in such a way as to make it consistent with European law unless expressly instructed by Parliament to do otherwise (*Garland v British Rail Engineering Ltd* [1982]);
  ➢ if Parliament wishes to enact legislation contrary to European law, it must expressly repeal or amend **s.2**. As a constitutional statute, the **1972 Act** is entrenched against implied repeal (*Thoburn v Sunderland City Council* [2002]). In the absence of any express instruction to do otherwise, English courts will give effect to European law, and disapply inconsistent English legislation (*Macarthys Ltd v Smith* [1979]);

NOTES

> ➢ in exceptional circumstances, English courts may suspend the operation of English legislation pending guidance from the Court of Justice on an apparent inconsistency (*R. v Secretary of State for Transport, Ex p. Factortame Ltd and others (No.2)* [1990]).

- There has, therefore, been a limited and temporary suspension of sovereignty, albeit for an unlimited period. Parliament retains, by virtue of **s.2(4)**, a residual power to re-assert its full sovereignty by repealing or amending **s.2**. However, as this would mean the United Kingdom repudiating its membership of the Union, it seems unlikely this would be done. In practice, therefore, the transfer, or pooling, of sovereignty would seem permanent.

The UK Courts and the Court of Justice

As we saw above, one of the main functions of the Court of Justice is to give definitive interpretations of European law. It does this in response to questions referred to it by national courts for a **preliminary ruling**. The national court then decides the case in light of that ruling. This emphasises that while it is the Court of Justice that **interprets** European law, it is the national courts of the Member States that **apply** it.

Under **Art.234** of the **Treaty of Rome**, any national court **may** request a ruling where it is necessary to enable it to give judgment—*i.e.* where the disputed point of European law is material to the decision, national courts have discretion to refer that point to the Court of Justice. Where the national court is one from which there is no appeal, then it has no choice—where a ruling is necessary to enable it to give judgment, **it must** make a reference.

In deciding whether a ruling is necessary to enable them to give judgment, English courts make use of the guidelines established in *H. P. Bulmer Ltd v J. Bollinger SA* [1974]—for example, a ruling is **not** necessary where the Court of Justice has previously given a ruling on the point in question (*i.e.* the point may be resolved by reference to case law of the Court of Justice) or where the point is reasonably clear and free from doubt (the *acte clair* doctrine).

Conclusion

UK membership of the European Union has had important and wide-ranging effects upon the English legal system, both in the creation and application of law. It has also had a number of less obvious effects—for example, the shift by English courts towards a purposive approach to the interpretation of legislation may have been influenced, at least in part, by the approach of the Court of Justice. This, together with notions such as indirect effect and incidental

NOTES

horizontal direct effect, indicates the capacity of EU law and practice to seep into all areas of domestic law and practice. As Lord Denning observed in *H. P. Bulmer Ltd v J. Bollinger SA* [1974], EU law is "like an incoming tide. It flows into the estuaries and up the rivers. It cannot be held back". Regarding the sovereignty question, while in theory the transfer or pooling of sovereignty could be reversed, in practice this is unlikely to occur. Assuming, therefore, the United Kingdom remains a member of the European Union, it is clear that the European legal order will continue to play an increasingly significant part in the development of English law.

Revision Notes

You should now write your revision notes for this topic. Here is an example for you and some suggested headings:

> ### *EU④—The Treaties*
>
> - primary source of EU law
> - establish aims & principles, empower institutions, enable legislation
> - can be viewed as EU constitution
> - not DA
> - may have both H & V DE provided provision is clear, precise, and uncondi- tional (*Van Gend en Loos*)

EU①—Introduction (Euro Legal Order etc)
EU②—Institutions
EU③—DA and DE
EU④—The Treaties
EU⑤—Regs, Dirs, Decs
EU⑥—Sovereignty—Euro view
EU⑦—Sovereignty—UK view
EU⑧—UK courts and CJEU

Using your cards, you should now be able to write a short paragraph in response to each of the following questions:

1. Explain the emergence of the EU.

2. Explain the role of the different EU institutions.

Notes

3. Explain the concepts of direct applicability and direct effect.

4. Discuss the Treaties as a source of EU law.

5. Discuss the different forms of EU legislation.

6. Evaluate the impact on UK sovereignty of EU membership.

7. Discuss the relationship between the CJEU and the UK courts.

Useful Websites

➤ BBC News A–Z of Europe—**http://news.bbc.co.uk/1/hi/in_depth/europe/euro-glossary/default.stm**

➤ information on the EU on the Europa website—**www.europa.eu.int/inst-en.htm**

➤ University of California, Berkeley, Library European Union Internet Resources—**www.lib.berkeley.edu/GSSI/eu.html**

➤ For more information on the European Court of Justice, visit **http://europa.eu.int/cj/en/index.htm**

NOTES

4   Statutory Interpretation

Key Points

What you need to know:

- The main approaches to statutory interpretation (literal, golden, and mischief approach).
- The minor principles of interpretation (rules of language and presumptions).
- Intrinsic and extrinsic aids to interpretation.

What you need to discuss:

- The advantages and disadvantages of the different approaches.
- The effectiveness of the courts in achieving the intentions of Parliament.

Introduction

Interpretation is an inevitable aspect of any form of communication as it is interpretation that gives information meaning. However, problems can arise where someone misinterprets information or where different people arrive at different interpretations of the same information. There are three reasons why legislation is likely to suffer from these problems:

- It tends to be complicated and is often a mixture of ordinary and technical language.
- It is often concerned with regulating future conduct. As the ability of the draftsman to anticipate the future is inevitably limited, problems will arise as to whether a particular provision applies to a particular case. For example, the courts recently had to decide whether a "Go-ped" (a type of motorised scooter) was a "motor vehicle" for the purposes of the **Road Traffic Act 1988** (*Chief Constable of North Yorkshire v Saddington* [2000]).

- It is often concerned with regulating competing interests (for example, employer and employee, landlord and tenant, trader and consumer) where the people concerned have a self-interest in promoting different interpretations.

While it is for Parliament (or those delegated by Parliament) to make legislation, it is the courts which provide the definitive interpretation when any of these problems arise.

Judicial Approaches to Interpretation

There are three traditional approaches (sometimes referred to as rules or canons):

The Literal Approach

Here, the courts should give the disputed words their ordinary, literal meaning, regardless of the outcome. If the outcome is absurd or repugnant, the remedy lies in parliamentary amendment, not judicial interpretation (*R. v Judge of the City of London Court* [1892]). For example, in *Whiteley v Chappell* [1868] it was held that impersonating a person who was deceased did not amount to the offence of impersonating someone entitled to vote at an election, because dead people are not entitled to vote.

The Golden Approach

Here, the courts should give the disputed words their ordinary, literal meaning unless the outcome is absurd or repugnant, when a more appropriate alternative interpretation may be used (*Grey v Pearson* [1857]). For example, in *R. v Allen* [1872], the word "marry" was interpreted as meaning "to go through a ceremony of marriage", because using its literal meaning would produce the absurd result that the offence of bigamy would be impossible to commit.

The Mischief (or Modern Purposive) Approach

Here, the court should give the disputed words the interpretation most likely to promote the purpose behind the legislation. Therefore, the court should consider not only the words themselves, but also what Parliament intended them to achieve (*Heydon's Case* [1584]). For example, in *Smith v Hughes* [1960], soliciting in a street or public place was interpreted to include soliciting from the window of a house. The court took the view that the nuisance caused by soliciting was the mischief aimed at, and that soliciting from house windows was just as much a nuisance as soliciting on the street. Nevertheless, even under a purposive approach, the starting point for interpretation must remain the actual words used by

Parliament (*Black-Clawson International Ltd v Papierwerk Waldhof-Aschaffenburg AG* [1975]). This preserves the proper constitutional balance between Parliament as the maker of legislation and the courts as its interpreters.

The Modern Unitary Approach

In recent years, the courts have developed an approach to interpretation which combines elements of all three of the traditional approaches—**the modern unitary approach**. Here, the courts must respect the actual words of the provision but, rather than adhere strictly to their literal meaning, should interpret them having regard to the context in which they are used and the purpose underlying the provision in which they appear. Of these three elements (words, context and purpose), it is the purposive that has become increasingly important. For example, in *Re Attorney-General's Reference (No.1)* [1988], Lord Lane C.J., having considered the literal meaning of the disputed word and the context in which it was being used, regarded the purpose of the legislation and the intention of Parliament as decisive. This may even, in exceptional circumstances, involve the addition, omission or substitution of words, though this must always be approached cautiously (*Inco Europe Ltd v First Choice Distribution* [2000]).

Subsidiary Principles and Presumptions of Interpretation

The courts are also guided in the interpretation of legislation by a number of minor principles and presumptions. Among the more significant are:

- the *ejusdem generis* **principle**—where general words follow a list of specific words, the general take their meaning from the specific. For example, a provision referring to "cats, dogs and other animals" would apply to domestic animals only, not to wild animals or livestock.

- the *expressio unius exclusio alterius* **principle**—the express inclusion of one member of a particular class excludes, by implication, all others not included. For example, a provision referring to "quarries and coal mines" would apply to all types of quarry and to coal mines, but not to any other type of mine.

Among the more significant presumptions are the presumption against retrospective effect, and the presumption of *mens rea* in criminal statutes.

We should also note that a new rule of interpretation was introduced by the **Human Rights Act 1998**. By **s.3(1)**, the courts must, so far as it is possible to do so, interpret legislation in

NOTES

such as way as to make it compatible with the Convention. Furthermore, as Lord Woolf has observed, **s.19** "requires . . . a statement as to the compatibility of the Bill with Convention rights. Where a positive statement of compatibility is made, it can be assumed that Parliament intended the legislation to comply with the Convention. If it does not do so on a literal interpretation, then using section 3 to achieve a compatible interpretation is indeed fulfilling Parliament's intention." However, the Act expressly preserves the full sovereignty of Parliament. Thus, while the courts may quash decisions or actions incompatible with Convention rights, or annul delegated legislation on grounds of incompatibility, they cannot disapply an Act of Parliament (**s.3(2)(b)**). By **s.4**, the courts may, in such circumstances, issue a declaration of incompatibility. Following this, the relevant minister may amend the offending legislation by statutory instrument (**Sch.2, para.1(2)**).

An Analysis of the Three Main Elements

The literal element—there are three main arguments for emphasising the literal element:

> ➢ it promotes certainty;

> ➢ it reduces litigation;

> ➢ it is constitutionally correct.

However, there are also arguments against:

> ➢ it ignores the natural ambiguity of language. Words rarely have one, single literal meaning. The correct meaning can only be decided by reference to the context in which the word is used. Therefore, there is frequently uncertainty that, constitutionally, has to be resolved by the courts;
> ➢ it fails to take account of the inevitable imperfection of draftsmanship;
> ➢ it is an automatic and unthinking response. The literal interpretation may often be the correct one, but it is not automatically so;
> ➢ it adopts a very narrow and legalistic view of sovereignty.

Therefore, it would be undesirable for the courts to over-emphasise the literal meaning of the disputed words.

The contextual (or golden) element—this at least avoids the most absurd or repugnant consequences of over-emphasising the literal meaning. However, it is unclear precisely what

NOTES

degree of absurdity or repugnance is required to justify abandoning the literal meaning. Therefore, according to Zander, it is an "unpredictable safety valve" which "cannot be regarded as a sound basis for judicial decision making".

The purposive element—this acknowledges the various factors that give rise to problems of interpretation and that the courts should seek to resolve them by arriving at the interpretation most likely to achieve the purpose of the legislation. This is clearly the most desirable approach for the courts to take and, therefore, the present emphasis on the purposive element within a unitary approach represents the most satisfactory balance of these three elements.

Intrinsic and Extrinsic Aids

However, there is a major obstacle to effective purposive interpretation. There are significant restrictions on the range of materials available to the courts to help them identify the purpose of the legislation. These materials fall into two categories:

- **Intrinsic aids to interpretation**—this is information within the statute itself. The courts can take into account:
  - ➢ long and short titles;
  - ➢ preamble;
  - ➢ headings;
  - ➢ schedules.

but may not make reference to marginal notes.

- **Extrinsic aids to interpretation**—this is information outside the statute. The courts can make reference to:
  - ➢ other statutes;
  - ➢ official government publications directly related to its enactment (for example, Green or White Papers, Law Commission reports), but only to identify the defect in the previous law, not the remedy the new law was intended to provide (the "*Black-Clawson*" rule);
  - ➢ where the legislation is related to an international treaty or convention, the treaty or convention itself (*Salomon v Commissioners of Customs and Excise* [1967]);
  - ➢ the official record of parliamentary debates and proceedings (**Hansard**), but only where:
    - – the words of the statute are ambiguous, unclear, or the literal meaning produces an absurdity; and

NOTES

– the parliamentary statement is made by the minister or other promoter of the Bill; and the words of the statement are clear (*Pepper (Inspector of Taxes) v Hart and others* [1993]). In this case, the House of Lords departed from its own previous decision in *Davis v Johnson* [1979]. In that case in the Court of Appeal, Lord Denning stated, "Some may say . . . should not pay any attention to what is said in Parliament. They should grope about in the dark for the meaning of an Act without switching on the light. I do not accede to this view." However, in the House of Lords, Lord Scarman observed that "such material is an unreliable guide to the meaning of what is enacted. It promotes confusion not clarity. The cut and thrust of debate . . . [is] not always conducive to a clear and unbiased explanation of the meaning of statutory language." The House was also concerned about an increase in cost and delay if reference to *Hansard* were permitted. However, since the relaxation of the exclusionary rule in *Pepper v Hart*, such fears appear to have been unfounded.

The court may not refer to:

➢ official publications not directly related to the enactment of the statute;
➢ unofficial publications (for example, pressure group reports).

These restrictions, particularly regarding extrinsic aids, may make it difficult for the court to identify the precise purpose of the legislation. The Law Commission, in a 1969 report, made a number of recommendations to remedy this:

● marginal notes should be available to the courts;

● official documents be available not only to identify the defect but also the remedy;

● an explanatory memorandum be attached to the statute for the guidance of the courts. This would be a combination of three existing documents:

➢ preamble;
➢ explanatory document prepared for MPs;
➢ detailed briefings prepared for ministers.

Although these recommendations have never been fully implemented, the explanatory notes have, since 1999, been expanded and published alongside the Act.

Conclusion

The present approach of the courts to statutory interpretation is a unitary one, with growing emphasis on the purposive element. This may be due in part to the influence of the Law

NOTES

Commission's 1969 report and also to the growing influence of the Court of Justice of the European Union. This is clearly the most satisfactory approach for the courts to adopt. Furthermore, the expansion and publication of explanatory notes should enable the courts to approach this task more effectively.

Revision Notes

You should now write your revision notes for this topic. Here is an example for you and some suggested headings:

SI②—Traditional Approaches

- *Literal*—words given ordinary, literal meaning *even if* outcome absurd—remedy in parl. amendment, not judicial interp. (*R. v Judge of City of London Court*)—e.g. *Whiteley v Chappell*

- *Golden*—words given ordinary, literal meaning *unless* outcome absurd (*Grey v Pearson*)—e.g. *R. v Allen*

- *Mischief/Purposive*—words given interp. most likely to advance purpose/achieve intention of Parl. (*Heydon's Case*)—e.g. *Smith v Hughes*

SI①—Introduction (need for interpretation)
SI②—Traditional Approaches
SI③—Modern Approach
SI④—Minor Principles
SI⑤—Evaluation of Elements
SI⑥—Intrinsic and Extrinsic Aids

Using your cards, you should now be able to write a short paragraph in response to each of the following questions:

1. Explain the need for statutory interpretation.

2. Describe the traditional approaches to interpretation

3. What approach to interpretation do the courts use currently?

4. Describe the minor principles of interpretation.

5. Evaluate the effectiveness of these approaches.

NOTES

6. Discuss the use of intrinsic and extrinsic aids.

Useful Websites

➢ For information about UK legislation and access to legislative texts and explanatory notes, use the HMSO site at **www.legislation.hmso.go.uk**

➢ For a report on the "Go-ped" case, visit **http://news.bbc.co.uk/1/hi/uk/964591.stm** and **www.guardian.co.uk/uk‾news/story/0,3604,388636,00.html**

Key Points

What you need to know:

- What is meant by a system of binding precedent.
- The court hierarchy.
- How a precedent can be altered or avoided.
- The limitations on judicial law-making.

What you need to discuss:

- The balance between certainty and flexibility in the operation of precedent.
- The law-making partnership between Parliament and the courts.

Introduction

The English legal system is a common law system. This means that many of its laws have developed over time through decisions of the courts. While this process began under Henry II, it was not truly formalised until a reliable system of case reporting was established in 1865 and the courts were reorganised under the **Judicature Acts 1873–1875**.

Stare Decisis

The basis of the doctrine of precedent is the principle of *stare decisis* (or, more accurately, *stare rationibus decidendis*). This means that a later court is bound to apply the same reasoning as an earlier court where the two cases raise substantially the same question of principle. Where there is no existing precedent to follow or modify, and no relevant

NOTES

legislation, then the court's decision on the point of law involved will establish an **original precedent**. This development of law according to principle is the hallmark of judicial law-making, as contrasted with the development of law according to policy by the legislature—legislative evolution rather than legislative revolution. The reasoning behind this approach is that it satisfies a basic requirement of justice—that similar cases should be decided according to similar principles. It also ensures judicial decisions are based on reason and principle, and not on arbitrary, individualised factors.

In order to operate a doctrine of binding precedent, the legal system must have three essential elements:

The Court Hierarchy

This is needed to establish which decisions are binding on which courts. The basic principle is that the decisions of higher courts are binding on lower courts. The highest court in the English system is the House of Lords. Decisions of the House of Lords are binding on all lower civil and criminal courts. It is itself bound by the decisions of no court except the Court of Justice of the European Union on matters of Union law only.

The next most authoritative court is the Court of Appeal, with two divisions, civil and criminal. Decisions of the Civil Division are binding on all lower civil courts, while those of the Criminal Division bind all lower criminal courts.

Below the Court of Appeal are the Divisional Courts, High Court, Crown Court, County Court and magistrates' courts. While both the Divisional Courts and High Court can establish precedents, in practice the great majority of common law is found in decisions of the House of Lords and Court of Appeal.

Law Reporting

An accurate system of law reporting is needed to allow these legal principles to be identified, collated and accessed. The earliest form of law reporting was the Year Books, first published in 1272. Modern reporting dates from the establishment of the Council on Law Reporting in 1865. The Council still publishes the **Law Reports** and, since 1953, has also published the **Weekly Law Reports**. Various private companies also publish both general and specialised series of reports, the best known being the **All England Law Reports** (published by Butterworths). Reports are also published in various newspapers (for example, *The Times*) and journals (for example, *New Law Journal*). The most recent development in this area has been the use of computerised reporting systems (for example, **LEXIS**), CD Roms, and the Internet.

NOTES

The Binding Element

A judgment of the court will generally contain four elements:

- a statement of the material (or relevant) facts of the case;
- a statement of the legal principles material to the decision (known as the *ratio decidendi*);
- discussion of legal principles raised in argument but not material to the decision (known as *obiter dicta*);
- the final decision or verdict.

It is the *ratio*, and *ratio* alone, that forms the binding element upon future courts when dealing with cases of a similar nature. *Obiter dicta*, while never binding, may have a strong persuasive force. Other forms of persuasive precedent include decisions of the Privy Council, other common law jurisdictions (notably Australia, Canada and New Zealand), and writings of legal academics.

Flexibility and Certainty in Precedent

The common law faces a dilemma between the competing but equally legitimate aims of flexibility and certainty. The law needs to be flexible in order to develop and evolve to meet changing times and demands. However, it must also be sufficiently certain to allow people to plan their affairs and lawyers to advise their clients. The binding nature of the *ratio* clearly creates a foundation of certainty. Therefore, it is necessary to consider how a degree of flexibility is introduced into the system.

Overruling, Reversing and Disapproving

Higher courts can always alter the law as developed by lower courts. Done on appeal, it is known as reversing. Where the lower decision is being cited as authority in another case, it is known as overruling. A case can only be overruled where its *ratio* is material to the decision in the later case. Where it is not material, the higher court can only disapprove the decision of the lower court. A case that has been disapproved, while strictly still valid precedent, is unlikely to be cited successfully in the future.

Distinguishing

Lower courts may be able to avoid following the *ratio* of a higher court where they can distinguish between the two cases, thereby developing exceptions to general principles. To distinguish means to find some material difference between the two cases that justifies the application of different principles. For example, in *R. v R (Rape—Marital Exemption)* [1991] Lord Lane C.J. reviewed the development of the marital exemption to rape through a series of cases that developed exceptions through distinguishing. He also observed that a point may be reached where the number and extent of the exceptions is such that the continuing validity of the original precedent must be reconsidered. However, this discretion to distinguish may be misused by lower courts in order to avoid an unwelcome precedent. This would be clearly unacceptable and was condemned by the Court of Appeal in *Lewis v Averay* [1972].

Departing

Departing refers to circumstances under which a court can depart from its own previous decisions. Until 1966, the House of Lords was bound by its own previous decisions (*London Tramways v London County Council* [1898]). This created a block at the top of the system of precedent, and meant that out-dated, incorrect or unacceptable decisions could only be rectified by legislation. Therefore, in 1966, the Lord Chancellor issued a **Practice Statement** that stated that while the House of Lords would regard its own previous decisions as normally binding, it would depart from them when it appeared right to do so. In exercising this discretion, it is required to consider:

- the danger of disturbing retrospectively existing civil arrangements;

- the particular need for certainty in the criminal law.

Consequently, the House of Lords has used this discretion sparingly, often preferring to distinguish from its own previous decisions rather than depart from them. Nevertheless, there have been occasions where the House has been prepared to depart from a previous decision:

- in *R. v Shivpuri* [1986] where the House departed from its own previous decision on attempts and impossibility in *Anderton v Ryan* [1985];

- in *R. v Howe* [1987] the House departed from the decision on duress and murder in *DPP for Northern Ireland v Lynch* [1975];

- in *Pepper (Inspector of Taxes) v Hart and others* [1993] the House departed from the decision on reference to *Hansard* when interpreting statutes in *Davis v Johnson* [1979];

- in *Arthur J. S. Hall & Co v Simons* [2000] the House departed from the decision on the advocate's immunity in negligence in *Rondel v Worsley* [1967].

The Court of Appeal (Civil Division) is normally bound by its own previous decisions, subject to exceptions established in *Young v Bristol Aeroplane Co Ltd* [1944]—for example, it is not

NOTES

bound where the previous decision was given *per incuriam*. This means the decision was given in ignorance or forgetfulness of relevant legislation or decision of the House of Lords, with the result that it is demonstrably wrong (*Morelle v Wakeling* [1955]; *Duke v Reliance Systems Ltd* [1988]).

The Court of Appeal (Criminal Division) is similarly bound by its own previous decisions subject to the *Bristol Aeroplane* exceptions and to that established in *R. v Taylor* [1950]—it is not bound where, in the previous decision, the law was misapplied or misunderstood resulting in a conviction and, therefore, to follow it would result in a manifest or obvious injustice. The Criminal Division has this additional element of flexibility because it is dealing with questions affecting the liberty of the citizen.

Following the announcement of the **Practice Statement** in 1966, Lord Denning led a move in the Court of Appeal to assert that the same discretion to depart from its own previous decisions should apply to the Court of Appeal. In *Davis v Johnson* [1978] he argued that the doctrine that the Court of Appeal was bound by its own previous decisions was a rule of practice and not of law and should be modified to allow the court to depart from an earlier decision if it was convinced that the earlier decision was wrong. He stated that:

"On principle, it seems to me that, whilst this court should regard itself as normally bound by a previous decision of the court, nevertheless it should be at liberty to depart from it if it is convinced that the previous decision was wrong. What is the argument to the contrary? It is said that, if an error has been made, this court has no option but to continue the error and leave it to be corrected by the House of Lords. The answer is this: the House of Lords may never have an opportunity to correct the error; and thus it may be perpetuated indefinitely, perhaps for ever . . . Even if . . . there is an appeal to the House of Lords, it usually takes 12 months or more for the House to reach its decision. What then is the position of the lower courts meanwhile? They are in a dilemma. Either they have to apply the erroneous decision of the Court of Appeal, or they have to adjourn all fresh cases to await the decision of the House of Lords. That has often happened. So justice is delayed, and often denied, by the lapse of time before the error is corrected."

However, the House of Lords took a contrary view, making it clear that the provisions of the **Practice Statement** only applied to the House of Lords, and the position of the Court of Appeal remained that stated in *Young*. Lord Diplock stated:

"In an appellate court of last resort a balance must be struck between the need on the one side for the legal certainty resulting from the binding effect of previous decisions and on the other side the avoidance of undue restriction on the proper development of the law. In the case of an intermediate appellate court, however, the second [consideration] can be

---

NOTES

taken care of by appeal to a superior appellate court, if reasonable means of access to it are available; while the risk to the first [consideration], legal certainty, if the court is not bound by its own previous decisions grows ever greater with increasing membership and the number of three-judge divisions in which it sits . . . So the balance does not lie in the same place as in the case of a court of last resort. That is why Lord Gardiner L.C.'s announcement about the future attitude towards precedent of the House of Lords in its judicial capacity concluded with the words: 'This announcement is not intended to affect the use of precedent elsewhere than in this House.'''

An Analysis of the Operation of Precedent

Advantages:

- it is a **just** system, ensuring similar cases are decided by similar principles;

- it is an **impartial** system, requiring decisions to be made according to established principles;

- it provides a **practical character** to the law, allowing it to develop in response to actual cases, rather than on an exclusively theoretical or abstract basis;

- it provides a **degree of certainty**, allowing individuals to order their affairs and lawyers to advise their clients;

- it allows a **measure of flexibility**—within the binding framework of *stare decisis*, the hierarchy of courts, the appellate process, the provisions of the Practice Statement, the *Bristol Aeroplane* and *R. v Taylor* exceptions, and the practice of distinguishing all allow the common law to develop and evolve to meet changing needs and times.

Disadvantages:

- there is a danger of **rigidity**, whereby necessary changes cannot occur because:

  - ➤ the system is contingent—changes depend upon appropriate cases reaching sufficiently superior courts (sometimes referred to as the "accidents of litigation");
  - ➤ the retrospective effect of overruling can discourage courts from changing the law.

- it is a **complex** system:

NOTES

➤ keeping track of valid authorities and the exceptions established through distinguishing is a difficult task;

➤ it can be difficult to identify the precise *ratio* of a decision, particularly in the multiple judgments of the House of Lords and Court of Appeal.

Reforms

There are two reforms that could enhance the flexibility of the system without significantly reducing the present level of certainty:

- **Public interest referrals**—at present, necessary changes may be delayed because individual litigants may be unwilling or unable to commit the time and money involved in taking their case to the superior courts. A public interest referral system would allow the trial judge to refer questions of law of general public importance, at public expense, to the superior courts. This would operate in a similar fashion to **Art.234** references to the Court of Justice of the European Union.

- **Prospective overruling**—at present, a court may be discouraged from overruling because of the retrospective consequences. Indeed, the House of Lords is specifically required to consider this under the Practice Statement. Under prospective overruling, any retrospective effect would be limited to the instant case and any similar case where proceedings had already commenced.

Conclusion

There is an inherent conflict in a system of binding precedent between the need for certainty and the desire for flexibility. Therefore, the system must seek to achieve the most satisfactory balance between these competing but equally legitimate aims. The English legal system largely achieves this, though we can argue that the introduction of public interest referrals and prospective overruling would enhance its success. We must always remember, however, that English law is not dependent upon precedent alone for its development. Precedent operates alongside and complements the contributions of the other sources. Parliament, the law reform agencies, the European Union and the English courts all work together to ensure that English law remains responsive to society's changing needs and demands.

Revision Notes

You should now write your revision notes for this topic. Here is an example for you and some suggested headings:

NOTES

Prec③—Law Reporting

- accurate reporting needed to enable principles to be recorded, collated and accessed
- earliest form = Year Books (from 1272)
- modern reporting—Council on Law Reporting (1865)—official reports/W.L.R.
- private (*e.g.* All E.R.); newspapers (*e.g. The Times*); journals (*e.g.* N.L.J.)
- on-line, CD-ROM, Internet

Prec①—Intro (*stare decisis*, etc.)
Prec②—Court Hierarchy
Prec③—Law Reporting
Prec④—*Ratio* & *Obiter*
Prec⑤—Overruling & Distinguishing
Prec⑥—Departing
Prec⑦—Advantages & Disadvantages
Prec⑧—Reforms

Using your cards, you should now be able to write a short paragraph in response to each of the following questions:

1. Explain the principle of stare decisis.

2. Describe the hierarchy of English courts.

3. Give a brief account of law reporting.

4. Discuss the binding and persuasive elements in a court judgment.

5. Explain the conflict between certainty and flexibility.

6. Describe how flexibility is introduced into a binding system.

7. Evaluate the effectiveness of the operation of precedent, including possible reforms.

Useful Websites

⊕ For information of the judicial work and judgments of the House of Lords, visit

---

NOTES

- For information on the judicial work of the Privy Council, visit **www.privycouncil.gov.uk/output/page5.asp**

- For information on the court system generally, access to judgements from various courts, and other useful links, visit, **www.lawreports.co.uk/index.htm** and **www.bailii.org**

NOTES

SECTION TWO: DISPUTE SOLVING

6 | Police Powers

Key Points

What you need to know:

- Police powers to stop and search.
- Police powers of arrest.
- Police powers of detention and the treatment of suspects at the police station.
- The balance of individual rights and the need for investigative powers.

What you need to discuss:

- Who gets stopped and searched?
- How effective is stop and search?
- How effective are the safeguards for suspects?
- Are any reforms needed?

Introduction

The role and powers of the police is the obvious starting point for any assessment of the criminal justice system, as the police have the responsibility for investigating crimes, gathering evidence, and dealing with suspects.

The role of the police in a democratic society is a sensitive one, balancing society's interest in the prevention of crime and the prosecution of offenders with the liberties of the individual. As the **Royal Commission on Criminal Procedure (the Philips Commission)** stated in 1981, a balance must be found between "the interests of the community in bringing offenders to justice and the rights and liberties of persons suspected or accused of crime". Consequently, police powers exist within a legislative framework, principally the **Police and**

Criminal Evidence Act 1984 (and accompanying **Codes of Practice**) and the **Criminal Justice and Public Order Act 1994**, designed to ensure that individual civil liberties are protected and respected. In this respect it is important to remember both that British criminal justice is founded upon a presumption of innocence, and that Britain has a long tradition of "policing by consent".

Pre-arrest powers

The police may always ask members of the public questions, but people are generally not obliged to answer those questions, stop and talk to the police, go to or subsequently remain at a police station unless they have been arrested (*Rice v Connolly* [1966]; *Ricketts v Cox* [1982]). However, the **Police Reform Act 2002 (S.50)** provides that if a constable in uniform has reason to believe a person has been or is acting in an anti-social manner, s/he may require that person to give their name and address. It is an offence, punishable by a fine, for that person to refuse to give their name or address or to give a false or inaccurate name or address.

While at common law the police cannot detain a person without arresting them (*Kenlin v Gardiner* [1967]), they may touch someone to attract their attention (for example, by tapping them on the shoulder—*Donnelly v Jackman* [1970]). However, the police do have statutory powers (**1984 Act, s.1**) to stop and search those they have reasonable grounds to suspect are carrying stolen or prohibited articles (*i.e.* offensive weapons or articles for use in robbery or burglary). The **Criminal Justice Bill 2003** proposes to extend the definition of prohibited articles to include articles intended to cause criminal damage. Other legislation (for example, **Misuse of Drugs Act 1971, s.23**) also grants specific stop and search powers, again based upon reasonable suspicion. More controversially, **s.60** of the **Criminal Justice and Public Order Act 1994** allows a senior police officer to authorise a general stop and search operation in a given area if s/he reasonably believes that serious violence may take place in the area (for example, a football match where there is a history of violence between the rival supporters). Such authorisation is operative for 24 hours, and may be extended by a further 24 hours. During this time, any person in the area may be stopped and searched for knives or offensive weapons—there is no requirement of reasonable suspicion.

Prior to conducting any search, the officer must inform the person to be searched of their name and the police station at which they are based. They must also state the purpose of the search, and the legal grounds for the search. A person cannot be required to remove any clothing in a public place other than a coat, jacket and gloves (**1984 Act, s.2**). If a more extensive search is required, this must be done in a private place and must be conducted by an officer of the same sex as the person being searched. The person searched is entitled to a copy of the written record of the search (**1984 Act, s.3**). The officer may use reasonable force in

NOTES

order to carry out the search (**1984 Act, s.117**). A person who believes they have been subjected to an unlawful or improper stop and search may complain to the **Police Complaints Authority** and/or pursue a civil remedy through the courts. The courts also have a general discretion to exclude evidence improperly obtained where they are of the view that it would have an adverse effect on the fairness of the proceedings (**1984 Act, s.78**).

Issues surrounding stop and search

Many reports and inquiries, such as Marian FitzGerald's *Final Report into Stop and Search* (1999) for the Metropolitan Police, and the Macpherson Report on the Stephen Lawrence Inquiry (1999), consistently recognise the value of stop and search to effective policing. FitzGerald's research demonstrated a considerable degree of consensus between the police and the community on the importance of stop and search in three main respects:

- Crime detection—stop and search accounts for almost all arrests for offensive weapons and "going equipped" to commit burglaries, etc.

- Intelligence gathering.

- Crime prevention and deterrence.

Nevertheless, there are a number of significant concerns regarding the *operation* of stop and search powers:

- Despite the fact that **Code of Practice A** makes it clear that personal factors alone (for example, colour, race, or a criminal record) cannot form the basis of a reasonable suspicion, there are concerns that stop and search powers are used disproportionately in relation to some groups (for example, black, and increasingly, Asian youths—2002 Home Office statistics show that black people are eight times more likely than whites to be stopped and searched, and Asians three times more likely).

- The manner in which some officers exercise their powers causes unnecessary bad feeling. Many people who report a negative experience of stop and search are angered by the *way* it was done, not by the *fact* that it was done at all.

- Contrary to the Code, a criminal record is still widely used as the reason for targeting individuals for stop and search.

- The power can be used, equally unjustifiably under the Code, for general social control. However, we should note the increasing public demands on the police to deal with "anti-social" behaviour.

NOTES

- Under the original rules, if the person consented to the search—a so-called "voluntary' search"—this did not constitute a **s.1** search and did not have to be recorded.

- Some argue that stop and search is ineffective and only a small proportion lead to arrest. However, we must always treat such statistics with caution—as one officer stated to FitzGerald, "You could be told by someone in the park that someone in a gang had been flashing a knife around—and there's 12 of them. So you search them and you find the one with the knife. But that's only 8 per cent. And that's rubbish isn't it? It was a successful search".

- There have been frequent concerns expressed regarding the independence and effectiveness of the Police Complaints Authority.

- The discretion given the court to exclude evidence obtained in breach of the Act or the Codes is exercised in inconsistent and unpredictable ways (contrast, for example, *R. v Canale* [1990] with *R. v Latif and Shahzad* [1996]).

Reforms

Following concerns raised by Macpherson and others, the Home Office issued a new Code of Practice A which came into force in April 2003. **Paragraph 1.5** insists all searches must fall within the scope of a legal power and prevents voluntary searches except of persons entering a sports ground or other premises where consent to the search is a condition of entry. **Paragraph 2.4** strengthens the guidance on "reasonable suspicion" and states that this should "normally be linked to accurate and current intelligence or information", and **para.2.5** points out that searches are "more likely to be effective, legitimate, and secure public confidence when reasonable suspicion is based on a range of factors". **Paragraph 3.1** provides that "all stops and searches must be carried out with courtesy, consideration and respect for the person concerned". Perhaps most significantly, **para.4** (following Recommendation 61 of the Macpherson Report) requires the recording of stops where an officer requests a person to account for themselves, but not to general conversations. A record must be made if the person questioned requests it, even if the officer believes a record is not required. **Paragraph 5** requires supervising and senior officers to monitor the use of stop, and stop and search, and to share this information with community representatives. Also, the **Police Reform Act 2002, s.9** provides for a new **Independent Police Complaints Commission** to replace the Police Complaints Authority from April 2004.

Responses to the changes have been largely supportive, with generally positive responses coming from both the Association of Police Authorities and the Mayor of London's Office. However, FitzGerald points out that simply redefining or clarifying the Code may have little

NOTES

impact on stop and search in practice. Of equal, if not greater importance, is to ensure effective training, monitoring and community liaison.

Powers of arrest

Arrest with a warrant

The police may obtain an arrest warrant by applying in writing to a magistrate and making an oral statement on oath. The warrant will specify the name of the person to be arrested and the general particulars of the offence. It allows the police to enter and search premises in order to make the arrest and to use such force as may be reasonable in the circumstances.

Arrest without a warrant

There are four main categories of arrest without warrant:

- reasonable suspicion concerning an arrestable offence (**1984 Act, s.24**)—a police officer may arrest without warrant anyone s/he reasonably suspects has committed, is committing, or is about to commit an arrestable offence (for example, one punishable by five or more years' imprisonment);

- general arrest conditions (**1984 Act, s.25**)—a police officer may arrest without warrant anyone s/he reasonably suspects has committed or attempted, or is committing or attempting any offence where service of a summons appears inappropriate or impracticable because either:

    - ➤ the suspect refuses to give his/her name and address, the police reasonably suspect the name and address given to be false, or the address is unsuitable for the service of a warrant;
    - ➤ the arrest is necessary to protect property, members of the public, or the suspect him/herself from harm.

- other statutory powers—other legislation (for example, **Public Order Act 1986**) also grant specific powers of arrest;

- arrest for breach of the peace—**1984 Act, s.26** preserves the old common law power of the police to arrest for a breach of the peace.

If necessary, the officer may use reasonable force in order to carry out the arrest (**1984 Act, s.117**). At the time of arrest or a soon as practicable thereafter, the person arrested must be

NOTES

informed of this fact and the grounds for arrest (**1984 Act, s.28**), though there is no precise form of words that must be used. They must be taken as soon as is practicable to a police station (**1984 Act, s.30**), where they may be detained and questioned, and subsequently either charged or released. The **Criminal Justice Bill 2003** proposes to allow police officers to grant "street bail" for some minor offences, enabling officers to spend more time on the beat rather than back at the police station. Only around 1 per cent of suspects are detained for more than 24 hours, and any detention beyond 36 hours (up to a maximum of 96 hours) must be authorised by a magistrate (**1984 Act, ss.43, 44**). A person can be detained prior to charge where the custody officer has reasonable grounds to believe this is necessary in order to secure or preserve evidence (including through questioning) (**1984 Act, s.37**). Otherwise, the person must be released either on bail or without bail. The custody officer must review the continuation of the detention no later than six hours after its commencement, and at periods of no longer than nine hours thereafter (**1984 Act, s.40**). A person should not normally be detained without charge for more than 24 hours (**1984 Act, s.41**). Any continuation of the detention after 24 hours must be authorised by an officer of the rank of superintendent or above and is only possible where the offence is a serious arrestable offence (for example, murder, rape) and the officer has reasonable grounds to believe the continuation is necessary in order to secure or preserve evidence (**1984 Act, s.42**). The **Criminal Justice Bill 2003** proposes to allow such an extension for any arrestable offence. Following charge, a person must normally be released with or without bail unless certain specified circumstances apply (for example, there are reasonable grounds to believe the person will not appear in court to answer bail) (**1984 Act, s.38**). A person in detention may be searched and samples taken (**1984 Act, ss.54, 63**), although intimate searches and the taking of intimate samples must be conducted by a doctor or nurse (**1984 Act, ss. 55, 62**), and his/her fingerprints may be taken (**1984 Act, s.61**). Any intimate search and the taking of any intimate samples must be authorised by an officer of the rank of superintendent or above.

The main safeguards for the suspect

That suspects in police custody need the safeguards now provided under PACE 1984 and Code of Practice C is clear from the case of Anthony Steel. In 2003, the Court of Appeal, following a reference from the Criminal Cases Review Commission (see **Chapter 7**), quashed Steel's 1979 conviction for murder. Mr Steel, who was mentally handicapped and at the borderline of abnormal suggestibility, had confessed to the crime in his sixth interview by detectives on his third day in custody. For the first day he had received no refreshments and went 37 hours without washing facilities. The present safeguards include:

- The caution—the suspect must normally be cautioned on arrest, and must always be cautioned before questioning.

- Detainees' welfare—**Code C** requires that questioning must take place in an appropriate interview room (comfortable, well-lit, ventilated, etc.) and the must be adequate rest and comfort breaks.

- Tape-recording of interviews (**1984 Act, s.60**).

- Informing someone of the detention—on arrival at a police station, the suspect is entitled to have someone of his/her choosing informed of his/her arrest (**1984 Act, s.56**). This may be delayed by a senior officer of the rank of inspector or above for up to 36 hours in certain specified circumstances (for example, if there is a reasonable belief that other suspects still at large may be alerted).

- The right to consult a solicitor—the suspect has the right to consult a solicitor in private and free of charge (**1984 Act, s.58**) (though again this right may be suspended for up to 36 hours on the same criteria as above).

- The custody record—the custody officer must maintain a custody record on all detainees and under **Code C** a solicitor or appropriate adult is entitled to consult the record at any reasonable time during the detention.

- Risk assessment—under **Code C**, the custody officer must conduct a proper and effective risk assessment of all those entering police custody to determine whether, among other things, they may be in need of medical attention or require an appropriate adult.

- Appropriate adults—under **Code C** any interview of a child or a vulnerable adult (someone who is or appears to be suffering from a mental disorder or is otherwise mentally vulnerable) must only be conducted in the presence of an appropriate adult (for example, a parent or social worker).

- Reviews of detention by the Custody Officer (see above).

- Exclusion of evidence—the courts must refuse to admit a confession where it may have been obtained by oppressive means (**1984 Act, s.76**). They also have a general discretion to exclude any evidence where they are of the view that it would have an adverse effect on the fairness of the proceedings (**1984 Act, s.78**).

- Complaints regarding treatment in custody, etc. can be made to the Police Complaints Authority.

- A civil remedy may be available through an action for wrongful arrest or false imprisonment.

Issues surrounding arrest and detention

- The notion of "reasonable suspicion" is excessively broad and allows excessive scope to the police to make arrests.

NOTES

- Just as black and Asian people are more likely to be searched if stopped than white people, they are also more likely to be arrested if searched. There are concerns, therefore, that the system operates in a discriminatory way.

- The ability of the custody officer to achieve an independent review of the detention is doubted as they generally have less information available to them than the investigating officers, and are often of a lower rank, especially when dealing with serious offences where extended detention and questioning is most likely. There is a risk, therefore, that custody officers simply "rubber stamp" decisions made by the investigating officers.

- The discretion given the court to exclude evidence obtained in breach of the Act or the Codes is exercised in inconsistent and unpredictable ways (contrast, for example, *R. v Canale* [1990] with *R. v Latif and Shahzad* [1996]).

- Some commentators have questioned the independence and effectiveness of the Police Complaints Authority. The **Police Reform Act 2002, s.9** makes provision for the replacement of the Police Complaints Authority by a new **Independent Police Complaints Commission** from April 2004.

- The **Police Reform Act 2002, s.51** also makes provision for **Independent Custody Visitors** (**ICVs**) as an additional safeguard for those in detention. The role of the ICV will be to inspect custody suites (in particular, cell accommodation, washing and toilet facilities and the facilities for the provision of food), and to meet with detainees to discuss their treatment and conditions.

Revision Notes

You should now write your revision notes for this topic. Here is an example for you and some suggested headings:

Police②—Stop & Search Powers

- PRA'02 (**s.50**)—give name/address—RB of anti-social behaviour
- PACE'84 (**s.1**)—S&S for stolen property/prohibited articles—RS required
- CJPOA'94 (**s.60**)—general S&S for knives/offensive weapons—RS not required BUT **s.60** needs authorisation of senior officer (RS of serious violence, geographic limits, time limits)
- Misc powers—*e.g.* MDA'71 (s.23)

Police①—Intro/Context
Police②—Police Stop & Search Powers
Police③—Stop & Search Issues
Police④—Arrest Powers and Issues
Police⑤—Detention & Questioning Powers
Police⑥—Detention & Questioning Issues

Using your cards, you should now be able to write a short paragraph in response to each of the following questions:

1. Explain why police powers are a sensitive issue in English Law.

2. Explain police powers of stop and search.

3. Explain police powers of arrest.

4. How adequate are the safeguards for the public regarding stop and search and arrest?

5. Explain police powers of detention and questioning.

6. How adequate are the safeguards for the suspect detained at the police station?

Useful Websites

- PACE Code of Practice A—**www.homeoffice.gov.uk/docs/pacecodea.pdf**

- PACE Code of Practice C—**www.homeoffice.gov.uk/docs/pacecodec.pdf**

- For information on police powers and the police generally—**www.homeoffice.gov.uk/crimpol/police/index.html**

- *Stop and Search: What You Should Know*—**www.met.police.uk/publications/stop_search/advice.htm**

- *Metropolitan Police Final Report into Stop and Search* by Marian FitzGerald—**www.met.police.uk/publications/stop_search/report.htm**

- For a series of articles on crime and policing in Britain, see the *Guardian* at **www.guardian.co.uk/crime/0,2759,339240,00.html**

NOTES

7 | Criminal Process

Key Points

What you need to know:

- The rules relating to bail.
- The procedure for determining mode of trial for either-way offences.
- Trials at magistrates', Crown, and youth courts.
- The appeal process following summary trial.
- The appeal process following trial on indictment.
- The role of the Criminal Cases Review Commission in investigating alleged miscarriages of justice.

What you need to discuss:

- The criteria for granting or refusing bail.
- The differences in trials at magistrates', Crown, and youth courts.
- The effectiveness of the Criminal Cases Review Commission.

The Criminal Process

Once a person has been charged by the police with an offence, the conduct of the prosecution passes from the police to the **Crown Prosecution Service (CPS)** (see **Chapter 10**). However, the **Criminal Justice Bill 2003** proposes to transfer responsibility for charging to the CPS, following pilot studies that resulted in a significant increase in both convictions and guilty pleas. Criminal offences fall into three categories:

- **Summary offences**—these are minor offences that are tried only in magistrates' courts.

- **Indictable offences**—these are serious offences that are tried only in the Crown Court.

- **Either-way offences**—these are intermediate offences, such as theft, that can be tried either summarily in the magistrates' court or on indictment in the Crown Court.

The role of the magistrates' court

Regardless of the category of offence, the accused person must be brought before the magistrates' court for an **Early Administrative Hearing (EAH)**. This is the first appearance in court by the defendant. The purpose of this hearing is to deal with any application for bail and/or legal aid, and to order any reports that may be required (for example, medical reports).

Bail

The question of whether someone accused of a crime is released on bail pending trial or remanded in custody is a difficult one. Once again, as with police powers, a balance must be struck between the rights of the individual (who at this stage has not been convicted of an offence) and the need to protect the public. The position regarding "street bail" and bail at the police station is explained in **Chapter 6**. We are concerned here with bail applications to the magistrates' court. Under the **Bail Act 1976**, there is a general right to bail, no matter how serious the offence concerned. However, the magistrates can refuse to grant bail where there are substantial grounds to believe the defendant will fail to surrender to bail, commit an offence, interfere with witnesses, or otherwise obstruct the course of justice. In making this determination, the magistrates must take into account the nature and seriousness of the offence, any past criminal record of the defendant, the community ties of the defendant, and the defendant's record of answering to bail previously. Also, bail need not be granted where the court takes the view that the defendant needs to be kept in custody for his/her own safety or welfare, or where there is insufficient information to make a decision. Conditions can be attached to the granting of bail, and among the more common are requirements to report to the police, reside at a specified address, or abide by a curfew. A financial security may be required of the defendant or a third party may provide a financial surety—either will be forfeited should the defendant subsequently fail to surrender to bail. If bail is refused, the defendant can renew the application at a subsequent hearing or appeal to a judge in chambers. Under the **Bail (Amendment) Act 1993**, the prosecution can appeal to a Crown Court judge against a grant of bail by magistrates where the defendant is charged with an offence punishable by at least five years imprisonment. The **Criminal Justice Bill 2003** proposes to extend this right of appeal to any offence punishable by imprisonment. Furthermore, under the **Criminal Justice and Public Order Act 1994** (as amended by the **Crime and Disorder Act 1998**), where the defendant is charged with a serious

NOTES

offence and has a previous conviction for such an offence, then bail will only be granted in exceptional circumstances. The main concern regarding bail appears to be substantial variations and inconsistencies in bail decisions in different parts of the country. Furthermore, approximately 15 per cent of those refused bail are subsequently not proceeded against or acquitted. However, this does not necessarily invalidate the bail refusal, as different criteria apply to a bail decision and a conviction. Finally, the relevant factors (such as community ties) for the granting of bail can discriminate against homeless defendants, demonstrating the need for the provision of more bail hostels.

Mode of Trial

Summary offences are then tried by either a District Judge sitting alone or by a bench of three lay magistrates. Regarding indictable offences, committal proceedings before examining magistrates ceased in January 2001. Instead, defendants are now "sent forthwith" to the Crown Court. Any submission of no case to answer will be part of the pre-trial procedure at the Crown Court. Regarding either-way offences, the magistrates' court will proceed to the **"plea before venue"** stage. Under the **Criminal Procedure and Investigation Act 1996**, if the defendant indicates that s/he intends to plead guilty, s/he loses the right to a Crown Court trial, and the magistrates then dispose of the case summarily. This can include committing the defendant for sentencing at the Crown Court if the magistrates believe their sentencing powers are inadequate. If the defendant indicates that s/he intends to plead not guilty, the magistrates must determine whether summary trial or trial on indictment is appropriate, although the defendant may elect for trial on indictment. Trials at the magistrates' court are quicker and cheaper than those at the Crown Court. Furthermore, from the defendant's point of view, there are lower possible penalties, although this must be balanced against a greater chance of conviction. Crown Court trials take longer, may be delayed and are more expensive, while from the defendant's point of view the advantages of a greater chance of acquittal and better legal representation must be weighed against the possibility of a higher sentence if convicted—judges are three times more likely than magistrates to impose an immediate custodial sentence, and that sentence is on average two and a half times as long as those imposed by magistrates.

Youth Courts

Apart from those charged with the most serious offences, young defendants (between 10 and 17 years of age) are tried by magistrates sitting as a Youth Court. The magistrates receive special training for this role and must sit as a mixed gender bench. The hearings are far less formal than those in an adult court and are held in private. Reporting restrictions apply and the press cannot identify the defendant even if convicted unless the court allows. This is a

NOTES

particularly important court as the peak age for offending is 17–18. The idea underlying a special court with an informal approach and reporting restrictions is to keep young offenders apart from adult offenders and maximise the possibility that early, sensitive and appropriate intervention will prevent the individual becoming trapped in a cycle of offending. This accords with the general emphasis on welfare and rehabilitation in the treatment of young offenders, including sentencing. However, the Government is considering removing reporting restrictions in relation to persistent young offenders—such a "naming and shaming" strategy has been criticised by Nacro, the crime reduction charity, as it may well stigmatise such offenders and make their rehabilitation more difficult.

The role of the Crown Court

If the trial takes place in the Crown Court, it will be before a judge alone if the defendant pleads guilty, or before a judge and jury where the plea is not guilty. The **Criminal Justice Bill 2003** proposes to allow defendants to choose a "bench trial" by a judge sitting without a jury, and also to allow the prosecution to request trial by judge alone where the case is complex or lengthy or where there is a risk of jury intimidation. The order of proceedings is generally as follows:

- The indictment is read.

- The jury is sworn in.

- The prosecution makes its opening speech.

- Prosecution witnesses are called, examined, cross-examined by the defence and, if necessary, re-examined by the prosecution.

- The defence, if it wishes, makes its opening speech.

- The defence, if it wishes, calls witnesses who are examined, cross-examined, and re-examined if necessary.

- The prosecution makes its closing speech.

- The defence makes its closing speech.

- The judge sums up the evidence to the jury and directs them on the relevant law.

- The jury retires to reach a verdict.

For more information on juries, see **Chapter 12**. The Crown Court also hears appeals from the magistrates' court (see below). For a more detailed discussion of sentencing, see **Chapter 20**.

NOTES

Appeals in criminal proceedings following summary trial

Appeals from the magistrates' court lie to either:

- The Crown Court. Where the accused pleaded guilty, s/he can only appeal against sentence. Where the plea was one of not guilty, s/he may appeal against conviction, sentence or both. The Crown Court can confirm, reverse or vary the decision of the magistrates (including increasing the sentence) or remit the case back to the magistrates' court with its opinion. Further appeal on a point of law can be made to the Queen's Bench Divisional Court by way of case stated.

- Alternatively, either the defence or prosecution can appeal directly, by way of case stated, from the magistrates' court to the Queen's Bench Divisional Court. The Divisional Court can confirm, reverse or vary the decision of the magistrates or remit the case back to the magistrates' court with its opinion.

Further appeal lies from the Divisional Court to the House of Lords, provided two requirements are met (**Administration of Justice Act 1960, s.1**):

- the Divisional Court certifies that the appeal raises a point of law of general public importance;

- the Divisional Court or the House of Lords grants permission on the basis that the point of law is one which ought to be considered by the House of Lords.

Appeals in criminal proceedings following trial on indictment

Appeal from the Crown Court to the Court of Appeal (Criminal Division) is possible where either (**Criminal Appeal Act 1995, s.1**):

- the trial judge grants an appeal certificate; or
- the Court of Appeal grants permission to appeal.

Unlike appeals following summary trial, a defendant convicted following trial on indictment can appeal against sentence, conviction or both, regardless of plea entered at trial. When dealing with an appeal against conviction only, the Court of Appeal has no power to interfere with the sentence passed by the Crown Court. The Court of Appeal must allow an appeal against conviction where it is satisfied that the conviction is unsafe (**Criminal Appeal Act 1995, s.2**). Regarding an appeal against sentence, the Court of Appeal may confirm, vary or

NOTES

reduce the sentence imposed by the Crown Court—it cannot increase the sentence. It may also use the opportunity to provide sentencing guidelines for the Crown Court.

Further appeal, by either the defence or prosecution, lies from the Court of Appeal to the House of Lords, provided two requirements are met (**Criminal Appeal Act 1968, s.33**):

- the Court of Appeal certifies that the appeal raises a point of law of general public importance;

- the Court of Appeal or House of Lords grants permission to appeal on the basis that the point of law is one which ought to be considered by the House of Lords.

While the prosecution cannot appeal against an acquittal, the Attorney-General can refer questions on a point of law to the Court of Appeal (**Criminal Justice Act 1972, s.36**). The opinion of the Court of Appeal has no effect on the acquittal. Nevertheless, this is an important additional mechanism for resolving doubtful points of criminal law. The Court of Appeal may, either of its own motion or on application, refer the question to the House of Lords.

Furthermore, while the prosecution cannot appeal against sentence, the Attorney-General may refer the sentence to the Court of Appeal where it is thought unduly lenient (**Criminal Justice Act 1988, s.36**). The Court of Appeal may confirm, vary, decrease or increase the sentence, and may again use the opportunity to issue sentencing guidelines.

The role of the Criminal Cases Review Commission

Once all avenues of appeal had been explored and a conviction upheld, that was the end of the matter unless the Home Secretary exercised his/her power to refer a case back to the Court of Appeal. Successive Home Secretaries were reluctant to do this. Following a series of highly publicised miscarriages of justice (for example, the "Guildford Four", the "Birmingham Six"), the **Royal Commission on Criminal Justice (1993)** recommended this power should pass to an independent review body and the **Criminal Cases Review Commission** was established in **1997** under the **Criminal Appeal Act 1995**.

The role of the Commission is to:

- consider suspected miscarriages of justice;

- arrange for their investigation where appropriate;

- refer cases to the Court of Appeal where the investigation reveals matters that ought to be considered further by the courts;

- respond to requests for assistance from the Court of Appeal;

NOTES

- advise the Home Secretary on the granting of pardons;

- refer cases to the Home Secretary where the Commission feels a pardon should be considered.

In its first Annual Report, the Commission reported that while the initial review procedure was being completed quickly, considerable delays were occurring in dealing with those cases taken forward for detailed review. It argued that more resources were required if unacceptably long delays were to be avoided. This call for more resources was supported by the Home Affairs Select Committee. Subsequently, the Commission has reported that increases in funding have allowed it to make significant inroads into the case backlog and to reduce delays. Finally, it seems that the Commission's review and referral procedures are working well, and 66 per cent of cases referred to the Court of Appeal have resulted in the conviction being quashed. Two recent examples are the cases of Robert Brown and Anthony Steel. Robert Brown was convicted of murder in 1977. However, police had fabricated interview notes and withheld key forensic evidence from the defence. Brown's conviction was quashed by the Court of Appeal in 2002. Anthony Steel was convicted of murder in 1979. Mr Steel, who was mentally handicapped and at the borderline of abnormal suggestibility, had confessed to the crime in his sixth interview by detectives on his third day in custody. For the first day he had received no refreshments and went 37 hours without washing facilities. His conviction was quashed by the Court of Appeal in 2003.

Revision Notes

You should now write your revision notes for this topic. Here is an example for you and some suggested headings:

Crim Process③—Mode of Trial

- Either-way offences—mags determine trial venue

- Plea before venue—D indicates guilty plea—loses right to CC trial—mags dispose summarily

- D indicates not guilty plea—mags determine, but D can elect CC trial

- Criminal Procedure and Investigation Act 1996

NOTES

Crim Process①—Categories of Offence

Crim Process②—Bail

Crim Process③—Mode of Trial

Crim Process④—Ads/Disads of mags/Crown Court trial

Crim Process⑤—Youth Courts

Crim Process⑥—Summary trial and Appeals

Crim Process⑦—Trial on Indictment and Appeals

Crim Process⑧—CCRC

Using your cards, you should now be able to write a short paragraph in response to each of the following questions:

1. Explain the different categories of criminal offence.

2. Explain the law surrounding the granting/refusal of bail.

3. Discuss the procedure for determining the trial venue for either-way offences.

4. Discuss the advantages and disadvantages of trial at the magistrates' court and the Crown Court.

5. Discuss the trial of young offenders in the Youth Courts.

6. Explain the procedure for summary trials and appeals.

7. Explain the procedure for trials on indictment and appeals.

8. Discuss the role of the Criminal Cases Review Commission in dealing with alleged miscarriages of justice.

Useful Websites

- The Court Service—**www.courtservice.gov.uk**
- Home Office Criminal Justice pages—**www.homeoffice.gov.uk/justice/index.html**
- Criminal Justice System website—**www.cjsonline.gov.uk/home.html**
- Criminal Cases Review Commission website—**www.ccrc.gov.uk**
- Youth justice—**www.youth-justice-board.gov.uk**
- Judges and Schools: A Guide to Court Visits—**www.lcd.gov.uk/judicial/schools/judgesandschools.pdf**

NOTES

8 | Civil Process

Key Points

What you need to know:

- The staffing and jurisdiction of the civil courts.

- The civil process and "three-track" system.

- Routes of appeal in civil proceedings.

What you need to discuss:

- The effectiveness of the Woolf reforms to the civil process.

The English Court System

The House of Lords

- **Staff**—the Lord Chancellor presides over the House of Lords, assisted by the Lords of Appeal in Ordinary (Law Lords) and any other peer who has held high judicial office. It must sit with at least three members, though they usually sit as a court of five, each of whom can deliver an "opinion". In extremely important cases, it may sit as a court of seven.

- **Jurisdiction**—the House of Lords has little remaining original jurisdiction. It is almost exclusively concerned with hearing appeals. Though it has full civil and criminal jurisdiction, in practice it is primarily concerned with civil business.

NOTES

The Court of Appeal

- **Staff**—the Civil Division is presided over by the Master of the Rolls and the Criminal Division by the Lord Chief Justice. They are assisted by the President of the Family Division of the High Court, the Vice-Chancellor, and the Lord Justices of Appeal. It may also call on any High Court judge to sit. It normally sits as a court of three, though in exceptionally important cases it may sit as a court of five or seven. In the Civil Division, each member is entitled to deliver a judgment—though in recent years there has been a growth in the use of single, "composite" judgments. In the Criminal Division, there is usually a single judgment delivered by the presiding judge. This is to prevent uncertainty arising in the criminal law from dissenting judgments.

- **Jurisdiction**—the Court of Appeal has exclusively appellate jurisdiction.

The High Court

- **Staff**—the High Court consists of three divisions: Queen's Bench; Chancery; and Family. The Queen's Bench Division is presided over by the Lord Chief Justice, the Chancery Division by the Vice-Chancellor, and the Family Division by the President. They are assisted by High Court judges. Each division may sit with a judge alone as a Division of the High Court, or with two or more judges as a Divisional Court. The distinction between these two formats is one of jurisdiction.

- **Jurisdiction**:

  - ➤ The High Court (Queen's Bench Division) has original civil jurisdiction (principally regarding large value claims in contract and tort). It may also sit as a Commercial Court, an Admiralty Court and an Election Court.
  - ➤ The Queen's Bench Divisional Court deals with the judicial review of administrative action. It also hears applications for the writ of *habeus corpus*, and exercises appellate criminal jurisdiction, hearing appeals by way of case stated from the magistrates' court or from the magistrates' court via the Crown Court.
  - ➤ The High Court (Chancery Division) has original jurisdiction over land matters, trusts, contentious probate, company, partnership and bankruptcy matters, and intellectual property. It also hears appeals from the County Court over taxation and insolvency. It may also sit as a Patents Court.
  - ➤ The Chancery Divisional Court hears appeals regarding taxation and land registration.

NOTES

> The High Court (Family Division) has original jurisdiction over matrimonial matters, family matters and non-contentious probate.
> The Family Divisional Court hears appeals regarding family matters from the magistrates' court.

The Crown Court

- **Staff**—cases will be heard by a High Court judge, circuit judge, or recorder, depending on the gravity of the offence.

- **Jurisdiction**—the Crown Court has exclusive original jurisdiction over criminal offences tried on indictment (the most serious offences) and also hears cases involving either-way offences (less serious offences) being tried on indictment, and hears appeals from summary conviction (for minor offences) in the magistrates' courts. It also has minor civil appellate jurisdiction (for example, regarding licensing appeals from the magistrates' court).

The County Court

- **Staff**—cases in the County Court are heard by circuit judges and district judges.

- **Jurisdiction**—the County Court has exclusively original civil jurisdiction. This principally involves lesser value claims in contract and tort, together with some equity and probate matters. Some county courts are also designated divorce county courts to hear undefended divorce cases.

The magistrates' court

- **Staff**—these courts are staffed primarily by lay magistrates, though the busier metropolitan areas also use District Judges. Lay magistrates sit as a bench of three, while District Judges sit alone.

- **Jurisdiction**:
  > civil—the magistrates court has a small amount of civil jurisdiction over minor family matters, some forms of statutory debt (for example, non-payment of Council Tax) and the granting of licenses (for taxis, public houses, etc.).
  > criminal—as a summary court, the magistrates' court deals with minor criminal offences or either-way offences where the defendant is being tried summarily (together these form approximately 95 per cent of criminal trials). Magistrates have limited sentencing powers (see **Chapter 12**). Where they think the offence merits a more severe sentence, they can commit the offender for sentencing at the

Crown Court. When dealing with young offenders, specially trained magistrates sit as a Youth Court (with different procedures and powers).

Civil Process and the Three-Track System

Since April 1999, following Lord Woolf's 1996 report **Access to Justice**, civil cases have followed a new, streamlined three–track procedure with an "overriding objective" of justice, efficiency, and proportionality. The "Woolf reforms" simplified the civil process by introducing a single set of Civil Procedure Rules, by modernising terminology (for example, "plaintiff" became "claimant", and "writ" became "claim form"), by encouraging early settlement (through pre-action protocols) and alternative dispute resolution (ADR), and by introducing a streamlined "three-track system" for civil litigation with improved case management.

Pre-Action Protocols

Pre-action protocols are intended to encourage early settlement of cases without recourse to litigation:

- The claimant must send two copies of a **letter of claim** to the defendant as soon as sufficient information is available to substantiate a realistic claim and before issues of quantum (the amount of compensation) are addressed in detail.
- The defendant must reply and identify his/her insurer within 21 days.
- The defendant or insurer must reply within three months stating whether liability is denied and, if so, giving reasons.
- If the defendant denies liability, this must be accompanied by any relevant supporting documentation.
- Either party may make an offer to settle and there may be serious costs consequences if the matter comes to court and it is found that a party has unreasonably failed to make or accept such an offer.

Going to Court

Where early settlement under the protocol has not occurred, the claimant must issue a claim form in the appropriate court:

- Claims for less than £15,000 (£50,000 in personal injury claims) issued in the County Court.

NOTES

- All other claims issued in the High Court (though straightforward cases will be transferred down to the County Court).

- The court (if requested) or the claimant will serve the claim form on the defendant.

- Within 14 days, the defendant must respond with either:

  ➢ an admission;
  ➢ a defence;
  ➢ an acknowledgement of service (giving him a further 14 days to file a defence).

- Failure to respond can lead to a judgement in default against the defendant.

- Where a defence is filed, the court will then send a detailed **allocation questionnaire** to the parties. Upon receipt of the completed questionnaire, the procedural judge will then allocate the case to one of three tracks—small claims, fast, or multi-track.

The Small Claims Track

This is for claims of £5,000 or less (£1,000 or less in personal injury claims). The emphasis is on an accessible and informal process and strict rules on costs are in place to discourage professional representation.

The Fast Track

This is for cases where:

- The amount claimed is between £5,000 and £15,000 (£1,000 and £15,000 in personal injury claims).

- The trial is not expected to last more than one day.

There are rules limiting the use of expert witnesses. A timetable is set geared towards a trial date not more than 30 weeks from the allocation to the fast track. There are also fixed costs for trial advocates, with no provision for any increase in these fees should the case last longer than the one day anticipated. This is intended to discourage time wasting and encourage efficient presentation and settlement.

The Multi-Track

This will be used for claims in excess of £15,000 and lower claims of unusual complexity deemed unsuitable for the fast track. The judge allocated to the case acts as a trial manager, setting a timetable and directing the legal work to be done. In particular, s/he will chair:

NOTES

- A **Case Management Conference**, to establish the timetable.
- A **Pre-Trial Review**—approximately 8–10 weeks prior to the hearing date, in order to explore the possibility of settlement before full trial costs are incurred and, if settlement is not possible, to prepare a trial agenda.

Evaluating the Woolf reforms

The Lord Chancellor's Department has conducted two reviews of the working of the Woolf reforms since their introduction in 1999. Putting the conclusions of these reviews together with the observations of other commentators, the general assessment of the effectiveness of the reforms seems to indicate that:

- The unified Civil Procedure Rules have reduced complexity but, to the annoyance of practitioners, have been subject to frequent amendment and revision. However, this is perhaps only to be expected in the early days following such major reforms, and the system should settle down. The most recent evidence suggests that this is, in fact, happening.
- The reforms have reduced the number of claims and encouraged early settlement. The use of pre-action protocols and the shift towards alternative dispute resolution (ADR) have been successful in creating greater openness and a less adversarial culture.
- The position regarding the impact on the cost of civil proceedings, according to the Lord Chancellor's Department, "remains relatively unclear with statistics difficult to obtain and conflicting anecdotal evidence. Where there is evidence of increased costs, the causes are difficult to isolate". While the costs of the trial phase may well have fallen, it may be that there has been a "frontloading" of costs onto the pre-trial phase. It may also be that some lawyers are delaying claims, thereby lengthening the pre-trial phase and delaying the point at which they become subject to judicial case management.
- There have been considerable delays in introducing the necessary information technology into the courts, and the Lord Chancellor's Department has been criticised for failing to keep adequate controls over the costs of this project.
- Enforcement proceedings, which were untouched by the Woolf reforms, remain complex and time-consuming.

Appeals in civil proceedings

The Woolf reforms also made significant changes to the civil appeals process. The Court of Appeal gave detailed guidance on this in *Tanfern Ltd v Cameron-Macdonald* [2000]:

NOTES

- As a general rule, appeal lies to the next level of judge in the court hierarchy. Thus, appeals from a District Judge lie to a Circuit Judge, from a Circuit Judge to a High Court Judge, and from a High Court Judge to the Court of Appeal.

- As a general rule, permission is required for an appeal. Permission may be granted either by the trial court or the appeal court.

- Permission to appeal will only be given where the court considers that the appeal would have a real prospect of success or that there is some other compelling reason why the appeal should be heard. Lord Woolf has explained that the word "real" means that the prospect of success must be realistic rather than fanciful (*Swain v Hillman* [1999]). However, permission to appeal is not required for an appeal from a District Judge to a Circuit Judge regarding a decision made in the small claims track.

- If the normal route of first appeal would be to a Circuit Judge or High Court Judge, then either the trial court or the appeal court may order the appeal to be transferred to the Court of Appeal if they consider it raises an important point of law or there is some other compelling reason for the Court of Appeal to hear it.

- The appeal court will only allow an appeal where the decision of the lower court was wrong, or where it was unjust because of a serious procedural or other irregularity.

- The appeal court has the power to affirm, set aside or vary any order or judgment made by the lower court.

- Where the first appeal is made to a Circuit Judge or High Court Judge, a second appeal to the Court of Appeal is only possible where the Court of Appeal considers that the appeal raises an important point of law or there is some other compelling reason to hear it (**Access to Justice Act 1999, s.55(1)**).

Further appeal from the Court of Appeal lies to the House of Lords. The permission of either court is required. While in civil appeals there is no statutory requirement that the appeal involve a point of law of general public importance, in practice permission is unlikely to be granted unless this is the case (**Procedure Direction** [1988]).

Revision Notes

You should now write your revision notes for this chapter. Here is an example for you and some suggested headings:

NOTES

Civil Process⑤—Evaluating Woolf

- unified Civil Procedure Rules have reduced complexity, **but** have been subject to frequent amendment

- reduced number of claims and encouraged early settlement—pre-action protocols and shift to ADR successful—less adversarial culture

- position on costs unclear—"frontloading" costs onto pre-trial stage; trial phase more efficient but some lawyers delaying claim?

- delays in introducing necessary IT

- enforcement proceedings still complex and inefficient

Civil Process①—Staffing

Civil Process②—Jurisdiction

Civil Process③—Civil Process

Civil Process④—3 Track System

Civil Process⑤—Evaluating Woolf

Civil Process⑥—Civil Appeals

Using your cards, you should now be able to write a short paragraph in response to each of the following questions:

1. Describe the staffing and jurisdiction of the civil courts.

2. Describe the Woolf reforms to the civil justice system.

3. Evaluate the effectiveness of the Woolf reforms to the civil justice system.

4. Describe the appeal routes in civil cases.

Useful Websites

- The Court Service website—**www.courtservice.gov.uk**
- The Civil Justice Council website—**www.civiljusticecouncil.gov.uk**

NOTES

- Lord Woolf's Final Report—**www.lcd.gov.uk//civil/finalfr.htm**

- A useful summary of the Woolf reforms of the civil courts—**www.compactlaw.co.uk/ woolf.html**

- "Further Findings: a continuing evaluation of the civil justice reforms"—**www.lcd.gov.uk/civil/reform/ffreform.htm**

- For information on the judicial work of the House of Lords, visit **www.parliament.the‾stationery‾office.co.uk/pa/ld/ldjudinf.htm**

NOTES

9 | Alternative Dispute Resolution

Key Points

What you need to know:

- The role of tribunals.
- The role of arbitration, mediation and conciliation.
- The role of inquiries and ombudsmen.

What you need to discuss:

- The limitations of the civil courts.
- The advantages and disadvantages of tribunals.
- The advantages and disadvantages of arbitration, mediation and conciliation.
- The advantages and disadvantages of inquiries and ombudsmen.
- Whether the public are given adequate advice and guidance on the range of alternatives available.

Introduction

Many disputes are resolved informally (for example, through negotiation, concession and compromise). However, where an informal approach is unsuccessful or inappropriate, formal mechanisms must be available to ensure the dispute is resolved fairly. The traditional formal mechanism is the court system. However, for a variety of reasons, the courts themselves are not always the most suitable or appropriate method. Therefore, a range of alternative mechanisms has been developed to supplement and complement the work of the courts.

Limitations of the courts

Despite the impact of the Woolf reforms (see **Chapter 8**), the civil courts still suffer from a number of significant limitations as a forum for dispute resolution:

- **Cost**—using the civil courts remains very expensive, both for the individuals concerned and for society as a whole, and may not be justified by the value of the dispute.

- **Delay**—court proceedings are still often very time-consuming and many disputes need a more urgent solution.

- **Inaccessibility**—in addition to the factors of cost and delay, many people (particularly the least-advantaged) still find courts intimidating and inaccessible.

- **Inappropriateness**—the adversarial nature of court proceedings is often inappropriate for the type of dispute (for example, family and matrimonial disputes, especially where children are involved).

- **Incapacity**—the court system simply could not cope with all the disputes requiring formal resolution.

Nevertheless, it is important to remember that the courts still have a valuable role to play, both in resolving those disputes not suited to any alternative mechanism (for example, criminal cases), and in overseeing the work of the alternative mechanisms to ensure justice and fairness.

The main forms of alternative dispute resolution

Tribunals

- **Administrative (public) tribunals**—these are designed to deliver justice quickly, cheaply, and informally. While the large number of tribunals makes it difficult to generalise, certain common characteristics can be identified:

  - ➤ All administrative tribunals are created by statute.
  - ➤ A tribunal will usually have three members—a legally-qualified chair and two lay experts.
  - ➤ Tribunal members can usually only be dismissed with the consent of the Lord Chancellor. This is an essential safeguard against executive interference in the independence of the tribunal.
  - ➤ Procedures are kept as informal as possible. However, some tribunals (for example, the Mental Health Review Tribunal) have to be quite formal because of the importance of the issues with which they are dealing.
  - ➤ The caseload of different tribunals varies widely. Some (for example, the Social Security Appeals Tribunal) deal with thousands of cases each year, while others (for example, the Plant Varieties and Seeds Tribunal) deal with only one or two.

NOTES

> ➤ Appeal on a point of law can generally be made to the High Court.
> ➤ Tribunals are subject to the supervisory jurisdiction of the Queen's Bench Divisional Court via judicial review.
> ➤ The work of tribunals is also monitored by the Council on Tribunals (established in 1958).

- **Domestic (private) tribunals**—these are concerned with the discipline of members of a particular profession or organisation (for example, doctors, solicitors, etc.). They are subject to the same rules of natural justice and fair procedure as administrative tribunals. There may also be specific provision for appeals to the courts (for example, to the Privy Council from the General Medical Council).

- **Advantages:**

> ➤ **Cost**—tribunal proceedings are inexpensive, both in absolute terms and relative to the cost of court proceedings.
> ➤ **Speed**—proceedings are quicker than court proceedings, also helping to minimise cost.
> ➤ **Informality**—proceedings are kept as informal as possible, making them less intimidating than court proceedings and, hence, more accessible.
> ➤ **Expertise**—lay members are appointed for their expertise in the area to which the tribunal relates. The specific jurisdiction of the tribunal develops this expertise further and helps ensure consistency.
> ➤ **Capacity**—tribunals, which deal with approximately 1,000,000 cases each year, relieve the courts of an otherwise unmanageable burden.

- **Disadvantages:**

> ➤ **Poor quality decision-making**—the speed and informality of tribunal proceedings creates a risk of poor quality decision-making. However, this is guarded against through the requirements of fair procedure and natural justice, supervision by the courts, and monitoring by the Council on Tribunals.
> ➤ **Bias**—there is a risk that the use of experts may create bias against the inexpert claimant. However, this is again met by the safeguards outlined above and the requirement of balance in the membership of many tribunals (for example, employment tribunals).
> ➤ **Representation**—this is a more significant problem. While professional representation is permitted before most tribunals, legal aid was rarely available. Although an increased use of lawyers runs a risk of increased formality, it is hard to avoid the conclusion that representation should be available equally to all. This situation may improve with the introduction of more flexible arrangements under the new Community Legal Service (see **Chapter 14**).

NOTES

Furthermore, the sheer variety of tribunals can cause confusion. Following concerns regarding the haphazard growth of the tribunal system, complex routes of appeal, and the need to ensure the coherent and consistent development of the law, the Lord Chancellor established a review of the system of administrative justice under Sir Andrew Leggatt.

The Leggatt Review of Tribunals

In August 2001, Sir Andrew Leggatt published his report: *Tribunals for Users—One System, One Service*. This was the first comprehensive review of the tribunal system for 44 years. He noted that in 1999, the system as a whole disposed of nearly one million cases, and that their collective contribution not only to administrative justice but to social welfare in general was enormous. The object of the review was to recommend a system that is independent, coherent, cost-effective and user-friendly.

In order to ensure independence, he recommended that all administrative tribunals should be supported by a Tribunals Service, analogous with, but separate from, the Court Service. This would raise the status of tribunals, while preserving their distinctiveness from the courts. The role of the Service would be to provide a high quality, unified service, to operate independently, to deal openly and honestly with the users of tribunals, to seek to maintain public confidence, and to report annually on its performance.

Regarding the tribunal system itself, tribunals should do everything possible to make themselves understandable, unthreatening and useful to users. Every effort should be made to reduce the number of cases in which legal representation is needed. This should be done by ensuring that tribunal decision-makers give comprehensible decisions; that users are provided with all necessary information; that voluntary and other advice groups are funded to provide legal advice; and that tribunal chairmen are trained to provide legitimate assistance to users in understanding proceedings and presenting their case. Where legal representation is unavoidable, voluntary and community bodies should be funded to provide it. Efficiency is to be encouraged by active case management and more effective use of information technology. Procedures should be designed to ensure that cases are dealt with economically, proportionately, expeditiously and fairly, and should be set out comprehensibly in guidance notes and leaflets. The system should be divided into logical and understandable divisions: education, financial, health and social services, immigration, land and valuation, social security and pensions, transport, regulatory and employment. Each division would have its own appellate tribunal, all being grouped together within an appellate division. There should be a right of appeal on a point of law, by permission, on the generic ground that the decision of the tribunal was unlawful. All chairmen and members should be appointed by the Lord Chancellor for renewable periods of five or seven years. A common, competency-based training system should be administered by the Judicial Studies Board. The system as whole

NOTES

should be overseen and represented by a Tribunals Board, consisting of the presidents of the divisions, the Chairman of the Council on Tribunals (which would retain its present role), the Chairman of the Tribunals Committee of the Judicial Studies Board, and the Chief Executive of the Tribunals Service.

The relationship of these proposals to the earlier Woolf reforms of the civil courts, and the reforms to funding of advice and representation under the Access to Justice Act 1999 is clear, and Sir Andrew's "watchwords" of informality, simplicity, efficiency and proportionality could be argued to mark out the present approach to the administration of justice as a whole. The Lord Chancellor has announced that the main Leggatt proposals would be in effect by 2008, with a White Paper giving the details being published in Summer 2003.

Arbitration

Arbitration is the reference of a dispute to an independent third party for determination. The arbitrator (often a member of the **Chartered Institute of Arbitrators**) makes a decision known as an award. While arbitration is essentially a private arrangement, it is subject to the supervisory jurisdiction of the courts and regulated by statute. There are three areas in which arbitration is particularly common:

- **Commercial arbitration**—many commercial contracts contain an arbitration clause. This avoids the cost, time and bad feeling that is often involved in litigation, and that could damage future business relations. It is also a private arrangement that protects commercially sensitive information. While such arbitration clauses have been recognised and enforced by the courts for some time, the courts have now held that more general ADR clauses are also enforceable (*Cable & Wireless plc v IBM UK Ltd* [2002]).

- **Industrial arbitration**—arbitration is frequently used to resolve industrial disputes. The Advisory Conciliation and Arbitration Service (**ACAS**), established by the **Employment Protection Act 1975**, offers a specialised service and helps to resolve approximately 85 per cent of the disputes referred to it.

- **Consumer arbitration**—many trade associations (for example, **ABTA**), in conjunction with the **Office of Fair Trading**, operate Codes of Practice which include arbitration schemes. These offer consumers an attractive low-cost alternative to court proceedings. However, they have three main failings:

  ➤ Many consumers are unaware they exist.
  ➤ Associations have limited sanctions against traders who breach the Code.

NOTES

> ➤ Those traders most likely to cause problems are also those least likely to subscribe
>   to the Code.

The courts themselves also offer an arbitration service in the County Courts for small claims
of £5,000 or less (for more details see **Chapter 8**).

- **Advantages**—arbitration shares many of the advantages of tribunals—cost, speed,
  informality, expertise. It has the additional advantages of privacy (as noted above in
  relation to commercial arbitration) and convenience (the arbitration takes place at a
  time and place to suit the parties).

- **Disadvantages**—the potential disadvantages of poor quality decision-making and bias
  are again safeguarded against through the framework of judicial and statutory
  regulation, and frequent use of professional arbitrators.

Mediation and Conciliation

Mediation and conciliation are essentially less formal versions of arbitration—while arbitration may be seen as a form of **alternative adjudication**, it is better to think of mediation and conciliation as forms of **assisted settlement**. Here, rather than make the decision, the role of the third party is to assist the disputing parties in reaching a mutually agreed settlement.

Inquiries

An inquiry is often used to resolve issues of general public or environmental concern (for example, accident inquiries, planning inquiries). However, the length of time and cost involved limits their usefulness as an alternative to the courts. They are a highly specialised mechanism for dealing with very specific issues.

The Ombudsman

The Ombudsman (or "grievance-man") is an independent official responsible for investigating complaints of maladministration or inefficiency. This concept (which originated in Scandinavia) was first used in Britain in 1967 with the introduction of an ombudsman for central government (the **Parliamentary Commissioner for Administration**). Public ombudsmen followed for both local government and the National Health Service. The **Courts and Legal Services Act 1990** introduced ombudsmen for both legal services and conveyancing. The private sector has also used this concept, particularly in the financial services sector. As it is the only mechanism for investigating complaints, not of wrongs *per se*, but of inefficiency or poor administration, the ombudsman is a valuable addition to the range of alternatives available. However, both the uncoordinated nature of the ombudsman network and the lack

NOTES

of a regulatory framework for private sector ombudsmen have given rise to concern. A Cabinet Office review of public sector ombudsmen in 2000 recommended a new Commission integrate the present ombudsmen for national and local government and the NHS, thereby providing a simple, single gateway for complaints. It also recommended that the present requirement for complaints to be referred via MPs be abolished, allowing the public direct access to the ombudsmen service. The government response to the recommendations is still under review. Regarding the private sector, the Government has reorganised the various financial services ombudsmen into a single, statutory Financial Services Ombudsman scheme, the largest in the world.

Advice and guidance

We can argue that the consumer of the services of these various dispute resolution mechanisms is not given adequate guidance in choosing the one most appropriate to their needs. In some parts of the USA a "multi-door" courthouse approach is used. Here, the person with a dispute is seen first by an "intake specialist" who advises them on the best method to use. Given that the local courthouse is not the focus of the community in Britain that it is in the USA, this is a service that might be best performed here by the Citizens Advice Bureaux. It may be that the introduction of the new Community Legal Service will facilitate such a development. The Lord Chancellor's Department published a consultation paper in 1999 on ways in which access to and use of ADR could be improved. Following this, the Government announced its "ADR pledge" in 2001, stating that Government Departments will go to court only as a last resort, and that Government legal disputes will be settled by mediation or arbitration whenever possible. In 2002, the Treasury Solicitor's Department has estimated an overall saving of legal costs of £2.5m through the use of ADR in the first year of the pledge. Finally, the potential of new information and communications technology has also opened the way for **Online Dispute Resolution (ODR)**, though this is still very much in its infancy.

Conclusion

The English legal system offers a wide range of mechanisms for the formal resolution of disputes. The various alternatives outlined above are an essential complement to the work of the courts, often offering the prospect of a remedy where otherwise none might exist. Nevertheless, the courts still perform a valuable role—both in resolving disputes not suitable for any alternatives (for example, criminal cases) and in supervising the work of the alternative mechanisms. However, more advice and guidance should be given to ensure the most appropriate use is made of the mechanisms available. We can only hope that the various

NOTES

reviews currently being undertaken, together with the new Community Legal Service, will bring this about.

Revision Notes

You should now write your revision notes for this topic. Here is an example for you and some suggested headings:

ADR⑦—*Inquiries*

- used to resolve issues of general public or environmental concern
- *e.g.* accident inquiries, planning inquiries
- cost and time involved limits usefulness
- highly specialised mechanism for specific types of dispute

ADR①—Intro

ADR②—Limits on Courts

ADR③—Admin Tribunals

ADR④—Domestic Tribunals

ADR⑤—Ads/Disads of Tribunals

ADR⑥—Arbitration, Mediation & Conciliation

ADR⑦—Inquiries

ADR⑧—Ombudsmen

ADR⑨—Advice & Guidance

Using your cards, you should now be able to write a short paragraph in response to each of the following questions:

1. What are the limitations of the courts as a forum for resolving disputes?
2. What important roles do the courts continue to play?
3. Discuss the contribution made by tribunals to dispute resolution.

NOTES

4. What are the advantages and disadvantages of arbitration, mediation and conciliation?

5. Discuss the role of inquiries.

6. How effective is the contribution made by the various ombudsmen schemes?

7. Do consumers receive adequate advice and guidance on the range of dispute resolution mechanisms available to them?

Useful Websites

- General information on resolving disputes without going to court—**www.lcd.gov.uk/civil/adr/index.htm** and **www.legalservices.gov.uk/leaflets/cls/alternatives-to-court-23.htm**
- The Leggatt review of tribunals—**www.tribunals-review.org.uk/leggatthtm/leg-00.htm**
- Government response to Leggatt—**www.lcd.gov.uk/civil/tribunals.htm**
- More information on arbitration and mediation—**www.arbitrators.org**, **www.acas.org.uk**, and **www.mediationuk.org.uk**
- More information on the various ombudsmen, and links to individual sites—**www.bioa.org.uk**
- Cabinet Office report, "Review of the Public Sector Ombudsmen in England"—**www.cabinet_office.gov.uk/central/ombudsmenreview.pdf**
- The Lord Chancellor's Department discussion paper and the summary of responses—**www.lcd.gov.uk/consult/civ_just/adr/indexfr.htm** and **www.lcd.gov.uk/consult/civ-just/adr/adrrespfr.htm**
- The Government "ADR pledge" and subsequent report—**www.lcd.gov.uk/civil/adr/index.htm**
- Information on ODR, **www.odrnews.com/whatis.htm**

10 The Legal Profession

Key Points

What you need to know:

- The role, training and work of barristers.
- The role, training and work of solicitors.
- The role of paralegals.
- The role of the Crown Prosecution Service.

What you need to discuss:

- The social, racial and gender composition of the profession.
- The efficiency of a formally divided profession.
- The accountability of the profession for the quality of the service it provides.

Introduction

The legal profession in England and Wales is divided into two branches—barristers and solicitors. In general terms, the **barrister** may be thought of as the **legal consultant** and the **solicitor** as the **legal general practitioner**. Solicitors are often assisted by **legal executives**.

Barristers

Work and organisation

There were approximately **10,300** practising barristers in 2003, most based in London. Their governing body is the General Council of the Bar (the **Bar Council**). The Bar Council is responsible for education and training, regulating professional conduct and ethics, handling complaints against barristers, and representing the interests of the Bar as a whole. The most visible aspect of their work is **advocacy** (presenting a case in court). However, barristers specialising in some areas of the law (for example, revenue law) rarely appear in court. Barristers also deal with a considerable amount of **pre-trial paperwork** (especially in civil cases), and giving **opinions** (a considered view of the merits of a case). They also spend time in **conferences** with solicitors and clients.

Training and career

The Bar is largely a graduate profession. Law graduates take a one-year vocational course (with an emphasis on skills)—the **Bar Vocational Course** (BVC)—organised by the Bar Council. Non-law graduates take the one-year **Common Professional Examination** (CPE) before going on to the BVC. This is followed by a further year of training (**pupillage**) with a qualified and experienced barrister. The trainee must also join one of the four **Inns of Court**.

Having completed training, newly qualified barristers must find a place in chambers from which to practise. **Chambers** is a set of offices from which a group of barristers practise (though they remain self-employed), sharing the running costs and the services of a clerk (who negotiates fees and allocates work). However, vacancies in chambers are limited, and in recent years some new barristers have had to accept unofficial residence as "squatters". New barristers must also undertake the **New Practitioners Programme** during their first three years' practice, and from 2001 all barristers have been required to undertake a programme of **Continuing Professional Development**.

Once qualified, the barrister will be known as a **junior** and remains so throughout his or her career unless promoted to the ranks of **Queen's Counsel** (Q.C. or "silk"). This is an honorific title awarded by the Queen on the advice of the Lord Chancellor. For the barrister, it means higher fees and an increased chance of becoming a judge. It is also said to indicate the most experienced and able barristers. However, as no interview or examination is held, it is difficult to regard it as a reliable indicator. In 2001, the Office of Fair Trading published a critical report, *Competition in Professions*, that expressed serious doubts over the value of the Q.C. system as a quality mark. In particular, it was concerned that there was no continuous quality appraisal to ensure that the award of Q.C. status remains justified, that there is inadequate peer review on selection, and that there are no professional examinations or assessment that must be taken in order to become a Q.C. In 2003, the Lord Chancellor announced a consultation exercise on the Q.C. system, with options including its abolition.

Most barristers remain self-employed, though some do go into employment in both the private and public sectors.

Notes

Solicitors

Work and organisation

This is the larger of the two branches, with approximately **89,000** practising solicitors in England and Wales in 2002 (with around 80 per cent working in private practice). Their governing body is the **Law Society**. The Law Society sees its role as threefold: as **regulator**, it oversees training, professional standards, and handles complaints; as **campaigner**, it represents the interests of solicitors in general; as **service provider**, it provides a range of services, including training and publications. In addition to self-regulation by the Bar Council and Law Society, the **Access to Justice Act 1999** established a new regulatory body for the profession as a whole—the **Legal Services Consultative Panel**. Solicitors' work involves giving general advice and the administration of clients' legal affairs. Typically, around 80 per cent of solicitors' work involves conveyancing, commercial, matrimonial and probate cases. Solicitors are also engaged in advocacy. Almost all advocacy in the magistrates' courts is undertaken by solicitors, and the abolition of barristers' monopoly of rights of audience in the higher courts was begun under the **Courts and Legal Services Act 1990**, with further measures following in the **Access to Justice Act 1999**, designed to make it easier for solicitor-advocates with appropriate qualifications and experience to appear in the higher courts.

Training and career

As with the Bar, most new entrants to this branch of the profession are graduates, though other possibilities exist (notably progression from a legal executive). Law graduates undertake a one-year vocational course, the **Legal Practice Course**, organised by the Law Society. Non-law graduates must precede this by taking the CPE (see above). This is followed by a two-year **training contract** with a qualified and experienced solicitor. During this period, the trainee solicitor must also complete the **Professional Skills Course**. All solicitors must undertake an on-going programme of **Continuing Professional Development**.

Newly qualified solicitors generally seek employment with an established practice as an assistant solicitor. They may then aspire to partnership or establish their own practice. Alternatively, they may obtain employment in both the public and private sectors.

Paralegals

Paralegals are people with some legal training, but who are not fully professionally qualified as either barristers or solicitors. Some paralegals (for example, **licensed conveyancers**) are of relatively recent creation. The longest established form of paralegal is the **legal executive**.

NOTES

Legal executives perform professional work under the guidance of a solicitor, tending to specialise in particular areas of law. Their governing body is the **Institute of Legal Executives**. Once qualified, they are entitled to undertake the Law Society training programme and qualify as a solicitor. Legal executives are also required to undertake an ongoing programme of **Continuing Professional Development**.

The Crown Prosecution Service

Since 1985, a new employment opportunity in the public sector for barristers and solicitors has been the **Crown Prosecution Service** (which also employs unqualified staff). The CPS, headed by the **Director of Public Prosecutions (DPP)**, was established by the **Prosecution of Offences Act 1985** to take over the greater part of the police role in prosecutions. The police are still responsible for charging a person with an offence. However, the **Criminal Justice Bill 2003** proposes to transfer responsibility for charging to the CPS, as pilot studies have shown that where the CPS has responsibility for charging, there is a significant increase in guilty pleas and convictions. Thereafter, the CPS is responsible for the conduct of the prosecution, including reviewing at all stages whether or not it should be continued.

The **Code for Crown Prosecutors** (issued by the DPP under **s.10** of the **1985 Act**) creates a two-part test for the continuation of prosecutions:

- **Evidential sufficiency**—there must be admissible, substantial and reliable evidence that the accused committed the offence. There must also be a realistic prospect of conviction, not merely a bare prima facie case.

- **Public interest**—the prosecution must also be in the public interest. The Code specifies a number of relevant considerations, including:

  - The likely penalty—the prosecutor must be satisfied that the likely penalty justifies the time and cost of proceedings.
  - Discrimination—whether the offence was motivated by discrimination against the victim on grounds of race, sex, religion, political views or sexual orientation.
  - Staleness—the prosecutor should be cautious in proceeding if the last offence was committed more than three years prior to the likely date of trial.
  - Youth—serious consideration should be given to the alternative of a caution (where appropriate) in cases involving young offenders.
  - Old age—except where the offence is a serious one, the prosecutor should be cautious in continuing proceedings against the elderly and infirm.

NOTES

> Mental illness—caution should be exercised in proceedings against the mentally ill, taking into account the likely effect of proceedings on the person's mental health.
> The attitude of the victim.
> Peripheral involvement—in general, proceedings should only be taken against those centrally involved in the offence.

If the prosecutor is still in doubt, he should consider the attitude of the local community and the prevalence of the offence. If still in doubt, the decision should be to prosecute.

There are special guidelines for the prosecution of juveniles. The prosecutor should consider the general issue of the juvenile's welfare, and there is a presumption in favour (where appropriate) of alternatives to prosecution (for example, cautions).

In 2001, an independent report by Sylvia Denman, commissioned by the CPS, condemned the CPS as "institutionally racist". It found that racist attitudes among CPS staff meant that a disproportionately high number of black and Asian people are being sent for trial.

An analysis of the present organisation of the profession

Social composition

Most entrants to the profession come from a middle-class background. Both women and the ethnic minorities have been significantly under-represented. We can argue that this deters able people from alternative backgrounds entering the profession and may also create a social distance between professional and client, contributing to the inaccessibility of the profession both as career and service.

However, the profession has taken some measures to address this. The Law Society has programmes to encourage women and ethnic minorities and the Bar Council has a number of scholarships. Also, the **1990 Act** places barristers under the obligations of the **Sex Discrimination Act 1975** and the **Race Relations Act 1976** when allocating pupillage and tenancies.

Furthermore, this situation is not unique to the legal profession. Where entry to higher education is still largely limited to the middle class, it is not surprising that this is reflected in an essentially graduate profession. Nevertheless, the situation has improved in recent years. Women now account for a third of all solicitors, and over half of all newly qualified solicitors are women and around 15 per cent from the ethnic minorities. However, it seems clear that discrimination still occurs. For example, Law Society statistics for 2002 show that the median

NOTES

salary for male assistant solicitors is approximately £42,000, whereas the median salary for female assistant solicitors is only approximately £32,000. Furthermore, an Inns of Court inquiry in 2002 found evidence of "systematic ethnic bias" at the Bar. In particular, the inquiry was highly critical of the disbursement of £2 million in discretionary funding for training, with almost 60 per cent of white applicants being successful as contrasted with only 26 per cent of ethnic minority applicants. Also, responding to critical reports by both the Office of Fair Trading and the Commission for Judicial Appointments, the Bar Council has acknowledged that the process for appointing Q.C.s needs radical reform to create a level playing field for female and ethnic minority applicants.

Therefore, further long-term measures need to be taken both to ensure the profession reflects more accurately the social, gender and ethnic composition of the society it serves, and to remove what might be termed the institutional discrimination that persists within the profession. However, recent and proposed changes to the funding of undergraduate and postgraduate study have fuelled fears that the progress of recent years may be quickly reversed. The prospect of university fees of around £20,000 together with fees in the region of £5,000 for the CPE and £6,000 for the LPC may well deter students from poorer backgrounds pursuing a legal career. Attempts have been made to counter this, such as the introduction of a minimum wage of £10,000 for pupil barristers. However, a survey by BDO Stoy Hayward found that this requirement is deterring chambers from recruiting. The survey estimated that that up to 139 out of 700 pupillages could be lost in 2003. Furthermore, the Bar Council has recently been forced to abandon plans to place a levy on barristers in order to widen access to the Bar. Opposition to the proposals was strongest from commercial and chancery barristers, the two best-paid areas of practice.

Efficiency of a divided profession

The formal division of the profession has been controversial for some years. Both the **Benson Commission** (1979) and **Marre Committee** (1988) argued for retaining the division. However, a significant body of opinion continues to argue for fusion into a single profession. While this may have some advantages (for example, some reduction in the cost of legal services) there are also potential disadvantages (for example, a possible decline in the availability of specialists). Also, in those jurisdictions (for example, the USA) where there is no formal (*de jure*) division, there still tends to be an informal (*de facto*) distinction between office lawyers and trial lawyers. It would seem, therefore, that the fusion debate is inconclusive. Further- more, both the **1990** and **1999 Acts** have removed many of the distinctions between the two branches, notably regarding advocacy rights, and the Bar Council has recently approved draft proposals to allow direct access by the public to barristers, and it will be some time before the consequences of these reforms can be fully assessed. That said, a report by the Office of Fair Trading in 2001 criticised the structure of the legal profession as anti-competitive and against the interests of consumers. It was also critical of the Q.C. system.

NOTES

Accountability

It has often been argued that the profession is insufficiently accountable for the quality of the service it provides. A particular concern related to the professional immunity in contract and tort for negligent advocacy (the "advocate's immunity"). This extended to the conduct of a case in court (*Rondel v Worsley* [1967]) and pre-trial work closely connected with it (*Saif Ali v Sydney Mitchell & Co* [1978]). The immunity was justified as being in the public interest—the advocate has a duty to the court as well as to the client, and should not be deterred in the performance of this duty by the threat of litigation. However, some argued that it was difficult to see why lawyers should be more privileged than other professional groups (*e.g.* doctors, accountants), particularly when it is remembered that the issue is liability for negligence, not mere errors of judgement. The House of Lords recently reviewed all the arguments for and against the immunity, together with the experience in other jurisdictions (*e.g.* Canada and South Africa) where there is no similar immunity, and held that it could no longer be justified (*Arthur J. S. Hall & Co v Simons* [2000]). Therefore, an advocate (whether barrister or solicitor) may now be sued for negligent advocacy in both civil and criminal cases.

The profession has sought to address public concerns over quality by introducing the **Barmark** and **Lexcel** quality assurance schemes, certified by the British Standards Institute. The dissatisfied client may also complain to the appropriate governing body. The Bar Council has a **Complaints Department**, and the Law Society has the **Office for the Supervision of Solicitors (OSS)**. This self-regulation was strengthened by the **1990 Act**, which established a **Legal Services Ombudsman** (to deal with complaints about the way in which the governing body has dealt with a complaint). The **1999 Act** extends the powers of the Ombudsman, in particular giving him the power to order compensation payments. Following concerns over the effectiveness of self-regulation, in particular the length of time complainants are waiting for decisions from the OSS, the **1999 Act** also makes provision for a **Legal Services Complaints Commissioner**. The Commissioner would have the power to set targets for the handling of complaints, require improvements to be made, and impose penalties on the professional bodies. However, the Government indicated it would not appoint a Commissioner for at least 18 months, and only then if the professional bodies have failed to improve performance. Nevertheless, the 2002 annual report of the Legal Services Ombudsman was highly critical of the performance of the OSS in dealing with complaints about solicitors' work. Without urgent and substantial improvement, the report stated, solicitors run the risk of losing their right to self-regulation. In this respect, the Law Society seems to have taken up permanent residence at the "last chance saloon". In a further attempt to improve the performance and image of the profession, the Law Society launched a "Client's Charter" in 2003. By contrast, the report praised the performance of the Bar Council in handling complaints about barristers. However, following an independent survey by MORI of complainants in 2003 which found that 74 per cent of complainants were very dissatisfied, the Bar Council has announced its intention to review and revise its complaints procedures.

NOTES

Conclusion

Both the profession and Parliament, through the **1990** and **1999 Acts**, have taken some measures to address criticisms made of its present organisation. These may hasten the decline of the "old professionalism" (that discouraged participation and accountability) and encourage the development of a "new professionalism" (committed to the provision of efficient, accessible and accountable services). Nevertheless, concerns remain, most notably regarding the status of women and ethnic minorities within the profession and the handling of complaints by both the Law Society and Bar Council.

Revision Notes

You should now write your revision notes for this topic. Here is an example for you and some suggested headings:

Prof④—Paralegals

- paralegal = some legal training but not fully prof. qualifed
- some recent—*e.g.* licensed conveyancers
- longest est. = legal execs (work with solicitors, often specialise, ILEX, CPD, can go on to become solicitor)

Prof①—Intro

Prof②—Barristers

Prof③—Solicitors

Prof④—Paralegals

Prof⑤—Crown Prosecution Service

Prof⑥—Social Composition

Prof⑦—Efficiency

Prof⑧—Accountability

Prof⑨—Conclusion

Using your cards, you should now be able to write a short paragraph in response to each of the following questions:

1. Briefly outline the different types of legal professional.

2. Describe the work and training of Barristers and the role of the Bar Council.

3. Describe the work and training of solicitors and the role of the Law Society.

4. Describe the role of paralegals.

5. Describe the functions of the Crown Prosecution Service.

6. Would you regard the present social composition of the profession as satisfactory?

7. Is the formal division between barristers and solicitors an efficient way to provide legal services?

8. Do you think the profession is sufficiently accountable to its clients?

Useful Websites

- Barristers and the Bar Council—**www.barcouncil.org.uk**

- Queen's Counsel—**www.lcd.gov.uk/judicial/qcinfofr.htm**

- Solicitors and the Law Society—**www.lawsociety.org.uk** and **www.research.lawsociety.org.uk**

- The Law Society Client's Charter— **www.lawsociety.org.uk/dcs/pdf/CCG_charter_english.pdf**

- A Recent History of Discrimination in the Legal Profession—Penny Darbyshire— **www.sweetandmaxwell.co.uk/online/eddey/13art.cfm**

- Legal executives and the Institute of Legal Executives—**www.ilex.org.uk**

- Council of Licensed Conveyancers—**www.theclc.gov.uk**

- Crown Prosecution Service—**www.cps.gov.uk**

- Code for Crown Prosecutors—**www.cps.gov.uk/Home/CodeForCrownProsecutors/**

- The Denman Report—Race Discrimination in the Crown Prosecution Service, by Sylvia Denman—**www.cps.gov.uk/Home/CPSPublications/denmanreport.pdf**

- Legal Services Ombudsman—**www.olso.org**

NOTES

11 The Judiciary

Key Points

What you need to know:

- The functions of the judge.
- The different types of judge and the courts in which they sit.
- The role of the Lord Chancellor.

What you need to discuss:

- The constitutional position of the Lord Chancellor.
- The effectiveness of the appointments and training process in producing a competent and representative judiciary.
- The nature and importance of judicial independence.

Introduction

The judge performs a number of important functions:

- The judge supervises the conduct of the trial.
- The judge decides any questions of law that arise during the trial.
- In most civil cases, the judge also decides questions of fact, reaches a verdict and awards a remedy.
- In serious criminal trials, the judge sums up the evidence to the jury and directs them as to the law they must apply in reaching their verdict. Following conviction, it is the judge who passes sentence.
- In performing the above, the judge must interpret and apply both statute and common law. This is a particularly important aspect of the work of judges in the superior courts.

Given this central role, both in the administration of justice and the development of the law, it is essential that the systems for the appointment, training and management of judges provide a judiciary that is competent, representative, and independent.

Judicial Appointments and Training

Most judicial appointees are barristers, and although recent legislation has increased the potential for solicitor-judges, this is likely to remain the case for the foreseeable future. Appointments (excluding senior judicial offices) are made by the Lord Chancellor. For junior judicial posts (District Judge, Recorder and Circuit Judge), appointment is by application and interview (with consideration being given to an assessment exercise including role-play). Applications are invited for appointment as a High Court Judge, although there is no interview and the Lord Chancellor is not restricted to appointing only those who apply. Appointment as Lord Justice of Appeal and Lord of Appeal in Ordinary (Law Lord) is by invitation.

Judge	Qualifications	Appointment	Court	Salary (as at April 1, 2003)
Lord of Appeal in Ordinary	Generally appointed from among the experienced judges of the Court of Appeal	By The Queen on the recommendation of the Prime Minister, who receives advice from the Lord Chancellor.	House of Lords	£ 175,055
Lord Justice of Appeal	The statutory qualification is a 10 year High Court qualification or to be a judge of the High Court. Appointment is usually on promotion from the ranks of experienced High Court Judges.	By The Queen on the recommendation of the Prime Minister, who receives advice from the Lord Chancellor.	Court of Appeal	£ 166,394

High Court Judge	The statutory qualification is a 10 year High Court qualification or to have been a Circuit Judge for at least two years.	By The Queen on the recommendation of the Lord Chancellor.	High Court	£ 147,198
Circuit Judge	The statutory qualification is a 10 year Crown Court or 10 year County Court qualification, or to be a Recorder, or to be the holder of one of a number of other judicial offices of at least three years' standing in a full-time capacity.	By The Queen on the recommendation of the Lord Chancellor.	Crown Court County Court	£ 110,362
Recorder	The statutory qualification for appointment as a Recorder is a 10 year Crown Court or 10 year County Court qualification.	By The Queen on the recommendation of the Lord Chancellor.	Crown Court County Court	
District Judge	The statutory qualification is a seven year general qualification.	By the Lord Chancellor.	County Court	£ 88,546 (£92,546 in London)
District Judge (Magistrates' Court)	The statutory qualification is a seven year general qualification.	By The Queen on the recommendation of the Lord Chancellor.	Magistrates' Court	£ 88,546 (£92,546 in London)

NOTES

The senior judicial offices are:

- **Lord Chancellor**—this is a political appointment, made by the monarch on the advice of the Prime Minister. The Lord Chancellor is a senior member of the Government, and the Lord Chancellor's Department is responsible for most aspects of the administration of justice (though some fall under the Home Office). Therefore, the Lord Chancellor is a senior member of the Executive, the head of the Judiciary, and an important figure in the Legislature (as Speaker of the House of Lords). This is a peculiar constitutional position and clearly at odds with the theory of the separation of powers (which holds that the three branches of the State should be separate, each acting as a check and balance on the others). Calls to reform the role of the Lord Chancellor have become increasingly widespread and well-founded. In 1999, the law reform group *Justice* referred to the Chancellor's dual role of justice minister and head of the judiciary as "inherently flawed". The implementation of the **Human Rights Act 1998** may well require reform of the judicial appointments process in order to comply with the right to a fair trial before an independent and impartial tribunal under **Art.6** of the **European Convention on Human Rights**. In 2000, an ESRC-funded report by Professor Diana Woodhouse called for the office of Lord Chancellor to be abolished, with a Minister of Justice taking over its political responsibilities, while the Lord Chief Justice would become head of the judiciary. Judges would be appointed by an independent commission. In 2003, a Bar Council working party headed by Sir Iain Glidewell called for an independent system for appointments to the High Court bench. Also in 2003, a report prepared for the Council of Europe by Erik Jurgens (a Dutch professor of constitutional law) stated that the Lord Chancellor's triple role contravened the European Convention on Human Rights, and that at the least the Lord Chancellor should give up his judicial role.

  The arguments for a Minister of Justice, accountable to the House of Commons in the same way as any other minister are difficult to counter. Similarly, the need for an independent Judicial Appointments Commission is arguably both clear and urgent. Not only is it likely to be required under **the Human Rights Act**, a 1999 study (*Paths to Justice*, funded by the Nuffield Foundation) by Professor Hazel Genn found that only 53 per cent of people interviewed believed they would get a fair trial in an English court, with two-thirds perceiving judges as out of touch with ordinary people. Reform of the way judges are appointed is essential in rebuilding public confidence in the judicial process itself.

  This need not, however, require the abolition of the ancient office of Lord Chancellor. It may be argued that the Lord Chief Justice already enjoys a very full role, and the House of Lords, effectively now a Supreme Court, will still need a presiding judge. It may be better to retain the office of Lord Chancellor in its judicial capacity, while

NOTES

divesting it of its executive and legislative responsibilities—a separation of powers many would argue is long overdue. In response to these concerns, the Lord Chancellor announced a consultation exercise in 2003 on the creation of an independent judicial appointments commission.

- **Lord Chief Justice**—this is the senior full-time judicial appointment. The Lord Chief Justice presides over the Court of Appeal (Criminal Division) and the Queen's Bench Division of the High Court.

- **Master of the Rolls**—presides over the Court of Appeal (Civil Division).

- **Vice-Chancellor**—while the Lord Chancellor is officially the head of the Chancery Division of the High Court, in practice he never sits as such, and the Vice-Chancellor is, therefore, its effective head.

- **President of the Family Division of the High Court**—presides over the Family Division of the High Court.

The Heads of Division (the Lord Chief Justice, the Master of the Rolls, the President of the Family Division and the Vice-Chancellor) are appointed by The Queen on the recommendation of the Prime Minister, who receives advice from the Lord Chancellor. Before giving advice the Lord Chancellor customarily consults senior members of the judiciary. The statutory qualification is to be qualified for appointment as a Lord Justice of Appeal or to be a judge of the Court of Appeal. In practice, Heads of Division are generally appointed from among the Lords of Appeal in Ordinary or Lords Justices of Appeal.

Judges hold office "during good behaviour". Judges in the High Court and above can only be dismissed for a breach of this obligation or by an address in both Houses of Parliament. Circuit Judges, Recorders, and District Judges may be dismissed by the Lord Chancellor for incapacity or misbehaviour. Otherwise, judges remain in office until either resignation or retirement at 70.

New judicial appointees receive little formal training. Since 1979, training has been administered by the **Judicial Studies Board**, and consists on a one-week residential course following appointment (with an emphasis on procedure and sentencing, though there are also presentations on issues such as racial awareness—a 2003 study by Oxford and Birmingham Universities for the Lord Chancellor's Department demonstrated significantly less dissatisfaction than expected from ethnic minority defendants, and has been taken as evidence of the success of racial awareness training for judges and magistrates). This is followed by at least one week sitting alongside an experienced judge. Thereafter, the judge will attend occasional refresher courses and seminars.

NOTES

Evaluation

The appointments process is too informal and secret. There is considerable support for the establishment of an independent Judicial Appointments Commission (with both professional and lay representation) to oversee a more formal and open process. In 1999, a report by Dr Kate Malleson, commissioned by the Lord Chancellor, criticised the present system as an "old boys' network" which favours barristers, and which puts solicitors, women and ethnic minorities at a disadvantage. It is argued that an independent commission is not only necessary to broaden the social, racial and gender composition of the judiciary, but also to comply with the **Human Rights Act 1998**. A survey by the Labour Research Department in 2002 demonstrated that the judiciary remains as white and public school-educated today as it was 10 years ago. 67 per cent of judges had received a public school education. Over the decade, while women judges had risen from 6 per cent to 8.9 per cent of the total, this is hardly remarkable progress, and less than 1 per cent of judges are drawn from the ethnic minorities. While it is unclear the extent to which, if at all, this social exclusivity damages judicial performance, it certainly seems to damage public confidence. As noted above, a 1999 study by Professor Hazel Genn found that two-thirds of people regarded judges as out of touch with the lives of ordinary people, and only 53 per cent thought they would get a fair hearing in an English court. Following a report by Sir Leonard Peach in 1999, the Lord Chancellor appointed a Judicial Appointments Commissioner to monitor the existing appointments system for judges and Q.C.s. This move was criticised as being only a half-hearted attempt at reform. Nevertheless, the first annual report of the Commissioner for Judicial Appointments in 2002 was highly critical of the appointments process—especially the lack of transparency in the consultation or "secret soundings" process regarding the suitability of applicants for appointment, referring to "anecdote, gossip, hearsay, irrelevant, self-indulgent comments". The process, the report stated, still produces a judiciary that is "overwhelmingly white, male, and from a narrow social and educational background". Responding to the report, Dr Kate Malleson observed that recent reforms to judicial appointments "may well help to improve the judicial appointments process, but they cannot address the core problem. Until the consultations process is removed or radically reformed there will never be a level playing field for all well-qualified applicants". Therefore, it remains the case that urgent steps need to be taken to broaden the social, ethnic and gender composition of the judiciary, and to restore public confidence in the administration of justice.

The age of the judiciary. Most judges are appointed in their early 50s and the retirement age is 70. It can be argued that this contributes to judicial remoteness. However, the only way of appointing younger judges would be to establish a career judiciary (such as that in France), where younger lawyers elect to undertake further training for a judicial career.

Judicial performance has been subject to increasing media criticism. Judges do, from time to time, make observations and pass sentences that seem to be out of step with public opinion.

NOTES

While such instances are rare, and the appeal process exists to correct any mistakes or unfairness that results, it is possible that this further damages public confidence in the judiciary. However, we must remember that media criticism is not always well-founded, with judges sometimes blamed for defects in the law over which they have no control.

The training programme is inadequate. Again, this could probably only be remedied with the establishment of a career judiciary.

Judicial Independence

The independence of the judiciary is a necessary condition of impartiality and, therefore, of a fair trial. This means that judges should be free from pressure by the executive, particular interest groups, and litigants.

Formal independence is guaranteed in a number of ways:

- Salaries and pensions are determined by an independent review body.

- Judges should not hold any other paid appointment or carry on any other profession or business while in office.

- Judges should disqualify themselves from any case where they might (or might appear to) be biased or in which they have a personal interest. This emphasises the importance of appearances—not only must justice be done, it must also be seen to be done. The importance attached to this is clear from the controversy surrounding the participation of **Lord Hoffmann** in the *Pinochet* case in 1998.

- Judges cannot be sued for acts either done within jurisdiction or which they honestly believed at the time to be within jurisdiction (*Sirros v Moore* [1975]). This immunity rests on the public interest justification that judges should not be deterred in the performance of their duties by the threat of litigation.

The **informal independence** of the judiciary from the other branches of the State is less certain. This independence is essential if the judiciary is to act as an effective check on the executive via judicial review. Some (for example, John Griffith in *The Politics of the Judiciary*) have argued that judges cannot, because of their background and position, be politically neutral and tend to be conservative in outlook. Others (for example, Lord Denning) have argued that the judges are perfectly capable of providing an effective check on government. While recent evidence, such as rulings on the legality of government policy regarding the entitlement of asylum seekers to welfare benefits, would seem to support the latter view, the introduction of the **Human Rights Act 1998** has ensured that this issue will continue to be debated.

Conclusion

It seems clear that in order both to restore and maintain public confidence in the judiciary, and meet the requirements of the **Human Rights Act 1998**, urgent steps need to be taken to:

- reform the role of the Lord Chancellor and the way in which judges are appointed;
- improve the scope and effectiveness of judicial training;
- broaden the class, gender, and racial composition of the judiciary,

in order to ensure we have a competent, representative, and independent judiciary capable of administering justice fairly, efficiently and effectively.

Revision Notes

You should now write your revision notes for this topic. Here is an example for you and some suggested headings:

> *Judges③—Lord Chancellor*
>
> - political appt by Queen on advice of PM
> - senior cabinet minister (LCD responsible for admin of justice)
> - also head of judiciary and senior member of H of L
> - contradicts separation of powers
> - recent suggestions (*e.g. Justice,* Woodhouse report) for new Minister of Justice—may well be necessary under HRA'98

Judges①—Intro

Judges②—Appointments

NOTES

Judges③—Lord Chancellor

Judges④—Training

Judges⑤—Evaluation

Judges⑥—Independence

Judges⑦—Conc

Using your cards, you should now be able to write a short paragraph in response to each of the following questions:

1. Identify the various functions performed by the judge.

2. Describe the appointment and training of judges.

3. Comment on the status and role of the Lord Chancellor.

4. Does the present appointments and training process produce and competent and representative judiciary?

5. What reforms might be made to improve or replace the present system?

6. Why is judicial independence important and how effectively is it ensured?

Useful Websites

- The appointment of judges, Sir Leonard Peach's report, and the Commission for Judicial Appointments—**www.lcd.gov.uk/judicial/judgesfr.htm**
- The training of judges and the Judicial Studies Board site—**www.jsboard.co.uk**

Notes

12 Magistrates and Juries

Key Points

What You Need to Know:

- The selection, appointment and role of the magistrate.
- The selection and role of the jury.

What You Need to Discuss:

- The social, racial and gender composition of the magistracy.
- The arguments for and against lay magistrates.
- The arguments for and against the use of the jury.

Introduction

One of the more remarkable features of the English legal system is the extent to which lay persons (people without formal legal qualifications) are involved in the administration of justice, particularly the criminal justice system. Some lay persons are brought into the system for their particular expertise (for example, tribunal members and lay assessors in the Admiralty Court). However, the principal justification for the two main lay institutions, the **magistracy** and the **jury**, is their **amateur** nature. This is intended to ensure the values and common sense of ordinary people have a role to play in the system, thereby preventing it becoming the property of a legal elite and remote from the concerns of ordinary citizens. Both these institutions have a long history. The first magistrates (also known as Justices of the Peace) were appointed in 1195 and assumed a judicial role in the fourteenth Century. The importance of the jury in deciding criminal trials dates from 1215 and the decision of the Fourth Lateran Council to withdraw Church support for trial by ordeal. By 1367 it was established that the jury's verdict had to be unanimous, and in **Bushell's Case** [1670] it was established the jury had the right to bring in a verdict according to its conscience.

NOTES

Magistrates

There are approximately 30,000 lay magistrates in England and Wales. While they do have some civil jurisdiction (for example, some family and licensing matters), their main responsibilities concern the criminal law. Approximately 95 per cent of all criminal trials take place in the magistrates' court. These summary trials mostly take place before a bench of three lay magistrates. In busy city courts, they may take place before a professional magistrate—a District Judge (Magistrates' Court)—sitting alone. In addition to summary trials, magistrates also deal with Early Administrative Hearings, applications for bail and warrants, and other associated matters. When dealing with someone convicted of a summary offence, the magistrates have the following sentencing powers:

- Maximum of 6 months' imprisonment. **[The Criminal Justice Bill proposes to increase this to 12 months]**

- Maximum fine of £1,000.

- Community sentences (for example, Community Rehabilitation Orders).

- Compensation order (maximum of £5,000).

- Absolute or conditional discharge.

Lay magistrates are part-time, amateur judges. They are unpaid, though they do receive allowances for travel, subsistence and loss of earnings. No formal qualifications are required, though some people (for example, undischarged bankrupts) are disqualified from becoming magistrates. Magistrates must live within 15 miles of the area served by the court, intended to ensure that magistrates' courts represent local justice by local people.

Magistrates are appointed by the Lord Chancellor on recommendation from a Local Advisory Committee. The committee must have one representative from each of the main political parties. However, most members are either serving or retired magistrates. Vacancies for new magistrates are sometimes advertised in the local press and volunteers are sought from local political parties and community groups. The majority of appointments, however, are made from those known personally or by reputation to members of the committee.

While lay magistrates are amateur justices, they have, since 1966, received some formal training. The initial training has concentrated on jurisdiction, procedure and sentencing. Thereafter, refresher training has continued the emphasis on sentencing exercises and also dealt with any relevant new legislation. This system has recently been replaced by the **Magistrates' National Training Initiative** (MNTI or "Minty"), involving a mentor system for new magistrates, under which experienced magistrates will assist new magistrates to achieve four basic competencies:

NOTES

- a knowledge of the framework within which magistrates operate;
- an understanding of basic law and procedure;
- the ability to think and act judicially;
- the ability to work as an effective team member.

Subsequently, all magistrates undergo regular appraisals and maintain a **Personal Development Log** (PDL). Magistrates receive further, specialist training to sit on either the Family or Youth benches.

Advantages

- **Cost**—using lay magistrates means that England and Wales has a much smaller bill for judicial services than any comparable country. However, a comparison of cost per case disposed between lay magistrates and District Judges (Magistrates' Courts) reveals less of a saving than might be anticipated.

- **Reflect local concerns**—using ordinary members of the local community means the magistracy should reflect the values, standards and concerns of that community.

Disadvantages

- Social composition—the Advisory Committee system, together with financial and employment constraints, produces a magistracy that is predominantly white and middle class. Most magistrates are from the professional and managerial classes, clearly contradicting the aim of a magistracy that is representative of the local community. The Lord Chancellor's Department intends to address this issue in a new National Recruitment Strategy for magistrates. In a speech to the 2002 Magistrates' Association AGM, the Lord Chancellor stated that this will "challenge the unjustified perception that to become a magistrate, you need to be white, middle-aged and middle-class; and it will seek to improve further the balance, within the magistracy, in terms of gender, disability, ethnicity, occupation and social background. It is, of course, vital to the continuing legitimacy of the lay magistracy, that it reflects the community it serves." Furthermore, to try and encourage more magistrates from the ethnic minorities, the Lord Chancellor's Department has piloted a successful Magistrates Shadowing Scheme in partnership with Operation Black Vote. In fact, in 2000/2001, the proportion of new appointments drawn from ethnic minority communities rose to 9.3 per cent—up from 8.6 per cent the year before, 6.5 per cent in 1997, and only 5 per cent in 1994.

NOTES

- **Inadequate training**—it is sometimes argued that magistrates receive insufficient training. The limited nature of their training is based on three arguments: first, magistrates are appointed for their existing qualities of judgement and responsibility; secondly, new magistrates learn their role sitting alongside experienced colleagues; thirdly, expert legal advice is available from the Clerk to the Court. This does, however, raise the danger that magistrates can become overly reliant on the Clerk. Hopefully, the recent new training initiative will meet these concerns.

- **Prosecution and conviction mindedness**—it is argued that many magistrates are, by virtue of their social background, too ready to side with the prosecution and police.

- **Inconsistencies in sentencing**—studies have shown considerable inconsistencies in sentencing from one Bench to another. While some degree of inconsistency is inevitable if magistrates are to reflect local concerns, Home Office statistics for 2001 show that there is still a disturbing level of inconsistency in sentencing between benches. For example, magistrates in Southeast Northumberland gave an absolute or conditional discharge to 45.6 per cent of those found guilty, against a national average of 21.2 per cent, while magistrates in Havering, East London discharged only 9.7 per cent.

However, alternatives to the lay magistracy, such as an increased use of District Judges, would be far more expensive than the present system. Also, and most significantly, it would remove an important element of community involvement. Nevertheless, if the lay magistracy is to continue, steps must be taken to reform the appointments process and ensure that social, racial and gender composition more accurately reflects that of the local community it serves. This is essential to maintain public confidence in the magistracy, and to make the ideal of local justice by local people a reality.

Juries

The use of juries in civil cases is now rare, being largely confined to actions for false imprisonment and defamation (where juries have been criticised for awarding excessively high levels of compensation). Our discussion, therefore, will focus on juries in serious criminal trials at the Crown Court.

A criminal jury consists of twelve members and their role is to decide questions of fact and reach a verdict. They receive no training, though they are shown a short explanatory video on how they have been selected, their role in the trial, and what to expect in court.

Qualifications for jury service are found in the **Juries Act 1974**. Anyone aged between 18 and 70, on the electoral register, and who has been a UK resident for at least five years is eligible for service. However, some people are or may be excluded:

NOTES

- **Ineligible for service**—for example, members of the clergy or religious orders, and the mentally ill.

- **Disqualified from service**—for example, those with a significant criminal record.

- **Excusal as of right**—some people (for example, doctors, nurses, those with previous service, those over 65 years of age) have a right to be excused service should they request this.

- **Excusal for good cause**—any person may request to be excused jury service for good cause, including where service would cause personal hardship (for example, during pregnancy).

If a juror becomes indisposed during the trial, the case continues unless the number of jurors remaining falls below nine. The jury must attempt to reach a **unanimous** verdict. However, where, following a minimum of two hours' deliberation, they are unable to do so, the judge may accept a **majority** verdict. With a jury of twelve or eleven members, at least ten must agree; with ten members, nine must agree; with the minimum of nine members, the verdict must be unanimous. If the jury falls below the minimum number or fails to reach a verdict, the case is discharged and may be re-tried before another jury.

It is difficult to research the workings of the jury, as the **Contempt of Court Act 1981** prohibits the questioning of jurors. However, studies of "shadow" juries reveal that while jurors generally take their role seriously, there is no standard pattern to their deliberations and the panel can be dominated by one or two strong-minded individuals.

Advantages

- **The symbolic value of community participation in the most serious criminal trials**—it is thought important that questions of this sort are decided by ordinary members of society, not a legal elite.

- **The "perverse" verdict**—the right of the jury to bring in a verdict according to its conscience is one of the few ways that ordinary citizens can comment directly upon the merits of a particular law or prosecution. When juries acquit in the face of the law and evidence, they are saying "We think the law is wrong" or "This prosecution should not have been brought". Recently, we can see this in the refusal of some juries to convict multiple sclerosis sufferers of cannabis offences. This attitude, together with the results of medical research, may well bring about a change to the law in this area.

- **Safeguard against oppression**—the perverse verdict enables the jury to reject prosecutions they regard as oppressive, leading Lord Devlin to describe the jury as "the lamp that shows that freedom lives".

NOTES

- **Spreads burden**—the burden of determining guilt or innocence in the most serious cases is spread across a group of people, rather than falling upon a single judge.

Disadvantages

- **The jury is open to intimidation**—this possibility has led to the removal of jury trial in Northern Ireland for terrorist offences, tried before a judge alone in a "Diplock" court. In November 2002, the Deputy Commissioner of the Metropolitan Police told the Home Affairs Select Committee that jury tampering was a major problem, costing the Metropolitan Police an average of £4.5 million per year in jury protection duties. The **Criminal Justice Bill 2003** proposes to allow the prosecution to apply for trial without jury where there is a danger of jury tampering.

- **Jurors cannot understand complex evidence**—this has been a particular concern regarding fraud cases. In **1986** the **Roskill Committee** recommended replacing the jury in such cases with two expert lay assessors, though this has not been implemented. Some commentators have also called for a raising of the lower age limit and for the introduction of some form of comprehension test. The **Criminal Justice Bill 2003** proposes to allow the prosecution to apply for trial without jury in complex or lengthy cases.

- **Susceptibility to persuasion**—jurors may be swayed by clever, persuasive or forceful advocacy rather than by the evidence in the case. In a rather bizarre example, a female juror was removed from a fraud trial in 2003 after sending a Valentine card to the prosecuting barrister.

- **Prejudice**—jurors may bring their own prejudices into the jury room. While the potential for majority verdicts should nullify any prejudice on the part of one or two jurors, in 2002 a trial had to be abandoned at a cost of £1.5 million due to racial antagonisms amongst the jury.

- **Unrepresentative**—in 2001, almost one-third of those summonsed were excused jury service, fuelling concerns that juries were increasingly unrepresentative of the community at large as most middle-class and professional people were able to avoid service. To overcome this, the **Criminal Justice Bill 2003** proposes to remove all categories of excusal as of right and significantly restrict discretionary excusal (in most instances, only a deferment, rather than excusal will be granted). Only the mentally disordered will be ineligible and those with a significant criminal record disqualified.

As with the magistracy, any alternative to the jury, such as a panel of judges, would tend to increase costs and remove the element of community participation. We should also note that in statistical terms, jury trial is far less significant than summary trial before magistrates.

NOTES

Conclusion

There is a long history of lay participation in the administration of justice in England and Wales. Besides the various practical benefits and advantages of this involvement (notably cost), arguably its greatest value lies in the symbolic quality of community participation. It is important for the maintenance of public confidence that the legal system is not seen as remote and the exclusive preserve of legal professionals. In this respect, both the lay magistracy and the jury are equally important. Nevertheless, a number of reforms could be made to improve the effectiveness of this involvement, most urgently in broadening the social composition of the magistracy.

Revision Notes

You should now write your revision notes for this topic. Here is an example for you and some suggested headings:

Lay⑤—Role of Juries

- Civil jury rare—defamation—criticised for excessive awards
- Criminal jury—12 members, randomly selected, shown video
- Hear evidence, decide questions of fact, reach verdict

Lay①—Intro

Lay②—Role/Powers of Mags

Lay③—Appt/Training of Mags

Lay④—Evaluation (Mags)

Lay⑤—Role of Juries

Lay⑥—Selection/Eligibility for Jury Service

Lay⑦—Evaluation (Juries)

Lay⑧—Conclusion

NOTES

Using your cards, you should now be able to write a short paragraph in response to each of the following questions:

1. Describe the reliance upon lay participation in the English legal system.

2. Describe the role and powers of lay magistrates.

3. Describe the appointment and training of lay magistrates.

4. How effective is the lay magistracy in delivering local justice by local people?

5. Describe the selection of jurors and their role in a trial.

6. Discuss the advantages and disadvantages of the jury.

Useful Websites

For more information on magistrates—**www.lcd.gov.uk/magist/magistfr.htm** and **www.magistrates-association.org.uk**

For more information on the Judicial Studies Board—**www.jsboard.co.uk**

For more information on jury service—**www.courtservice.gov.uk/using_courts/jury/index.htm** and **www.juror.cjsonline.org**

For a series of interesting articles on juries, visit the *Guardian* at **www.guardian.co.uk/jury/** and **www.guardian.co.uk/jury/article/0,2763,426241,00.html**

For information on research into jury trial undertaken for the New Zealand Law Commission, visit **www.guardianunlimited.co.uk/Archive/Article/0,4273,4041149,00.html**, **www.lawcom.govt.nz/documents/publications/PP32.pdf**, **www.lawcom.govt.nz/documents/publications/PP37Vol1.pdf**, **www.lawcom.govt.nz/documents/publications/PP37Vol2.pdf** and **www.lawcom.govt.nz/documents/publications/r69.PDF**

For Penny Darbyshire, Andy Maughan and Angus Stewart's work on jury research for the Auld Review of the Criminal Courts, visit **www.kingston.ac.uk/ku00596/elsres01.pdf**

Notes

13 Access to Legal Services

Key Points

What You Need to Know:

- The different sources of legal advice.
- The different methods of funding legal advice.

What You Need to Discuss:

- The problems some people face in obtaining legal advice.
- The effectiveness of the measures intended to overcome these problems.

Introduction

The principle of the rule of law is at the heart of the English legal system. This states, *inter alia*, that all citizens are equal before the law. Nevertheless, for this notional equality to have any practical meaning, individuals must have access to the systems and institutions that uphold it. Equal access to legal services is a fundamental issue if all citizens are to benefit from the law and its protections. However, this equality of access does not exist. Rather, there is what has been termed an **unmet need** for legal services. Research in the 1970s by Abel-Smith, Zander and others identified three forms of unmet need:

- where someone does not recognise their problem as a legal one;
- where the problem is recognised as legal, but the person is unable to access the services available;
- where the problem is recognised as legal, but no developed service exists to provide the appropriate help.

The Reasons for the Unmet Need

There are four main factors that create the unmet need:

- **the geographical factor**—lawyers tend to be located in areas convenient to their traditional client-base (the propertied and commercial classes). This has led to an imbalance in the distribution of legal services, both locally and nationally. Locally, lawyers tend to be based in the business area of town, rather than in industrial or residential areas, making it difficult for the non-propertied classes to access their services. This will often require taking time off work and additional expense, over and above the cost of the lawyer's services. Nationally, there tends to be far more lawyers per head of population in the commercial and light industrial south than in the heavy industrial north. This does not mean that people in the northern communities have less need of legal services. Rather, it means that the profession has been more concerned with providing for the needs of prosperous, home-owning business communities than those of urban, working class, industrial communities. Concerns have also been expressed regarding an urban-rural, as well as a North-South, divide in the availability of legal services. Law Society statistics for 2002 show the following geographical distribution of firms and solicitors:

Region	Population (%)	Firms (%)	Solicitors (%)
Greater London	13.8	26.0	42.0
Rest of South East	15.4	15.5	10.1
South West	9.5	8.7	7.9
Wales	5.6	5.3	3.3
West Midlands	10.1	7.8	6.6
East Midlands	8.0	4.8	4.1
Eastern	10.4	9.9	6.5
North West (inc Merseyside)	12.9	11.8	10.1
North East	4.8	3.5	2.5
Yorkshire and Humberside	9.5	6.6	6.8
Total	100.0	100.0	100.0

- **the psychological factor**—the essentially middle-class nature of the profession can create a social distance between lawyer and non-propertied client. For many people this makes the law seem an alien and intimidating world with which they are reluctant to become involved.

NOTES

- **the knowledge factor**—relatively few lawyers have a detailed knowledge of areas of law not directly relevant to the needs of their traditional clients. Therefore, they are frequently ill-equipped to meet the needs of non-propertied clients.

- **the cost factor**—many people simply cannot afford the cost of private legal services. Civil litigation, for example, involves costs of many thousands of pounds—a financial risk clearly beyond the means of many people and a considerable deterrent to many more.

We can argue, therefore, that the legal profession has systematically failed to provide a range of services appropriate and affordable for all sections of society, preferring, perhaps understandably, to concentrate on the needs of the propertied and commercial classes.

Alternative Providers and Funding

Obtaining legal services from the legal profession, and paying for those services privately is only one of the options open to someone with a legal problem. There are a number of other providers and sources of funding available:

- **Local authority advice units**—typically covering housing, benefit and consumer issues.

- **Charities**—many charity organisations offer advice on issues relating to their area of work.

- **Trade unions**—offer advice to members on employment law issues, and increasingly offer a range of other services.

- **The motoring organisations**—both the AA and RAC offer advice to members.

- **The broadcast and print media**—offer general advice through phone-ins and advice columns.

- **Citizens Advice Bureaux**—there are approximately 2,000 CAB outlets throughout Britain, frequently located in high streets and other accessible locations such as hospitals and health centres. They deal with approximately 6 million enquiries per year, of which it is estimated that around one-third involve legal issues. Given their geographical distribution, informal atmosphere, specialist knowledge of issues such as welfare, housing, and immigration, together with the fact that their advice is free, CAB address all the factors giving rise to the unmet need. Therefore, they would appear to have a key role to play in any successful strategy to resolve it. The **Benson Commission** in **1979** viewed CAB as excellently placed to provide a preliminary advice and referral service. However, they would require significant increases in funding to perform this role effectively.

NOTES

- **Law Centres**—there are approximately 50 law centres, located in London and the other major metropolitan areas. They share the advantages of CAB, with the additional benefit of being specifically concerned with legal issues. Their work was similarly praised by the Benson Commission, and could make a major impact, together with CAB, in a co-ordinated approach to addressing the unmet need. However, inadequate and insecure funding limits their ability to do so.

- **Private insurance schemes**—this is becoming increasingly popular in its own right, and some element of legal insurance is frequently included in car and home insurance policies. It is estimated that currently around 17 million people have some form of legal insurance, and the Government is keen to see this increase further.

- *pro bono* **work**—both branches of the profession (through the Free Representation Unit, the Bar Pro Bono Unit, and the Solicitors' Pro Bono Group) are increasingly concerned to establish *pro bono* work—providing some services free of charge—as an important aspect of lawyers' duties. In an effort to try and raise awareness of this type of work, the term *pro bono* has recently been replaced by the term "law for free".

- **conditional fees**—the **Courts and Legal Services Act 1990** made provision for the first time for lawyers to enter into conditional fee arrangement for a limited range of cases. Under a conditional fee arrangement, the lawyer agrees to take a reduced fee or even no fee if they lose the case (hence the term "no-win, no-fee"), but can charge an additional "success fee" if they win. Therefore, the only financial cost to the claimant at the outset of the case is the insurance policy they must take out to cover the other side's costs should they lose the case. The main argument against such arrangements was that it was undesirable for a lawyer to have a direct financial interest in the outcome of a case. The main arguments in favour were that they would relieve some of the burden on the legal aid system, and also widen access to justice by addressing the "middle income trap" (see below). The **Access to Justice Act 1999** widened the range of cases that could be taken under a conditional fee arrangement, and also addressed two of the main concerns regarding the operation of the original scheme by allowing successful claimants to recover both the success fee and the insurance premium for the losing side.

Resolving the unmet need

The **Legal Aid** system (state subsidies for private legal services) was first introduced in 1949. For the following 50 years (together with the **Green Form Scheme**, established in 1972, and **ABWOR**—assistance by way of representation—established in 1979) this was the main strategy to ensure access to justice. This covered assistance with the cost of litigation and representation (legal aid) and cost of preliminary and non-contentious work (legal advice and assistance).

However, the demand-led nature of the scheme saw costs escalate while the proportion of the population eligible for help declined dramatically (creating the "middle-income trap"). The **1998 Modernising Justice White Paper** detailed the main failings of the scheme:

- Civil legal aid was too heavily biased towards expensive court-based solutions and sometimes used to fund undeserving cases (despite the merits test).

- As lawyers were paid by work claimed, there was no incentive to deal with cases quickly and efficiently.

- Most significantly, while gross spending from 1993 to 1998 grew by 35 per cent (to approximately £800 million per year), the number of cases funded fell by 31 per cent—a third more money to help a third less people.

- Similarly, spending on criminal legal aid in the same period rose by 44 per cent while the number of cases funded rose by only 10 per cent.

- The means test for criminal legal aid was a waste of time and money—it did not stop apparently wealthy defendants making successful claims, and 94 per cent of defendants in the Crown Court paid no contribution anyway.

The White Paper proposed the most widespread reform of access to legal services since the introduction of legal aid 50 years previously. These proposals formed the core of the **Access to Justice Act 1999**. The Act abolishes the legal aid scheme. In its place, a **Legal Services Commission** will oversee a **Community Legal Service** (for civil matters) and a **Criminal Defence Service** (for criminal matters).

The Community Legal Service will fund access to civil legal services through contracts with lawyers and other providers (for example, in 2001–2002, the CLS made 24 grants to CAB for legal and advice partnership projects), subject to rigorous quality assurance mechanisms. It will work with local authorities and others to establish **Community Legal Service Partnerships** in each local authority area to plan and co-ordinate the funding of local advice and other legal services. By March 2002 there were 202 Community Legal Service Partnerships, involving 379 Local Authorities covering over 95 per cent of the population. This means the CLS has exceeded its target, which was to cover 90 per cent of England and Wales with a CLS Partnership by this date. A key task of partnerships is to establish effective local referral networks so people with problems will end up in the right place, no matter where they enter the system. Using the Community Legal Service's **"Just Ask"** website, anyone with a problem is able to enter a simple query and receive answers from among 400 other sites. There is also

NOTES

an electronic directory of 15,000 sources of help (including solicitors, advice centres and specialist resources) that will produce a list of the nearest helpers speaking a particular language and knowledgeable about the particular area of law. Commuters and shoppers are able to access this at **TownPages** information booths in train stations and supermarkets around the country. Other initiatives have included video-links between advice centres and remote communities. The old merits test for litigation and representation has been replaced by a new, more flexible **funding assessment**, placing greater emphasis on alternative approaches (for example, mediation) and funding (for example, conditional fees), though "litigation funding" will still be available in appropriate cases. These reforms are closely allied to the Woolf reforms to civil justice. As noted above, the Act also took steps to improve and extend conditional fee arrangements, particularly by allowing the winning side to recover the success fee and legal insurance premiums from the losing side.

The Criminal Defence Service will use a mixture of in-house salaried public defenders and contracts (mostly fixed-price) with lawyers in private practice who meet minimum quality standards. This is intended to cover the full range of defence services, from advice at the police station to representation in court. The existing Duty Solicitor schemes at both police stations and magistrates' courts were unaffected by the reforms but have been incorporated within the range of CDS services. Very complex and expensive cases, where the trial is expected to last at least 25 days, will be covered by individual contracts with lawyers on a special panel who have demonstrated their competence to deal with such cases (for example, complex fraud). The merits test is unchanged. Administered by the Clerk to the Court, this requires the granting of aid to be desirable in the interests of justice. This is decided by the application of the **Widgery criteria** (established in 1966 by the Widgery Committee on Legal Aid in Criminal Proceedings). For example, aid is desirable where the charge is so serious the applicant is at serious risk of losing his/her liberty; where it is in the interests of someone other than the accused (for example, in sexual offences, where it is undesirable that the victim be cross-examined by the alleged perpetrator). The means test, however, is abolished. Instead, the judge will have the power to order convicted defendants to pay some or all of their defence costs. This means that assets frozen or that come to light during proceedings can be taken into account, meaning that wealthy criminals should pay much more than under the previous law.

The future for legal services

While we can hope that the new arrangements under the CLS and CDS will overcome many of the problems associated with the old legal aid system, there is no doubt that the problem of the unmet need remains. In 2001, the Lord Chancellor's Department issued a report (*Legal and Advice Services: A pathway out of social exclusion*), building on Professor Hazel Genn's

NOTES

groundbreaking 1999 study *Paths to Justice*, on the role of legal services in addressing social exclusion, including a commitment to measure and characterise levels of unmet legal need every three years. The report points out that "legal rights are useless if people do not know what those rights are or do not know how to enforce them, and they unable to receive expert independent help", and that "lack of access to reliable legal advice can be a contributing factor in creating and maintaining social exclusion". The report goes on to emphasise the need for a multi-agency approach to addressing these problems and the central role of CLS Partnerships in coordinating these activities, illustrating how this can help overcome social exclusion by reference to a number of case studies in the areas of homelessness, mental health problems, debt and money problems, welfare benefit issues, family and relationship difficulties, education problems and diversity issues.

Regarding the more mainstream legal services, following the Office of Fair Trading's critical 2001 report *Competition in Professions*, the Lord Chancellor's Department issued a consultation paper, *In the Public Interest?*, in 2002. The main proposals are to implement those sections of the Courts and Legal Services Act 1990 that would allow banks, building societies and other "authorised practitioners" to offer conveyancing and probate services. The main arguments in favour are that this would increase competition and consumer choice and lower the costs of these services. However, there is a concern that this might have an adverse effect on small firms of solicitors, particularly those in rural areas, and thereby damage the overall provision of legal services.

Conclusion

The previous emphasis on the use of subsidies to the private sector via legal aid offered no real, long-term solution to the unmet need for legal services. With the **Access to Justice Act 1999**, it has finally been recognised that any successful strategy must employ a broader range of providers and funding. Overall, the changes introduced by the Act mark a radical move towards the development of a more diverse, flexible and accessible range of services, funding and providers.

Revision Notes

You should now write your revision notes for this topic. Here is an example for you and some suggested headings:

NOTES

Access②—Reasons for Unmet Need

- Geographical imbalance in distribution—lawyers tend to congregate in prosperous, home-owning areas (North-South, Urban-Rural divide)

- Social gap between lawyers and non-propertied client can make services seem inaccessible

- Few lawyers have detailed knowledge of law outside issues concerning propertied and commercial classes

- Cost of private legal services beyond the resources of most people

---

Access①—Intro

Access②—Reasons for Unmet Need

Access③—Alternative Providers/Funding

Access④—Legal Aid and MJWP'98

Access⑤—AJA'99 and the CLS

Access⑥—AJA'99 and the CDS

Access⑦—Conclusion

Using your cards, you should now be able to write a short paragraph in response to each of the following questions:

1. Why is access to legal services an important issue?

2. Why is there an unmet need for legal services?

3. Apart from the legal profession, what other providers and sources of funding for legal services are available?

4. Discuss the reasons for the replacement of the legal aid system.

5. Describe the new Community Legal Service.

6. Describe the new Criminal Defence Service.

Useful Websites

For information on the Legal Services Commission—**www.legalservices.gov.uk**

NOTES

- ⊕ For information on the Community Legal Service—**www.justask.org.uk**

- ⊕ For information on Citizens Advice Bureaux—**www.citizensadvice.org.uk** and **www.adviceguide.org.uk**

- ⊕ For information on the Law Centres Federation—**www.lawcentres.org.uk**

- ⊕ For information on the Bar Pro Bono Unit—**www.barprobono.org.uk**

- ⊕ For information on the Solicitors' Pro Bono Group—**www.probonogroup.org.uk**

- ⊕ For the Lord Chancellor's Department report "Legal and Advice Services: A pathway out of social exclusion"—**www.lcd.gov.uk/laid/socex/index.htm**

- ⊕ For the Lord Chancellor's Department consultation paper, "In the public interest?"—**www.lcd.gov.uk/consult/general/oftrept.htm**

NOTES

SECTION THREE: CRIMINAL LAW

14 | Criminal Law—General Principles of Liability

Key Points

What you need to know and discuss:

- The concept of the *actus reus*.
- The requirement of causation.
- The concept of the *mens rea* and intention.
- The concept of the *mens rea* and recklessness.
- The requirement of coincidence.
- The concept of transferred malice.
- The role of strict liability in the criminal law.

Introduction

It is difficult, if not impossible, to produce a comprehensive definition of a crime. Commonly, people think of crimes as acts that threaten public safety, security or morality. Alternatively, crime can be defined as anti-social conduct that is sufficiently serious to require state intervention and punishment. While both these definitions account for the more serious offences against person and property, there are a number of acts (for example, parking offences), and some omissions, which are subject to the criminal law yet do not cause such a threat. Thus, to be accurate, we can only say that a crime is any act or omission that is contrary to the criminal law. However, while this identifies what conduct *is* a crime, it is of no help in identifying what conduct *ought* to be a crime.

Nevertheless, the popular definition is useful in illustrating the general nature of criminal liability. One of the main reasons for having a criminal justice system is the belief that those who engage in anti-social conduct should be held responsible for their actions and punished. In order to be deserving of punishment, a person must have acted in a blameworthy manner—*i.e.* have been at fault in acting as they did. Though not a universal requirement, this notion of fault is a very important aspect of most criminal offences, and helps to explain the basis of many of the defences to criminal liability. It is sensible, therefore, to keep this idea of fault or individual responsibility in mind throughout the following discussion of the criminal law.

This idea of fault is present in the principal maxim of the criminal law: *actus non facit reum nisi mens sit rea* (the act is not guilty unless the mind is also guilty). However, this must be treated cautiously. As implied above, *mens rea* is not required for all offences. Furthermore, the idea of a "guilty mind" can be misleading—a person can have the required *mens rea* without being morally guilty, and vice versa. Nevertheless, most criminal offences contain both these elements and this means that for most crimes the prosecution must prove beyond a reasonable doubt that the defendant committed the *actus reus* of the crime, while at the same time having the required *mens rea*.

The *actus reus*

The *actus reus* is the physical element of a crime. It can include conduct, circumstance and consequence. For example, the *actus reus* of murder contains all three: an unlawful act (conduct), under the Queen's Peace (circumstance), which causes the death of another human being (consequence). By contrast, the *actus reus* of rape contains only two: sexual intercourse (conduct), without the person's consent (circumstance). Thus, some offences, such as rape, are termed **conduct** crimes, while others, such as murder, are termed **consequence** or **result** crimes.

Liability for Omissions

Generally, the *actus reus* must be a voluntary positive act. In this sense, an act is voluntary if it consciously willed and deliberate. However, there are limited circumstances where an omission (rather than an act) will give rise to liability. The general position in English law is that omissions do not attract criminal liability. For example, if A watches B (a complete stranger) drown and does nothing to save him, A has committed no crime. In these circumstances, A's omission is a **pure** omission. Nevertheless, there have been circumstances where criminal liability has been imposed for an omission:

- *R. v Pitwood* [1902]—here P was employed as a railway crossing keeper and failed to close the crossing gates. A cart driver was killed when hit by a train. P's manslaughter conviction was upheld as he was under a contractual duty to close the crossing gates.

NOTES

- *R. v Dytham* [1979]—here D was a police officer who failed to intervene when a person was being fatally assaulted outside a nightclub. D's conviction for misconduct in a public office was upheld on the basis that he was under a duty as a police officer to act to preserve the peace.

- *R. v Gibbins and Proctor* [1918]—here G and P failed to feed G's daughter and she died. G and P's murder conviction was upheld on the basis that they owed a duty of care to the daughter.

- *R. v Stone and Dobinson* [1977]—here S and D failed to care properly for S's sister who subsequently died. S and D's manslaughter conviction was upheld on the basis that they had accepted a duty to care for the sister.

- *R. v Miller* [1982]—here M, a vagrant, fell asleep while smoking in a squat. Waking up, and finding the mattress on fire, M simply moved to the next room and went back to sleep. M's conviction for arson was upheld on the basis that having caused the fire through his carelessness, he was under a duty to raise the alarm.

What all these cases have in common is that D has accepted or been placed under a duty to act, and his/her omission constitutes a failure to discharge that duty—the omission is no longer pure. We should also note that legislation may impose liability for omissions (for example, failing to report a road traffic accident—**Road Traffic Act 1988, s.170**).

While the person in the drowning example given above may be regarded as morally culpable in failing to do anything to save the person drowning, there would be considerable difficulties in placing a general legal obligation on people to act to prevent harm to others or to property, particularly in establishing the precise nature of that duty (such uncertainty being highly undesirable in the criminal law). Furthermore, we can argue that the proper role of the criminal law is to discourage and punish wrongful acts, to seek to prevent people being actively bad, rather than to compel them to acts of heroism or to act in a morally virtuous manner (for a more detailed discussion of the relationship between law and morality, see **Chapter 39**). Finally, on a purely practical level, the criminal justice system is kept busy enough dealing with those who are actively bad, without also having to deal with those who are responsible for morally dubious omissions.

Causation

An aspect of the *actus reus* that can cause problems is the requirement of causation. Where the *actus reus* consists of both conduct and consequence (*i.e.* it is a consequence or result crime), the prosecution must establish a clear and unbroken causal link between them—*i.e.* must prove the defendant's conduct caused the unlawful consequence. This is approached in two stages:

- **Cause in fact**—the conduct must be a *sine qua non* of the consequence. This is established by applying a "**but for**" test, showing that without the defendant's conduct, the unlawful consequence would not have occurred. If the consequence would have occurred in any event, then it cannot be said to be the defendant's fault. This applies even where the defendant's conduct was intended, unsuccessfully, to cause the consequence (*R. v White* [1910]).

- **Cause in law**—not every act that is a *sine qua non* of the consequence will attract criminal liability. In some circumstances, the conduct will be too remote (or distant) from the consequence, while in others the actions of a third party (a *novus actus interveniens*) will intervene and break the chain of causation. Thus, it is not sufficient to show that the defendant's conduct was a *factual* cause of the unlawful consequence. It must also be a *legal* cause. The first point to note here is that the defendant's conduct need not be the sole or even the main cause of the unlawful consequence (*R. v Pagett* [1983]). It is sufficient that it made a contribution. This raises the question as to what *degree* of contribution is required. In *R. v Cheshire* [1991], it was stated that the defendant's conduct must have made a **significant contribution** to bringing about the unlawful consequence. The existence of a second cause will only break the causal link where its effect is so **potent** that it makes the defendant's contribution **negligible**.

There are two further aspects of causation that we need to note:

- The defendant must take his/her victim as s/he finds s/he—the defendant cannot rely on some unusual characteristic of the victim in order to avoid liability for the consequences of his/her conduct. This applies to both physical and psychological characteristics (*R. v Blaue* [1975]).

- The defendant will be held to have caused all the reasonably foreseeable consequences of his/her conduct (for example, where a person is threatened with an assault by the defendant and, seeking to escape, is injured, the defendant will be held to have caused those injuries provided the victim's attempt to escape was reasonably foreseeable) (*R. v Pagett [1983]; R. v Williams* [1992]). However, this only shows that the defendant *caused* the consequence, not that s/he *intended* it. Intention is a state of mind and, therefore, is part of the mental element of the crime, not the physical.

The *mens rea*

The *mens rea* is the mental element of a crime. For most crimes, it is not sufficient to prove only that the defendant committed the unlawful act. It must also be shown they had a particular state of mind. The need to show a criminal state of mind emphasises the **subjective** nature of criminal liability and highlights the central role of fault.

NOTES

While the precise *mens rea* required varies from one offence to another, it will usually incorporate one of four general states of mind: intention; recklessness; negligence; and blameless inadvertence. Negligence and blameless inadvertence rarely give rise to criminal liability, and will be examined in the discussion of strict liability below. Therefore, discussion here will concentrate on intention and recklessness.

Intention

The issue here is whether or not the defendant intended to bring about the unlawful consequence. The test for intention is:

- a person **must** be held to intend a consequence where it is his/her **purpose** in acting to bring that consequence about (referred to as **direct** intent).

- a person **may** be held to intend a consequence where:
    - ➤ it was virtually certain to result from his/her actions; and
    - ➤ s/he knew it was virtually certain to result (referred to as **oblique** intent).

(*R. v Moloney* [1985]; *R. v Hancock and Shankland* [1986]; *R. v Nedrick* [1986]; *R. v Woollin* [1998]).

In this context, it is important to distinguish between intention/purpose and motive/desire. A person may intend a particular consequence without either desiring it or it being the motive for his actions. For example, in so-called "mercy killings", where a person gives an overdose of medication to a terminally-ill relative, while s/he does not desire the death of his/her loved one, and the motive is to relieve suffering, s/he nevertheless intends to kill—*i.e.* it is the **purpose** in giving the overdose to cause death.

Finally, we should note that proof of intention is always a sufficient condition of criminal liability. For some offences, such as murder, it is also a necessary condition—*i.e.* **only** proof of intention is sufficient to give rise to liability.

Some commentators have expressed the view that the definition of intention should be limited to that of direct intent. There are two main arguments for this:

- oblique intent is more properly regarded as recklessness—*i.e.* a "virtually certain" consequence is not an "absolutely certain" consequence and, therefore, a person who knowingly takes the risk of causing such a consequence should be regarded as highly reckless rather than as intending that consequence.

- The fact that a consequence is virtually certain is merely evidence on which a jury *may* find intention. That the jury has a **discretion** to find the required intent in the latter

NOTES

circumstances is confirmed by the **Criminal Justice Act 1967, s.8**. This may lead to inconsistent and possibly unjust results, as it means that juries may find the necessary intention where they believe the defendant's conduct warrants a criminal conviction.

However, given that the vast majority of offences can be committed intentionally or recklessly, this debate is really only of importance in relation to offences that can only be committed intentionally, most notably murder. In this respect, it may be argued that oblique intent serves a useful purpose in enabling those whose conduct shows such a high degree of disregard for human life to be convicted of murder rather than manslaughter.

Recklessness

A person is reckless where s/he takes an unjustified risk of committing the offence. Whether or not a risk is justified is decided by an **objective** test—*i.e.* would a reasonable person regard the risk as unjustified (*R. v Lawrence* [1982]; *R. v Sangha* [1988]). Therefore, the defendant cannot avoid liability by arguing that in his/her **subjective** opinion the risk was justified.

However, the defendant's subjective perception is relevant in deciding whether criminal liability will flow from taking that risk. This again emphasises the importance of fault and responsibility. The law has developed two different tests for recklessness:

- **Subjective (or Cunningham) recklessness**—under *R. v Cunningham* [1957], a person is reckless where:

  - ➤ s/he is subjectively aware of the risk; and
  - ➤ s/he nevertheless goes on to take that risk; and
  - ➤ the taking of the risk is objectively unjustified in the circumstances.

- **Objective (or Caldwell) recklessness**—under *R. v Caldwell* [1981], a person is reckless where:

  - ➤ the risk is a serious one; **and either**
  - ➤ s/he is subjectively aware of the risk and nevertheless goes on to take it (essentially subjective recklessness); **or**
  - ➤ s/he gives no thought to the possibility of the risk and the risk was an obvious one to a reasonable person; **and**

  - ➤ the taking of the risk is objectively unjustified in the circumstances.

While the objective test was at one point extended to include liability for manslaughter, concerns were frequently expressed regarding the undesirability of the second, objective limb of the test (see below). Following *R. v Adomako* [1994], the objective test was once again largely

NOTES

limited to the offence of criminal damage (for which it was first introduced). For almost all other offences (except those which can only be committed intentionally), the subjective test applies.

Criticisms of Objective Recklessness

- It is absurd and illogical to have two different definitions/tests for the same concept.

- Objective recklessness is more properly regarded as negligence. While a person who knowingly takes a risk may clearly be regarded as being reckless, it is difficult to view the inadvertent risk-taker in the same light. Surely the difference between recklessness and negligence must be the difference between conscious and deliberate risk-taking on the one hand and unconscious or inadvertent risk-taking on the other.

- Following from the above, the objective test extends negligence liability by the back door. Regarding criminal damage, if Parliament had intended this to be an offence of negligence liability, it would have been very easy to them to say so clearly in the 1971 Act.

- The objective test, taking no consideration of the subjective qualities of the defendant, can produce very harsh results. For example, in *Elliott v C (a minor)* [1983] a 14–year-old girl with learning difficulties lit a fire in a shed to keep warm, thus causing the shed to burn down. Her conviction for arson was upheld on the basis that the risk would have been obvious to a reasonable person. It was irrelevant that the girl herself was incapable of appreciating the risk.

- The illogicality, complexity, and potential unfairness of the test makes it difficult for juries to understand and apply.

Reforms

- The harshness of the objective approach could be mitigated by allowing subjective characteristics of the defendant to be grafted onto the notion of the reasonable person. However, this is hardly likely to make to test easier for juries to understand and has certainly proved complex and unsatisfactory in relation to the partial defence to murder of provocation (see **Chapter 16**).

- Abolish the notion of objective recklessness and revert to a single, subjective test which, as Professor Sir John Smith has pointed out, appears to have been entirely trouble-free in practice. The Law Commission, while generally in favour of this approach, has expressed reservations regarding manslaughter where death is caused by the inadvertent taking of a serious risk of death or serious injury. However, such concerns would be met by the offence of killing by gross carelessness proposed by the Home Office in its consultation paper on involuntary manslaughter published in 2000 (see **Chapter 16**).

NOTES

The relationship between the *actus reus* and *mens rea*

Here we must consider the **requirement of coincidence**. For liability to arise, the defendant must have committed the *actus reus* while, at the same time, having formed the required *mens rea*—*i.e.* the criminal act and criminal state of mind must coincide. However, the courts have allowed a degree of flexibility in satisfying this requirement:

- **continuing offences**—where the *actus reus* of the offence is of a continuing nature (for example, rape), it is sufficient the defendant forms the required *mens rea* at some point during its commission—*mens rea* need not be present from the outset (*Fagan v Metropolitan Police Commissioner* [1968]).

- **the transaction principle**—where the defendant has committed a series of related acts (one of which is the *actus reus* of the offence), constituting a single transaction, it is sufficient the defendant forms the required *mens rea* at some point during this transaction (*Thabo Meli v R* [1954]; *R. v Church* [1965]). This applies even where there is an appreciable interval between the commission of the *actus reus* and formation of the *mens rea* (*R. v Le Brun* [1991]).

Transferred malice

The concept of transferred malice applies where a criminal act directed at one person or item of property results, in fact, in injury, loss or damage to another person or item of property—for example, where A aims a blow at B but misses and strikes C instead. In such circumstances, the malice toward the anticipated victim is transferred to the actual victim, preventing the defendant from avoiding liability (*R. v Latimer* [1886]).

However, this principle will only apply where the anticipated and actual offences are of the same nature. Where this is not the case, the malice cannot be transferred—for example, where A throws a stone at B but misses and breaks C's window instead—here, A's malice which forms the basis for the *mens rea* of the anticipated assault cannot be transferred to form the basis for the *mens rea* of criminal damage. Nevertheless, in such circumstances, the defendant may also have the required *mens rea* for the actual offence—in the above example, A may have been reckless regarding the risk of damage to C's window.

Where the defendant would have a defence against the anticipated victim, this will also be transferred and operate against the actual victim (*R. v Gross* [1913])—for example, were A to aim a blow in self-defence at B but miss and strike C, A would be able to raise self-defence to any charge of assaulting C.

NOTES

Strict liability in the criminal law

Offences of strict liability are those for which there is no requirement of *mens rea* regarding one or more elements of the *actus reus*—for example, with possession of a prohibited substance, it is sufficient to show the defendant knew of the existence of the substance—it is not necessary to show he knew what that substance was (*R. v Marriott* [1971]).

Almost all strict liability offences are created by statute. The courts have been reluctant to develop such offences at common law (blasphemous libel being one of the few examples) and employ a presumption of *mens rea* when interpreting criminal statutes. The House of Lords has recently reaffirmed this reluctance in very clear terms in *B (a minor) v DPP* [2000] and *R. v K* [2001]. Thus, Parliament must use very clear words if it wishes to create an offence of this type. The reason for this reluctance is clear—the imposition of strict liability is contrary to the general principles of the criminal law that, as we have seen, focus on issues of fault (*Sweet v Parsley* [1970]).

Lord Scarman (in *Gammon (Hong Kong) Ltd v Attorney-General of Hong Kong* [1984]) provided valuable guidance for the identification of statutory offences of strict liability:

- There is a presumption in favour of a requirement of *mens rea* when interpreting criminal statutes.
- This is particularly strong where the offence is "truly criminal".
- This can only be displaced where the offence was clearly intended to be one of strict liability.
- This can only occur where the statute deals with an issue of social concern.
- Even then, the presumption can only be displaced where the imposition of strict liability would encourage greater care to prevent the commission of the unlawful act.

Therefore, in identifying such offences, two main factors must be considered:

- **the wording of the statute**—some words (for example, "use") are generally regarded as strict liability words, while others (for example, "knowingly") are generally regarded as *mens rea* words. However, there are no hard and fast rules here, and some words (for example, "cause" and "permit") have been interpreted differently in different contexts.
- **the nature (or context) of the offence**—given the above, this element would seem to be the decisive factor. Here, the courts have tended to draw a distinction between acts that

NOTES

are, in Lord Scarman's words, "truly criminal" (for which *mens rea* is required) and acts that merely happen to be regulated by the criminal law (for which strict liability may be appropriate).

Therefore, it would seem that strict liability offences fall into two categories:

- **the regulatory offence (or quasi-crime)**—for example, parking offences.

- **the public interest (or social danger) offence**—for example, dangerous drugs, environmental pollution (*Alphacell Ltd v Woodward* [1972]).

As strict liability represents a significant departure from the general principle of fault-based criminal liability, we must be considered whether its use can be justified at all in the criminal law.

Arguments against:

➤ It is contrary to general principle.

➤ It is objectionable and serves no useful purpose to punish someone who has taken reasonable care to comply with the law.

➤ It may result in unnecessary social stigmatisation.

Arguments for:

➤ While it may be generally desirable that criminal liability should depend upon proof of individual fault, there are circumstances where the collective or public interest in prohibition outweighs that individual interest.

➤ The imposition of strict liability may encourage positive steps to comply with the law, rather than merely negative action to avoid non-compliance.

➤ The use of strict liability avoids the complications that would otherwise arise in seeking to establish corporate liability (for example, in relation to pollution offences).

➤ While fault (or the degree of fault) may not be relevant to liability with such offences, it is still highly relevant in sentencing.

Furthermore, while liability for such offences may be strict, it is not absolute. The defendant may be able to raise one of the general defences outlined below. Furthermore, a statutory defence of due diligence or reasonable precautions is often provided, thereby making the offence, effectively, one of negligence liability.

NOTES

Therefore, it may be argued that the use of strict liability in the criminal law may be justified in these limited and exceptional circumstances. However, its extensive use would be clearly unacceptable.

Revision Notes

You should now write your revision notes for this topic. Here is an example for you and some suggested headings:

SL⑧—Strict Liability (evaluate)

- arguments against: contrary to general principle; achieves little; unnecessary stigmatisation

- arguments for: situations where collective interest prevails over individual; encourage greater vigilance; avoids complications in corporate liability; fault still relevant to sentencing

- can be justified in limited and exceptional circumstances—widespread use unacceptable

---

AR①—*Actus Reus* (Acts and Omissions)
AR②—*Actus Reus* (Causation)
MR③—*Mens Rea* (Intention)
MR④—*Mens Rea* (Recklessness)
MR⑤—*Mens Rea* (Coincidence with AR)
TM⑥—Transferred Malice
SL⑦—Strict Liability (describe)
SL⑧—Strict Liability (evaluate)

Using your cards, you should now be able to write a short paragraph in response to each of the following questions:

1. What is meant by the term *actus reus*?

2. How satisfactory is the law relating to liability for omissions?

3. Explain and evaluate the requirement of causation.

4. What test does the law use to establish intention?

NOTES

5. How satisfactory is this approach to intention?

6. Describe both subjective and objective recklessness.

7. How satisfactory is the law's approach to the issue of recklessness?

8. To what extent must the *actus reus* and *mens rea* coincide?

9. Explain the concept of transferred malice.

10. Can the use of strict liability in the criminal law be justified?

NOTES

15 | Criminal Law—General Defences

Key Points

What you need to know and discuss:

- The defence of non-insane automatism.
- The defence of insanity.
- The defence of mistake.
- The defence of intoxication.
- The defence of incapacity.
- The defence of duress by threats.
- The defence of duress of circumstances.
- The defence of self-defence.
- The defence of consent.

Introduction

Proof of commission of the *actus reus* together with formation of the required *mens rea* will give rise to prima facie criminal liability. However, the defendant may rebut this prima facie case by establishing a defence. The operation of these defences again highlights the importance of fault as they show the defendant either did not commit the *actus reus* voluntarily, or did not form the required *mens rea*, or his/her actions were in some way justified or excusable.

Non-insane automatism

Here, the defendant argues that at the time of committing the *actus reus* s/he had no conscious, voluntary control over his/her actions—s/he was acting as an automaton. This is a defence because a person cannot be held at fault regarding conduct over which s/he had no control.

NOTES

This defence is termed "non-insane" automatism to distinguish it from the defence of insanity. The essential distinction between the two defences is that with non-insane automatism the cause of the automotive state must be **external** (for example, medication or a blow to the head), while with insanity the cause must be **internal** (for example, illness or disease). For example, in *R. v Quick* [1973] a diabetic suffered a hypoglycaemic blackout through not taking his medication properly. As this was an external factor (the medication), conduct during the blackout was regarded as automatism. By contrast, in *R. v Hennessy* [1989], the blackout occurred when the diabetic had not taken his medication at all. Here, the blackout was attributed to an internal factor (the diabetes) and, hence, the appropriate defence was insanity. We should also note that, despite earlier *dicta* to the contrary, in *R. v Burgess* [1991] it was held that acts done while sleepwalking were to be regarded as acts done while insane rather than under a state of automatism. Finally, this defence is not available where the automotive state is self-induced through the voluntary consumption of dangerous drugs (*R. v Lipman* [1969]).

Insanity

Insanity, in this context, is a legal, not medical concept. It is designed to cover those situations where, because of some mental infirmity, the defendant should not be held responsible for his/her actions. Where raised successfully, it results not in an acquittal, but in a special verdict of "not guilty by reason of insanity". This allows the court considerable discretion in dealing with the defendant, ranging from an absolute discharge to detention in hospital (**Criminal Procedure (Insanity and Unfitness to Plead) Act 1991**).

This defence is governed by the **M'Naghten Rules** (established in *M'Naghten's Case* [1843]). The defendant must show that, at the time of committing the offence, he was:

- suffering from a defect of reason,

- caused by a disease of the mind,

- with the result that either:

  ➢ s/he did not know the nature and quality of his/her act; or
  ➢ s/he did know this, s/he did not know that it was wrong.

___

NOTES

Definitions

- **Defect of reason**—the defendant must have been totally deprived of the power to reason (*R. v Clarke* [1972]).

- **Disease of the mind**—this is not limited to recognised mental illnesses, but includes any disease or internal factor which impairs mental function, and has been held to include arteriosclerosis (*R. v Kemp* [1957]), epilepsy (*R. v Sullivan* [1983]), diabetes (*R. v Hennessy* [1989]), and somnambulism (*R. v Burgess* [1991]). Thus, it is a far broader notion than simply mental illness or diseases of the brain.

- **Did not know the nature and quality of the act**—this refers to the **physical** nature of the act, not its legal or moral status. This requirement is met where the defendant is either acting as an unconscious automaton (as in Kemp where the arteriosclerosis caused a mental blackout) or where s/he was suffering from insane delusions (for example, cutting someone's throat under the delusion that he was slicing a loaf of bread).

- **Did not know that it was wrong**—wrong, in this context, means contrary to law (*R. v Windle* [1952]). This requirement is met where, although the defendant knew what s/he was doing, s/he was suffering from insane delusions that, if true, would have made his/her conduct lawful (for example, where the defendant kills in "self defence" while suffering from the delusion that the victim is an assassin sent to kill him/her).

The relationship between insanity and automatism

The distinction between automatism and insanity is important because while the former results in an acquittal, the latter results in the special verdict. The purpose (or policy) behind this distinction is to allow those whose mental condition does not represent a continuing danger to the public to go free, while permitting the detention of those who, though they are not criminally responsible for their actions, do remain a threat.

Unfortunately, the principles evolved to implement this policy (primarily the internal/ external cause distinction) has led to some undesirable consequences—for example, the categorisation of conditions such as epilepsy and diabetes as insanity—and to some (arguably) unsustainable distinctions—for example, between the situations in *Quick* and *Hennessy*.

A better approach might be to have a single defence resulting in a special verdict of "not guilty by reason of automatism", thereby allowing the court discretion to deal with the

NOTES

individual in the most appropriate way, following consideration of medical and social reports. The courts have, however, made it clear that any such development must be legislative, rather than judicial (*R. v Sullivan* [1983]).

Mistake

A mistake of fact (but not of law) may operate as a defence where, as a result of the mistake, the defendant did not form the required *mens rea*—for example, it is not theft when a person appropriates property belonging to another in the honest, though mistaken, belief that it is his/hers. This applies whether s/he mistook the property for his/her own or whether, due to a mistaken belief regarding the civil law concerning the transfer of ownership, s/he honestly thought the property was now his/hers—these are both mistakes of fact. However, it would not be a defence to argue that s/he honestly, though mistakenly, believed it was not against the law to appropriate someone else's property—this is a mistake of law.

In all cases the mistake must be an **honest** one. In some cases it must also be **reasonable**. The present position was established in *R. v Williams* [1987]:

- Where the *mens rea* required is either intention or subjective recklessness, the mistake need only be honest. There is no requirement that it also be reasonable—though the less reasonable the mistake, the less likely a jury is to believe it was honestly made.

- Where the *mens rea* required is either objective recklessness or negligence, the mistake must be both honest and reasonable. The law will not invest the reasonable man with the defendant's unreasonable mistake.

- Where the offence is one of strict liability (see above), mistake is no defence, even where both honest and reasonable.

- Mistake is no defence where it results from voluntary intoxication (*R. v O'Grady* [1987]).

Intoxication

Whether intoxication (by drink or drugs) should be a defence raises a dilemma between policy and principle. As a matter of policy, it is wrong that an intoxicated offender should be able to avoid responsibility for his/her actions simply because of his/her intoxication. As a matter of principle, however, there can be no doubt that intoxication can prevent someone forming the required *mens rea*. In an attempt to resolve this, the law has developed rules

NOTES

based partly on the distinction between voluntary and involuntary intoxication, and partly upon the type of offence committed.

Involuntary intoxication

This is where the person is either forced to consume the intoxicating substance against his/her will, or where s/he consumes it in complete ignorance of its intoxicating properties (for example, where a soft drink has been spiked with alcohol). Intoxication is not involuntary where a person voluntarily consumes a substance, knowing it to be intoxicating, but is mistaken as to its strength (*R. v Allen* [1988]).

Involuntary intoxication is a defence to any crime where, taking his/her intoxicated state into account, the defendant did not form the required *mens rea* (*R. v Sheehan* [1975]; *R. v Pordage* [1975]). It is important to note that intoxication is not a defence where, despite the intoxication, the defendant did form the required *mens rea*, even if the effect of the intoxication was to reduce sober inhibitions (*R. v Kingston* [1994]).

Voluntary intoxication

This is where a person voluntarily consumes a substance, knowing it to be intoxicating. While (as might be expected) the law shows less sympathy for the voluntarily intoxicated offender, this may still be a defence where, taking his/her intoxicated state into account, s/he did not form the required *mens rea*. Whether it will, in such circumstances, be allowed as a defence depends upon the type of offence committed. Voluntary intoxication may be a defence to crimes of **specific intent**, but not to crimes of **basic intent** (*DPP v Majewski* [1976]; *R. v Lipman* [1969]). Crimes of specific intent include murder, all attempts to commit a crime and all offences where the *mens rea* extends beyond the *actus reus* (crimes of **ulterior intent**—for example, the *mens rea* of theft extends beyond the dishonesty of the appropriation because of the additional requirement of an intention to permanently deprive). Crimes of basic intent include all other crimes, including manslaughter.

There are two further points regarding intoxication that we should note:

- **Dutch courage**—voluntary intoxication will not be a defence to crimes of specific intent where the defendant, having formed the intention to commit the crime, becomes intoxicated in order to overcome sober inhibitions (*i.e.* to acquire Dutch courage) that would otherwise prevent him/her from carrying out that intention (*Attorney-General for Northern Ireland v Gallagher* [1963]).

- *Bona fide* **medical treatment**—voluntary intoxication may be a defence to any crime where the intoxicating substance is consumed in pursuance of *bona fide* medical

---

NOTES

treatment or prescription. This applies where the effect of the substance is usually sedative or stabilising, provided the defendant was not subjectively reckless to a risk the substance might induce aggressive, unpredictable or uncontrollable conduct (*R. v Bailey* [1983]; *R. v Hardie* [1984]). The substance concerned need not have been medically prescribed.

While a number of criticisms may be levelled against the present law relating to intoxication, most notably that it is both illogical and complex, it nevertheless represents a serious attempt by the courts to reconcile the competing interests of principle and policy indicated earlier, with the strict application of legal principle being tempered by a necessary dose of pragmatism. Arguably the only acceptable alternative would be that put forward in a minority recommendation in the Criminal Law Revision Committee's Fourteenth Report for a special verdict that the offence was committed while intoxicated. The relevance of the defendant's intoxication would then be shifted from the issue of liability to that of sentencing.

Incapacity

The position regarding the criminal capacity of minors is:

- **Children under ten years of age** are not criminally responsible for their actions (**Children and Young Persons Act 1963, s.16**). They are presumed incapable of forming *mens rea*. However, the courts and local authorities do have powers outside the criminal law to deal with such children. Furthermore, where a child under ten commits an offence at the instigation of an adult, the adult may be liable through the innocent agency of the child.

- **Children over the age of ten** have (following the abolition of the presumption of *doli incapax*—**Crime and Disorder Act 1998, s.34**) full criminal responsibility. However, as might be expected, there are important differences in approaches to the punishment of young and adult offenders.

Duress by Threats

A person may have a defence where s/he can show he was forced to commit the crime because of threats made to him/her by another person. This is known as acting under duress. For this defence to be successful, the defendant must show:

- that s/he was (or may have been) forced to act as s/he did because, as a result of what s/he reasonably believed the threatener to have said or done, s/he had good reason to fear that if s/he did not act in this way, the threatener would kill him/her or cause him/her serious physical injury; and

- that a reasonable person, acting in the circumstances as the defendant reasonably believed them to be and sharing those characteristics of the defendant that would influence the effect of the threat upon him/her, would not have responded differently. (*R. v Graham* [1982]; *R. v Howe* [1986])

This defence is also available where the threat of death or serious injury is aimed not at the defendant him/herself, but at someone whom s/he is under a duty to protect (*R. v Shayler* [2001]). This obviously includes members of his/her family and may, in appropriate circumstances, include strangers—for example, where an armed robber threatens the life of a customer in order to force a bank cashier to hand over money. The defence may also be available where a threat of death or serious injury is combined with other threats or pressures (*R. v Valderrama-Vega* [1985]).

Duress will not be a defence where:

- the defendant had an opportunity before the commission of the offence to avoid the threatened consequences—*i.e.* the threat must be imminent but need not be immediate—what matters is that the threat was operating to overbear the defendant's will at the time of the offence. (*R. v Hudson and Taylor* [1971]; *R. v Abdul-Hussain and others* [1999]).

- the source of the threat is an organisation (for example, a criminal gang or terrorist group) which the defendant joined voluntarily and with the knowledge that threats of this kind (*i.e.* threats of death or serious injury in order to force the defendant to commit an offence of the type charged) might be made (*R. v Sharp* [1987]; *R. v Shepherd* [1988]; *R. v Z* [2003]).

- there is an insufficiently close and direct connection between the threat and the offence (*R. v Cole* [1994]).

- the offence concerned is murder (*R. v Howe* [1987]) or attempted murder (*R. v Gotts* [1992]).

Duress of Circumstances and Necessity

There is no general defence of necessity (*R. v Dudley and Stephens* [1884]; *London Borough of Southwark v Williams* [1971]). However, the courts have recognised a limited form of necessity defence, often referred to as **duress of circumstances**. This covers situations where the

---

NOTES

defendant has been forced to act, not as a result of threats made by another person, but in response to the circumstances in which s/he finds him/herself (*R. v Willer* [1986]; *R. v Conway* [1988]; *R. v Martin* [1989]; *R. v Pommell* [1995]). The causative circumstances must be external to the defendant (*R. v Rodger and Rose* [1998]). Therefore, it seems that this defence is subject to the same two-part (subjective/objective) test and the same limitations as the defence of duress by threats (see above).

However, the situation regarding duress by threats, duress of circumstances and necessity has been cast into some uncertainty by two recent decisions—*Re A (children) (conjoined twins: surgical separation)* [2000] and *R. v Shayler* [2001]. In *Re A* the court had to decide whether it would be lawful for doctors to operate to separate conjoined twins, knowing that if they did not both would die, but that if they did that one would die. Given the urgency of the situation and the complexity of the issues, it is hardly surprising that the judgment lacks absolute clarity. In sanctioning the operation, the court relied, *inter alia*, on a defence of necessity. In doing so, Brooke L.J. identified three requirements for that defence:

- that the act was necessary to avoid inevitable and irreparable evil;
- that no more should be done than was reasonably necessary for the purpose to be achieved;
- that the evil inflicted was not disproportionate to the evil avoided.

This left two important questions open: was there a general defence of necessity in the criminal law? Was necessity a defence to murder? In *Shayler*, Lord Woolf, using the terms duress of circumstances and necessity interchangeably, refined this test as follows:

- the act was necessary to avoid an imminent peril of death or serious injury to the defendant or someone for whom s/he reasonably regards him/herself as being responsible;
- the act done should be no more than is reasonably necessary to avoid the harm feared;
- the harm resulting from the act should not be disproportionate to the harm avoided.

This appears to resolve the first question by making it clear that there is no general defence of necessity—a person cannot plead the necessity of hunger to a charge of stealing food, etc. It does, however, leave the second question open. On its facts, *Re A* would seem to indicate that necessity is available to a charge of murder. However, Ward L.J. was at pains to emphasise the unique circumstances of that case, and it remains uncertain the extent to which it will be regarded as authority in less uncommon circumstances. Furthermore, on its facts, the court in *Shayler* was unable to address the issue of necessity and murder directly and did not make

NOTES

any *obiter* comments on the point. It is in this context that we must consider the issues surrounding these defences.

The existence of a defence of duress as a limited form of a necessity defence is a consequence of a desire to recognise that in some circumstances a person's will may be overborne either by threats or the desperate circumstances in which s/he finds him/herself and that s/he may, in such circumstances, be forced to choose the lesser of two evils. It is, in this sense, a concession to human frailty. However, as a matter of policy it is undesirable to allow people to avoid the consequences of their criminal conduct on grounds of necessity except in the most extreme of circumstances. It is for this reason that the defence is subject to the variations limitations outlined above. The question is, therefore, to consider whether the courts have been able to reconcile these competing imperatives in a satisfactory way. The first point to note in this regard is the complexity of the defence and the difficulties this may present to juries. Secondly, there is the question of inconsistency—it is difficult to see why duress by threats/duress of circumstances/necessity should be a potential defence, for example, to a charge of causing grievous bodily harm with intent but not to murder, given that the *mens rea* required for the former offence is also sufficient for the latter. It may also be argued that excluding murder from the scope of the defence requires an unreasonable level of heroism from individuals who find themselves in the most horrible dilemma. The Law Commission, in 1977, recommended that duress should be available as a defence to murder, but Parliament has failed to act upon this recommendation. A further possibility would be to allow duress as a partial defence to murder, resulting in a conviction for voluntary manslaughter. This would at least have the merit of enabling the judge to have regard to the element of duress when determining sentence. This leads to the final possibility—to abolish the defence entirely, taking the view that, as Lord Griffiths put it in *R. v Howe* [1987], "it would have been better had this development not taken place and that duress had been regarded as a factor to be taken into account in mitigation" (a view echoed by both Lords Keith and Jauncey in *R. v Gotts* [1992]).

Self-defence (and its variations)

Where a person is faced with a violent, unlawful or indecent assault, s/he may be justified in using force in self-defence to repel that assault. *Both* the decision to use force *and* the degree of force used must be (objectively) reasonable in the circumstances as s/he (subjectively) believed them to be (*R. v Williams* [1987]; *R. v Owino* [1995]). In deciding the question of reasonableness regarding both issues, the following factors must be taken into account:

- the circumstances as the defendant honestly believed them to be, even if this belief was mistaken (*R. v Williams* [1987]) (except where the mistake was due to voluntary intoxication—see above);

Notes

- the time available to the defendant to consider what to do (*Palmer v R.* [1971]).

Thus, a decision to use force or a degree of force which may appear unreasonable with hindsight may be regarded as reasonable when the circumstances as the defendant believed them to be and the time available for reflection are taken into account.

There is no requirement that the degree of force used is objectively proportionate to that threatened, or that the defendant sought to retreat or avoid the confrontation (*R. v Bird* [1985]). These are simply factors to be taken into account in deciding whether the defendant's conduct was reasonable.

The main criticism of the present law on self-defence is that a person who is reasonably entitled to use *some* force, but then in fact uses *excessive* force, is deprived of any defence. This is partly tempered by the requirement to take the time available for reflection (the "heat of the moment" factor) into account in determining whether the degree of force used was reasonable. In any event, even where the defendant is deprived of the defence, the full circumstances of the case remain relevant to sentencing. However, this still leaves one major problem—where the defendant uses excessive and fatal force in self-defence (as in *R. v Clegg* [1995] and *R. v Martin* [2001]), he may be convicted of murder and subject to the mandatory life sentence. This problem could be dealt with in two ways—by creating a further category of voluntary manslaughter or by abolishing the mandatory life sentence for murder (see **Chapter 16**).

Using force in defence of others or in defence of property is governed by the same principles as outlined above, although it is doubtful today whether it would ever be reasonable to use fatal force in defence of property alone.

Acting in the prevention of crime

This is a statutory defence under the **Criminal Law Act 1967**. **S.3(1)** provides:

"A person may use such force as is reasonable in the circumstances in the prevention of crime, or in effecting or assisting in the lawful arrest of offenders or suspected offenders or of persons unlawfully at large."

This clearly has considerable overlap with self-defence and its variants (outlined above) and its application is governed by the same principles.

Consent of the victim

Generally, the consent of the victim affords no defence. However, there may be a defence to a charge of common assault where it is shown both that the victim consented and that the

NOTES

activity involved is not contrary to the public interest (*R. v Donovan* [1934]; *R. v Brown* [1993]). Furthermore, consent may be a defence to a charge of even a serious assault arising out of:

- **Surgical treatment**—consent is necessarily a defence here to conduct that would otherwise amount to grievous bodily harm. Emergency surgical treatment without consent would appear to be justified either on grounds of public policy or necessity.

- **Sports**—it would seem that players are held to have consented to contact incidental to the sport. This may include some instances of foul play, but not the deliberate (or "professional") foul (*R. v Billingshurst* [1978]) or conduct which has nothing to do with the sport (for example, throwing a punch in a rugby scrum). The position of boxing is more unusual, in that the violent contact is not incidental to the sport but is rather its primary objective. However, it seems the same principles apply. Finally, it seems this exception extends beyond organised games to include rough and undisciplined play, provided there was no intent to cause injury (*R. v Jones* [1987]).

It must, of course, be shown that the victim did, in fact, genuinely consent to the assault. Where the victim's consent is procured by duress, then clearly there will be no defence. More difficult are cases where consent is procured by a deception. The deception will not vitiate the victim's consent provided the victim had genuinely consented to both the nature and quality of the act, though this may involve making some very fine, and arguably unsustainable distinctions (see, for example, *R. v Richardson* [1999] and *R. v Tabassum* [2000]).

There are two main areas of controversy regarding the present law on consent:

- **Consensual sexual activity in private**—while some would argue that the law has no business interfering in such circumstances, others would support legal intervention on moral or public health grounds (for a more detailed discussion of the relationship between law and morality, see **Chapter 39**).

- **Euthanasia**—while the courts have had to deal with some difficult and distressing cases, such as *R. v Cox* [1992] and *R. v DPP, Ex p. Diane Pretty* [2001], it has remained clear that euthanasia or "mercy killing" remains murder at common law and that any alteration to this position would be a matter for Parliament.

Revision Notes

You should now write your revision notes for this topic. Here is an example for you and some suggested headings:

NOTES

Def①—Automatism

- D an automaton—no conscious, voluntary control over his actions
- Cause of the automotive state must be external (*Quick, Hennessy*)
- Not available where automotive state self-induced by drink or drugs (*Lipman*)

Def①—Automatism

Def②—Insanity

Def③—Mistake

Def④—Intoxication (involuntary)

Def⑤—Intoxication (voluntary)

Def⑥—Incapacity

Def⑦—Duress by Threats

Def⑧—Duress of Circumstances and Necessity

Def⑨—Self-Defence

Def⑩—Consent

Using your cards, you should now be able to write a short paragraph in response to each of the following questions:

What requirements must be met (and how satisfactory are those requirements) for a successful defence of:

1. Automatism?
2. Insanity?
3. Mistake?
4. Intoxication?
5. Incapacity?
6. Duress by threats/duress of circumstances/necessity?
6. Self-defence?
8. Consent of the victim

NOTES

16 | Criminal Law—Murder and Manslaughter

Key Points

What you need to know and discuss:

- The *actus reus* and *mens rea* of murder.
- Voluntary manslaughter by diminished responsibility.
- Voluntary manslaughter by provocation.
- Voluntary manslaughter by suicide pact.
- Constructive (or unlawful act) manslaughter.
- Gross negligence manslaughter.
- The reforms proposed to the law of involuntary manslaughter.

Murder

Murder is an offence at common law subject to a mandatory sentence of life imprisonment.

The *actus reus* of murder

This is:

- an unlawful act,
- that causes the death of another human being.

The unlawful act is usually a direct assault on the victim's person, though this is not necessarily the case—for example, in *R. v Hayward* [1908] it was held that causing death from fright alone was sufficient. Similarly, under the rules relating to causation discussed earlier, it could be murder where the victim, seeking to escape a murderous assault, jumped from a window and died from the fall, provided the escape attempt was reasonably foreseeable.

NOTES

The victim must be a living human being. It is not possible to murder someone not yet born or already dead. Regarding birth, in order to be a victim of murder, the child must be wholly expelled from the mother's body and have an independent existence. Thus, where a child, having been born, dies as a result of injuries sustained in the womb, this may be murder. Where, however, the child is born dead as a result of those injuries, the appropriate offence would be child destruction. Where a child is killed during the first year of its life by its mother, the appropriate offence may be infanticide rather than murder. Regarding death, the courts adopt a test of brain death (*R. v Malcherek* [1981]).

Historically, for both murder and manslaughter, death had to occur within a year and a day of the injury being inflicted. This rule was originally introduced to resolve problems of causation. Subsequent medical advances removed this justification and the rule was abolished by the **Law Reform (Year and a Day Rule) Act 1996**. However, the Attorney-General's consent is required for proceedings where the death occurs more than three years after the injury or where the person has already been convicted of an offence committed in circumstances connected with the death.

The *mens rea* of murder

This is traditionally referred to as **malice aforethought**. While this may be misleading (as neither ill-will nor premeditation are required), it is a vital concept as it is the presence of malice aforethought which distinguishes murder from manslaughter. There are two forms of malice aforethought (*R. v Moloney* [1985]):

- an intention to kill (known as **express** malice);
- an intention to cause grievous bodily harm (known as **implied** malice).

The test for intention is that outlined earlier in the general discussion of *mens rea*. Regarding implied malice, there is no need to show that the defendant knew or foresaw any risk of death resulting from his/her actions. It is sufficient that s/he intended to cause grievous bodily harm and that death in fact resulted (*R. v Vickers* [1957]).

There are two main issues regarding the present state of the law on murder:

- it has been argued that the *mens rea* of murder should be limited to an intention to kill (express malice) and that any other killings should be regarded as manslaughter.
- the mandatory life sentence should be replaced by a discretionary life sentence. The present position treats all murders as equally blameworthy, which is manifestly not the case—contrast, for example, the position of the contract killer or terrorist on the one

NOTES

hand and that of the mercy killer on the other. Furthermore, it may be argued that the mandatory life sentence is less a matter of principle and more a matter of historical accident, a consequence of building the parliamentary coalition necessary to abolish the death penalty. A discretionary life sentence would enable judges to impose a sentence fitting to both the offence and the offender. It would have the added advantage of removing the need for the categories of voluntary manslaughter detailed below, leaving factors such as provocation to be treated as mitigation.

Manslaughter

There are two general categories of manslaughter: **voluntary** and **involuntary**.

Voluntary manslaughter

Killings which would amount to murder (*i.e.* the defendant has malice aforethought) but for the operation of three partial defences:

- diminished responsibility;
- provocation;
- killing in pursuance of a suicide pact.

(**Homicide Act 1957**)

Involuntary manslaughter

Killings without malice aforethought—takes two forms:

- constructive (or unlawful act) manslaughter;
- gross negligence manslaughter.

(*R. v Adomako* [1994])

Voluntary manslaughter

At common law there was only one form of voluntary manslaughter—killing under provocation. The **Homicide Act 1957** gave statutory force to this category and added a further two—killing while suffering from diminished responsibility and killing in pursuance of a suicide pact.

Diminished responsibility (Homicide Act 1957, s.2)

It is voluntary manslaughter where a person kills another while "suffering from such abnormality of mind (whether arising from a condition of arrested or retarded development

of mind or any inherent causes or induced by disease or injury) has substantially impaired his/her mental responsibility for his acts or omission in doing . . . the killing".
Thus, the defendant must show that:

> ➢ s/he was suffering from an abnormality of mind (whether due to an internal or external cause);

> ➢ this substantially impaired his/her mental responsibility for the killing.

A person's state of mind is abnormal if it is so different from that of ordinary people that a reasonable woman/man would regard it as abnormal (*R. v Byrne* [1960]). This includes not only questions of perception and reason but also the ability to exercise will-power. Thus, it may be diminished responsibility where a person, though they know it to be wrong, cannot control an irresistible impulse. A substantial impairment is one that is more than trivial, but need not be total (*R. v Lloyd* [1967]).

This special defence clearly has similarities with both automatism and insanity and it is useful to contrast the differing requirements and effects of these mental state defences:

	Defence to:	Cause of:	Degree of impairment required:	Result:
Automatism	All crimes	External	Total	Acquittal
Insanity	All crimes	Internal	Total	Special verdict
Diminished Responsibility	Murder only	Either	Substantial	Voluntary manslaughter

There are three main issues regarding diminished responsibility:

● It can cause difficulties for juries. For example, while diminished responsibility can be caused by the effects of long-term alcoholism or drug addiction (*R. v Tandy* [1988]), it cannot be caused by temporary intoxication. Therefore, where the defence raise the issue of diminished responsibility (due, for example, to clinical depression) and the defendant was also intoxicated, the jury must attempt to consider what they defendant would or may have done in the circumstances had s/he not been intoxicated (*R. v Gittens* [1984]; *R. v Dietschmann* [2003]).

● The defence is open to misuse by both the prosecution and juries, in that a plea of diminished responsibility may be accepted or a voluntary manslaughter verdict returned on minimal evidence where there is sympathy for the defendant, as may be

NOTES

the case in some mercy killings. Equally, a murder conviction may be returned in the face of compelling evidence of diminished responsibility, as occurred in *R. v Sutcliffe* [1981].

- The defence was originally introduced in the era of the death penalty for murder, and enabled mentally disturbed killers who did not satisfy the very strict requirements of an insanity defence to be convicted of manslaughter rather than murder. Since the abolition of the death penalty, the defence simply serves to allow the court discretion in sentencing rather than impose a mandatory life sentence. It may be argued that a better solution today would be to abolish the mandatory life sentence for murder (see above).

Provocation (Homicide Act 1957, s.3)

It is voluntary manslaughter where the killer was "provoked (whether by things said or things done or by both together) to lose his self control" and that "whether the provocation was enough to make a reasonable man do as he did shall be left to . . . the jury; and . . . the jury shall take into account everything both said and done according to the effect, in their opinion, it would have on a reasonable man".

Thus, the defendant must satisfy two elements:

- **the subjective element**—that as a result of things said or done or both together, s/he was provoked to lose his/her self-control. The loss of self-control must be **sudden and temporary** (*R. v Duffy* [1949]). This is intended to distinguish between genuinely uncontrollable reactions and calculated acts of revenge. However, it has caused a number of difficulties, particularly where women have delayed (albeit for a brief period) in striking back against abusive partners. However, it is now clear that this requirement does not mean that the response has to follow immediately upon the provocative conduct—what matters is that when the defendant does react to the provocation, s/he is suffering from a loss of self-control (so-called "slow-burn" provocation) (*R. v Ahluwalia* [1992]). Furthermore, it is also recognised that any history of prior provocation is relevant in deciding whether the defendant lost his/her self-control—what might be termed "last-straw" provocation (*R. v Thornton* [1992]).

- **the objective element**—that a reasonable person in those circumstances (including any history of provocation) would (or may) have been provoked to lose his/her self-control and would (or may) have responded in the same way as the defendant. In *DPP v Camplin* [1978], Lord Diplock stated that a reasonable man for these purposes is:

  "a person having the power of self-control to be expected of an ordinary person of the sex and age of the accused, but in other respects sharing such of the accused's characteristics as . . . would affect the gravity of the provocation to him; and that the question is not merely whether such a person would in like circumstances be provoked to lose his self-control but also whether he would react to the provocation as the accused did".

It seems clear from this that particular characteristics of the defendant may be relevant to the reasonableness both of the loss of self-control and the subsequent response. However, some later decisions (*e.g. R. v Morhall* [1995]; *Luc Thiet Thuan v R.* [1997]) drew a distinction between these "control" and "response" elements, arguing that age and sex only were relevant to the control element but that other characteristics may be relevant to the response element. This caused much concern and confusion, requiring juries to engage in the "mental gymnastics" of an arguably unworkable distinction. However, in *R. v Smith* [2000], the House of Lords (by a 3–2 majority) held that it did "not understand . . . a distinction . . . between matters affecting the gravity of the provocation and matters affecting self-control" (Lord Clyde) and that, therefore, "the particular characteristics of the accused may be taken into account at both stages of the inquiry" (Lord Slynn). According to Lord Hoffmann, "the jury may think that there was some characteristic of the accused, whether temporary or permanent, which affected the degree of control which society could reasonably have expected of him and which it would be unjust not to take into account". The provocation need not be aimed at this characteristic, though it will clearly be of particular relevance where it is—for example, where an impotent man is taunted about that condition.

Finally, we should note that the provocation need not come from the victim nor be aimed at the defendant. It may still be a defence where the provocation comes from a third party (*R. v Davies* [1975]) or is aimed at a third party (*R. v Pearson* [1992]). It may still be raised even where the provocation is self-induced by the defendant's own conduct (*R. v Johnson* [1989]). These are simply factors to be considered in deciding whether the loss of self-control and subsequent response were reasonable.

There are three main issues regarding the present law on provocation:

- The requirement of a sudden and temporary loss of self-control, despite the interpretation placed on this requirement in *R. v Ahluwalia*, may still operate to discriminate against women who delay in reacting to abusive partners. It may also provide an unjustified excuse for men who kill their female partners (there are approximately 100 domestic killings per year, 95 per cent of which are committed by men). It is for these reasons that the Solicitor-General has announced that the Government is reviewing whether provocation should continue to be a defence to murder.

- There continues to be debate regarding the proper interpretation of the objective element. In *R. v Smith*, Lord Millett (in the minority) observed that "introducing a

NOTES

variable standard of self-control ... subverts the moral basis of the defence" by effectively removing any objective standard against which the defendant's conduct can be measured. However, Lord Clyde (in the majority) stated that "Society should require that [the defendant] exercise a reasonable control over himself, but the limits within which control is reasonably to be demanded must take account of characteristics peculiar to him which reduce the extent to which he is capable of controlling himself ... This is not to destroy the idea of the reasonable man nor to reincarnate him; it is simply to clothe him with a reasonable degree of reality."

- While *R. v Smith* appears to have settled the law, the lack of any clear guidance on when and whether the defendant's subjective characteristics may be relevant (this is left almost entirely to the discretion of the jury) has left problems for both judges and juries. In *R. v Weller* [2003], Mantell L.J. observed that "appeals concerning the appropriate direction on provocation seem to have increased since the decision in *Smith*." He went on to recommend that judges give their proposed direction in writing to both the prosecution and defence for their consideration, and stated that "there may also be considerable advantages in giving the direction to the jury in writing at the appropriate moment in the summing up before taking them through it. It is asking a lot of a jury to absorb the direction as they listen to it and to carry it in their minds with them into the jury room."

Given the above, perhaps the best solution, as discussed earlier, would be to abolish the notion of voluntary manslaughter altogether, accompanied by the abolition of the mandatory life sentence for murder.

Suicide pacts (Homicide Act 1957, s.4)

It is voluntary manslaughter where one person kills another as part of a suicide pact between them. A suicide pact is "a common agreement between two or more persons having for its object the death of all of them, whether or not each is to take his own life" and "nothing done by a person who enters into a suicide pact shall be treated as done by him in pursuance of the pact unless it is done while he has the settled intention of dying in pursuance of the pact".

Involuntary manslaughter

This is killing without malice aforethought and takes two forms (*R. v Adomako* [1994]):

Constructive (or unlawful act) manslaughter

The *actus reus* of this offence is:

- an unlawful act,

- that is dangerous, in that it exposes others to the risk of some harm, albeit not serious harm (*R. v Church* [1965]). It is important to note that the act must be *both* unlawful *and* dangerous (*R. v Slingsby* [1995]).

- and that causes the death of the victim.

The *mens rea* is that required for the unlawful act. It is not necessary to show that the defendant knew the act was either unlawful or dangerous or that s/he was aware of the circumstances which made it dangerous. It is sufficient that a reasonable man would have been aware of those circumstances (*R. v Watson* [1989]) and have regarded the act as dangerous (*DPP v Newbury and Jones* [1976]).

Gross negligence manslaughter

The *actus reus* of this offence is:

- a duty of care owed by the defendant to the victim (this is a question of law for the judge to determine—*R. v Singh* [1999]),

- a breach of that duty by the defendant,

- that causes the death of the victim.

The *mens rea* is gross negligence that the jury considers justifies a criminal conviction. Lord Mackay, in *R. v Adomako* [1994], stated that this was "supremely a jury question", the question being whether, having regard to the risk of death involved, the defendant's conduct was so bad in all the circumstances as to amount, in the jury's opinion, to a criminal act or omission. Subsequently, the Court of Appeal in *R. v Lidar* [1999] stated that there had to be a high probability of serious physical injury, and that the defendant may have run this risk either advertently (in effect, reckless manslaughter) or inadvertently.

Involuntary Manslaughter—Criticisms and Reforms

The complexity of the law in this area has long given cause for concern, and in **1996** the **Law Commission** published a report containing recommendations for reform and a draft bill. In **May 2000** the **Government** published its own **proposals** based on the Commission's report, although there are no current plans for legislation.

The two main criticism of the present law are that:

NOTES

- the test for gross negligence manslaughter is circular, in that the jury is directed to convict the defendant if they think his/her conduct was criminal;

- the scope of constructive manslaughter is too broad, encompassing both conduct which is little short of murder and that which is little more than an accident. This creates problems for judges in determining the appropriate sentence, and the public in understanding why a particular sentence has been passed.

Therefore, the Government is considering three new offences:

- **reckless killing**—a person would commit this offence if:

  ➢ his/her conduct causes the death of another;

  ➢ s/he is aware of a risk that his/her conduct will cause death or serious injury;

  ➢ it is unreasonable for him/her to take that risk having regard to the circumstances as s/he knows or believes them to be.

The maximum penalty would be life imprisonment.

- **killing by gross carelessness**—a person would commit this offence if:

  ➢ his/her conduct causes the death of another;
  ➢ a risk that his/her conduct will cause death or serious injury would be obvious to a reasonable person in his/her position;
  ➢ s/he is capable of appreciating that risk at the material time but did not in fact do so;

  and either:

  ➢ his/her conduct falls far below what can reasonably be expected in the circumstances;

  or

  ➢ s/he intends by his/her conduct to cause some injury, or is aware of, and unreasonably takes, the risk that it may do so, and the conduct causing (or intended to cause) the injury constitutes an offence.

The maximum penalty would be 10 years' imprisonment.

- **death resulting from the intentional or reckless causing of minor injury**—a person would commit this offence if:

NOTES

➢ his/her conduct causes the death of another;

➢ s/he intended or was reckless as to whether some injury was caused (although death or serious injury was not foreseeable);

➢ the conduct causing, or intended to cause, the injury constitutes an offence.

The maximum penalty would be between five and ten years (possibly seven).

Revision Notes

You should now write your revision notes for this topic. Here is an example for you and some suggested headings:

Murder②—Mens Rea

- malice aforethought (two forms—*Moloney*):
- express malice (intention to kill)
- implied malice (intention to cause GBH)
- test for intention (*Moloney, Nedrick, Hancock & Shankland, Woollin*)
- re. implied—no need to show foresight of risk of death—sufficient that D intended GBH and death resulted (*Vickers*)

Murder①—Actus Reus

Murder②—Mens Rea

M'slaughter③—Diminished Responsibility

M'slaughter④—Provocation

M'slaughter⑤—Suicide Pact

M'slaughter⑥—Constructive

M'slaughter⑦—Gross Negligence

M'slaughter⑧—Criticisms and Reforms

Using your cards, you should now be able to write a short paragraph in response to each of the following questions:

NOTES

1. Explain the *actus reus* and *mens rea* of murder.

2. Describe and discuss the partial defence of diminished responsibility.

3. Describe and discuss the partial defence of provocation.

4. Describe and discuss the partial defence of suicide pacts.

5. Explain the *actus reus* and *mens rea* of constructive manslaughter.

6. Explain the *actus reus* and *mens rea* of gross negligence manslaughter

7. What criticisms may be made of the present law of involuntary manslaughter and what reforms have been proposed?

Useful Websites

- For the Law Commission report "Legislating the Criminal Code: Involuntary Manslaughter" (Law Com. No. 237), visit **www.lawcom.gov.uk/library/lc237/lc237.pdf**

- For the consultation paper "Reforming the Law on Involuntary Manslaughter: The Government's Proposals", visit **www.homeoffice.gov.uk/docs/invmans.html**

17 Criminal Law—Non-Fatal Assaults

Key Points

What you need to know and discuss:

- The *actus reus* and mens rea of common assault.

- The *actus reus* and *mens rea* of assault occasioning actual bodily harm.

- The *actus reus* and *mens rea* of unlawful and malicious wounding or inflicting grievous bodily harm.

- The *actus reus* and *mens rea* of unlawful and malicious wounding or causing grievous bodily harm with intent.

- The criticisms of the present law regarding offences against the person and proposed reforms.

Common assault

Under **s.39** of the **Criminal Justice Act 1988**, common assault is punishable by up to six months' imprisonment (up to two years if racially aggravated—**Crime and Disorder Act 1998, s.29**) and/or a fine. At common law, assault and battery were two separate offences and **s.39** appears to preserve this distinction. However, **s.40** refers only to common assault and in *R. v Lynsey* [1995] this was held to include both assault and battery. Thus it seems that either assault or battery (in their common law sense) are now both to be regarded as common assault. The *actus reus* is either:

- **assault**—placing another in fear of immediate and unlawful personal violence. This may be done by acts alone (for example, raising one's fists at someone) or by acts and words together (for example, raising one's fists, saying "I'm going to thump you!"). Words alone (and even menacing silence) can amount to an assault, provided the victim fears immediate violence (*R. v Ireland, R. v Burstow* [1997]). However, words can also negate the effect of acts (for example, it would not be an assault to raise one's fists while saying "If you were a younger man, I would thump you!") (*Tuberville v Savage* [1669])—though this is not the case where the words merely announce a condition by which the victim can avoid the threatened violence (for example, raising one's fists while saying "Unless you give me your money, I will thump you!") (*Blake v Barnard* [1840]); or

- **battery**—the application of unlawful personal violence on another. Any degree of physical contact (however slight) without consent is sufficient. However, a person is held to have impliedly consented to everyday physical contact (for example, an accidental collision in a busy street, tapping on someone's shoulder to attract their attention). The application of force is usually direct (for example, by hitting or spitting) but need not be so—for example, it would be a battery if A pulls B's chair away as B is sitting down. This also emphasises that a battery does not have to be accompanied by an assault.

The *mens rea* is either:

- an intention to place another in fear of immediate and unlawful personal violence or subjective recklessness as to the risk of doing so; or

- an intention to apply unlawful personal violence to another or subjective recklessness as to the risk of doing so.

   (*R. v Venna* [1976]; *R. v Savage and Parmenter* [1991])

Assault Occasioning Actual Bodily Harm

This is an offence under **s.47** of the **Offences Against the Person Act 1861**, punishable by up to five years' imprisonment (up to seven years if racially aggravated—**Crime and Disorder Act 1998, s.29**). The *actus reus* of this offence is:

- a common assault,
- that caused actual bodily harm.

"Actual bodily harm" is harm that is more than trivial but not really serious (*DPP v Smith* [1961]). This indicates that the victim must be caused some noticeable discomfort, albeit of a minor and/or temporary nature. "Harm" includes not only physical, but also psychiatric, harm (but not mere emotions, such as fear, distress or panic) (*R. v Chan-Fook* [1994]).

   Regarding the *mens rea*, it is sufficient to show that the defendant had either formed an intention or was subjectively reckless with regard to the assault and that actual bodily harm

NOTES

was in fact caused. It is **not** necessary to show the defendant either intended or foresaw that actual bodily harm would or might be caused (*R. v Savage and Parmenter* [1991]).

Unlawful and malicious wounding or infliction of grievous bodily harm

This is an offence under **s.20** of the **1861 Act**, punishable by up to five years' imprisonment (up to seven years if racially aggravated—**Crime and Disorder Act 1998, s.29**). The *actus reus* of this offence is either:

- an unlawful wounding. For wounding to occur, both the inner and outer skin must be broken (*Moriarty v Brookes* [1834]); or

- the unlawful infliction of grievous bodily harm. "Grievous bodily harm" means really serious bodily harm (*DPP v Smith* [1961]). Again, "harm" includes psychiatric harm (*R. v Ireland, R. v Burstow* [1997]).

Either of the above is sufficient—there may be a wounding without there also being grievous bodily harm, and vice versa.

Regarding the *mens rea*, it is sufficient to show either:

- an intention to inflict some harm, albeit not serious harm; or

- subjective recklessness as to the infliction of some harm, albeit not serious harm.

It is **not** necessary to show that the defendant intended or foresaw that wounding or really serious harm would or may result (*R. v Savage and Parmenter* [1991]).

Unlawful and malicious wounding or causing grievous bodily harm with intent to do grievous bodily harm or resist lawful arrest

This is an offence under **s.18** of the **1861 Act**, punishable by up to life imprisonment. The elements of this offence are:

- *actus reus*—as for **s.20** (see above).

- *mens rea*—either:

Notes

> an intention to do grievous bodily harm (recklessness is **not** sufficient); or
> an intention to resist lawful arrest, and either intention or subjective recklessness as to the causing of some harm, albeit not serious harm.

Criticisms and Reforms

The **Offences Against the Person Act 1861** has been subject to many criticisms:

- It was an Act consolidating existing law and much of its language is archaic and confusing.

- In particular, there are inconsistencies is the terms used to indicate the conduct required for the various offences—"occasioning", "inflicting', "causing", etc.

- the specific mention of "wounding" alongside "grievous bodily harm" confuses the manner by which the harm is caused with the degree of harm caused.

- while the police merit special protection, as the very nature of their job places them a greater risk of assault, it is confusing to include this within the general offence in **s.18**.

- There have also been difficulties over the scope of the term "bodily harm"in particular, the extent to which this covers psychological as well as physical harm.

- Furthermore, there is frequently a confusing lack of congruence between the *actus reus* and *mens rea*. For example, for a **s.20** GBH, the defendant must have caused serious injury, but the *mens rea* only requires intention or foresight of some harm being caused (*R. v Savage and Parmenter* [1991]).

These complexities and confusions create additional burdens for the police and courts, and create a risk of injustice for defendants. Significant reforms were proposed in a **Law Commission report** in **1993**. In **1998**, the Home Office issued a **draft Bill**, based on the Law Commission's proposals, for consultation. The aim of the Bill is not to make the law either tougher or more lenient, but rather to make it clearer and easier to use. The main offences proposed are:

- intentionally causing serious injury (**clause 1**), to replace **s.18** GBH with intent. This also removes any separate reference to wounding.

- recklessly causing serious injury (**clause 2**), to replace **s.20** GBH (the proposed maximum penalty is seven years' imprisonment—the increase from the present maximum of five years is justified as the new offence would require foresight of serious harm, not merely some harm as at present).

NOTES

- intentionally or recklessly causing injury (**clause 3**), to replace **s.47** ABH (it would be necessary to prove intention or recklessness in relation to the injury, not merely the assault as at present).

- assault (**clause 4**).

- **Clause 15** makes it clear that injury includes both physical and mental harm. It also proposes that for **clause 1** offences only, harm would include the transmission of a disease, though this is likely to prove controversial.

- the Bill also contains separate offences intended to afford greater protection to the police.

While this bill would bring much needed clarity and consistency to this area of the law, due to pressure on the legislative timetable, there are no current plans for legislation.

Revision Notes

You should now write your revision notes for this topic. Here is an example for you and some suggested headings:

OAPA②—ABH

- s.47—5yrs imprisonment

- ar – common assault that causes ABH (more than trivial, not really serious—*DPP v Smith*—inc. psychiatric harm—*Chan-Fook*)

- mr = intention/subjective recklessness re. assault—not necessary to show intention or foresight re. ABH (*Savage & Parmenter*)

OAPA①—Common Assault

OAPA②—ABH

OAPA③—GBH

OAPA④—GBH with intent

OAPA⑤—Criticisms

OAPA⑥—Reforms

Using your cards, you should now be able to write a short paragraph in response to each of the following questions:

NOTES

1. Explain the elements of common assault.

2. Explain the elements of assault occasioning ABH.

3. Explain the elements of unlawful and malicious wounding or inflicting GBH.

4. Explain the elements of unlawful and malicious wounding or causing GBH with intent.

5. What criticisms may be made of the current law regarding offences against the person and what reforms might be introduced?

Useful Websites

For the consultation paper "Violence: Reforming the Offences Against the Person Act 1861", visit **www.homeoffice.gov.uk/docs/vroapa.html**

For the draft Offences Against the Person Bill, visit **www.homeoffice.gov.uk/docs/oapdb.html**

NOTES

18 | Criminal Law—Property Offences

Key Points

What you need to know and discuss:

- The *actus reus* and *mens rea* of theft.
- The *actus reus* and *mens rea* of robbery.
- The *actus reus* and *mens rea* of burglary.
- The *actus reus* and *mens rea* of obtaining property by deception.
- The *actus reus* and *mens rea* of obtaining services by deception.
- The *actus reus* and *mens rea* of evading a liability by deception.
- The *actus reus* and *mens rea* of making off without payment.
- The *actus reus* and *mens rea* of criminal damage.

Theft

Under **s.1** of the **Theft Act 1968**, theft is the dishonest appropriation of property belonging to another with an intention to permanently deprive the other of it. The maximum sentence is seven years' imprisonment. Therefore, the *actus reus* of theft is:

- **appropriation**—by **s.3**, this is "any assumption . . . of the rights of an owner". Following *R. v Morris* [1983], *any* assumption of *any* of the rights of the owner is sufficient—it is *not* necessary that the thief assumed *all* the rights of the owner. Thus, doing anything in relation to property which may properly only be done by the owner may be an appropriation (for example, in *Morris*, switching price labels in a super-market). We might have thought that an appropriation had to be something done without the consent or authority of the owner. The **Criminal Law Revision Committee**, whose report formed the basis of the Act, certainly thought so, and the inclusion of the specific offence of obtaining property by deception (**s.15**) lends weight to this argument. However, the interpretation of "appropriation" and "assumption" has caused the House of Lords no end of difficulty. In *Lawrence v Commissioner of Police for the Metropolis* [1971], the victim, an Italian tourist, showed an address on a piece of paper to Lawrence, a taxi driver. Lawrence told the victim it was very far and would be expensive—both of which were untrue. The victim offered Lawrence £1 who then, indicating this was not enough, took a further £6 from the victim's wallet. The correct fare was, in fact, approximately 55 pence. The defence argument was that as the victim had consented to Lawrence taking the £6, this could not be an appropriation and, hence, not theft. In the House of Lords, Viscount Dilhorne, speaking for a unanimous court, took a different view, stating "an appropriation . . . may occur even though the owner has permitted or consented to the property being taken". However, in *R. v Morris* [1983] (see above), Lord Roskill, again speaking for a unanimous court, stated "the concept of appropriation . . . involves an element of adverse interference with or usurpation of some right of the owner". So which view was correct, *Lawrence* or *Morris*? The House of Lords in *R. v Gomez* [1993] (Lord Lowry dissenting) adopted the position in *Lawrence*—an act could be an appropriation notwithstanding that it was done with the consent or authority of the owner. In *Gomez* the owner's consent had again been procured by a deception. In this regard it is worth noting that if Lawrence, Morris and Gomez had each been charged with obtaining property by deception contrary to **s.15** of the **1968 Act**, then none of these problems would have arisen. Speaking for the majority in *Gomez*, Lord Keith stated "*Lawrence's* case makes it clear that consent to or authorisation by the owner of the taking by the rogue is irrelevant. The taking amounted to an appropriation within the meaning of s.1(1) of the 1968 Act. *Lawrence's* case also makes it clear that it is no less irrelevant that what happened may also have constituted the offence of obtaining property by deception under s.15(1) of the 1968 Act." However, Lord Lowry, in a powerful dissenting judgement, stated the "act of appropriating property is a one-sided act, done without the consent or authority of the owner. And, if the owner consents to transfer property to the offender or to a third party, the offender does not appropriate the property, even if the owner's consent has been obtained by fraud", noting that "there is no problem (and there would have been none in *Lawrence, Morris* and the present case) if one prosecutes under s.15 all offences involving obtaining by deception and prosecutes theft in general under s.1. In that way some thefts will come under s.15, but no "false pretences' will come under s.1." However, Lord Keith's view prevailed and, on its broadest interpretation, the *ratio* in *Gomez* means that anything we do to someone else's property is potentially theft, depending on our state of mind at the time—it effectively reduces theft to an offence of dishonesty. This appears to be the view taken by the House of Lords (by a 3–2 majority) in *R. v Hinks* [2000]. Here the defendant had befriended an elderly man of limited intelligence and, over a period of six months, he transferred approximately £60,000 from his building society account into that of the defendant. The difficulty here

NOTES

was that unlike Lawrence, Morris, and Gomez, Hinks did nothing to deceive—there was no possibility of a successful s.15 prosecution—and had been made a valid gift of the money. It was clear that everyone involved with the case took the view that Hinks was "up to no good" but this is, unsurprisingly, not an offence known to the criminal law—could it be theft? Lord Steyn, speaking for the majority, was clear: "it is immaterial whether the act was done with the owner's consent or authority. It is true of course that the certified question in *R. v Gomez* referred to the situation where consent had been obtained by fraud. But the majority judgments do not differentiate between cases of consent induced by fraud and consent given in any other circumstances. The ratio involves a proposition of general application." To hold otherwise, he argued, would "place beyond the reach of the criminal law dishonest persons who should be found guilty of theft." However, Lord Hobhouse, in his dissenting judgment, observed that such an approach "depends upon the disturbing acceptance that a criminal conviction and the imposition of custodial sanctions may be based upon conduct which involves no inherent illegality and may only be capable of being criticised on grounds of lack of morality . . . An essential function of the criminal law is to define the boundary between what conduct is criminal and what merely immoral . . . To treat otherwise lawful conduct as criminal merely because it is open to such disapprobation would be contrary to principle and open to the objection that it fails to achieve the objective and transparent certainty required of the criminal law by the principles basic to human rights." Furthermore, regarding the point that there is no difficulty in reducing theft to an offence of dishonesty because the honest have nothing to fear from this, Lord Hobhouse observed that dishonesty has received "no greater definition than consciously falling below the standards of an ordinary and decent person and may include anything which such a person would think was morally reprehensible. It may be no more than a moral judgment", concluding that "it will not suffice simply to invite the jury to convict on the basis of their disapproval of the defendant's conduct and their attribution to him of the knowledge that he must have known that they and other ordinary and decent persons would think it dishonest. Theft is a crime of dishonesty but dishonesty is not the only element in the commission of the crime." Nevertheless, the majority view prevailed and it may be that the House of Lords has, in its interpretation of appropriation and theft, managed to create an offence of "being up to no good". Whether this is desirable is, of course, another matter. Finally, **s.3** states that it may be an appropriation where a person comes by the property (whether innocently or not) without stealing it, but subsequently assumes a right to it by keeping or dealing with it as the owner (for example, where a person initially borrows a book from another and subsequently sells it to a second-hand bookshop rather than returning it—though the initial borrowing may now itself, under *Gomez* and *Hinks*, amount to an appropriation!).

Notes

- **property**—by **s.4**, property includes "money and all other property, real or personal, including things in action and other intangible property". Intangible property refers to property that does not physically exist, such as a debt or copyright. This means that almost anything can be stolen. However, land (and things severed from land) generally cannot be stolen unless:

  ➢ the person is acting as a trustee or personal representative and deals with the land contrary to the obligations imposed by this status;

  ➢ a person not in possession of the land takes something from the land (for example, cultivated flowers or fruit—wild flowers, etc. cannot be stolen unless picked for commercial purposes; nor can wild animals be stolen);

  ➢ a tenant appropriates any fixture or structure let with the land (for example, if the tenant sells a garden shed or greenhouse).

- **belonging to another**—by **s.5**, property belongs to "any person having possession or control of it, or having in it any proprietary right or interest". This means that, in appropriate circumstances, we can even steal our own property—for example, if someone takes their car from a garage without paying for repairs (*R. v Turner* [1971]). Property will also be regarded as belonging to another where:

  ➢ the property is the subject of a trust (it belongs to the beneficiaries);

  ➢ a person receives property from another and is under an obligation to retain and deal with it in a particular way (it belongs to that other)—for example, A receives money from his flatmates to pay household bills but spends the money on himself (*Davidge v Bunnett* [1984]). This is now only relevant where A forms his dishonest intent after receiving the money. If he never intended to pay the bills then, following *Hinks*, he commits theft when he is given the money;

  ➢ a person receives property by another's mistake and is under a legal obligation to make restoration to that other—for example, A receives an over-payment of wages through his employer's mistake (*Attorney-General's Reference (No.1 of 1983)* [1984])

The *mens rea* of theft is:

- **dishonesty**—the Act does not provide a definition of dishonesty. However, **s.2** states that a person is **not** dishonest where:

  ➢ s/he appropriates the property in the belief that s/he has a legal right to deprive the other person of it;

  ➢ s/he appropriates the property in the belief that the other person would consent if they knew of the appropriation and its circumstances;

NOTES

> s/he appropriates the property (except as trustee or personal representative) in the belief that the person to whom it belongs cannot be discovered by taking reasonable steps.

In all other circumstances the test for dishonesty is that established in *R. v Ghosh* [1983]—a person is dishonest if:

> what s/he did is regarded as dishonest according to the ordinary standards of reasonable and honest people; **and**

> the defendant knew it was so regarded—it is irrelevant whether the defendant him/herself regarded his conduct as dishonest.

This test has the merit of avoiding the possibility of so-called "Robin Hood" defences, where the defendant believes his conduct to be justified but acknowledges that others may regard it as dishonest. Nevertheless, it has been criticised for placing the definition of dishonesty on the moral judgement of the jury, and that this may lead to inconsistency and injustice. However, the Law Commission, in its report on Fraud (2002), points out that the jury is required to apply not their own personal standards but what they perceive to be the standards of society at large and that, furthermore, they are not aware of any research or evidence to show that verdicts are in fact significantly inconsistent when dishonesty is a live issue in a case.

- **intention to permanently deprive**—**s.1** makes it clear that it is "immaterial whether the appropriation is made with a view to gain, or is made for the thief's own benefit". What is important is that the defendant intends the other person to be permanently deprived of the property—for example, it will be theft where A, in an act of malice, takes and destroys a treasured possession belonging to B. Therefore, it will not be theft where A appropriates property belonging to B but intends, at some point, to return it, except where (**s.6**):

  > s/he treats the property as his/her own to dispose of regardless of the other's rights. Borrowing and lending may be included here where it is "for a period and in circumstances making it equivalent to an outright taking or disposal"—for example, A "borrows" B's weekly bus pass and returns it after it has expired. While B has not been permanently deprived of the thing itself, s/he has been permanently deprived of its value—the effect is the same as if A had never returned the pass itself. However, in *R. v Lloyd* [1985], Lord Lane held that this would only apply where the "goodness, the virtue, the practical value . . . has . . . gone out of the article", and that the defendant's intention must be to "return the 'thing' in such a changed state that it can truly be said that all its goodness or virtue has gone.' The problem here is in the use of the word "all". What if, in the above example, A returns B's bus pass a day before it expires? Clearly not "all"

NOTES

its value has gone, but would this nevertheless be regarded as "equivalent to an outright taking or disposal"? Many people in B's position might well think so. This requirement may also be problematic where A appropriates and subsequently abandons B's property—for example, A takes B's bicycle from outside B's house and later abandons it some miles away. It seems that if A abandons the property in circumstances where it is likely to be returned to B, there is no theft, but if the circumstances are such that return is unlikely then this may be theft. Whether this is so is clearly a question of degree and will depend on the circumstances of the particular case;

➢ s/he parts with the property subject to a condition as to its return that s/he may not be able to perform—for example, where A pawns property belonging to B.

Robbery

Under **s.8** of the **Theft Act 1968**, robbery is theft with violence or the threat of violence. The maximum sentence is life imprisonment. Therefore, the *actus reus* of robbery is:

- the appropriation of property belonging to another (theft); **and**
- the use of force on any person; **or**
- putting or seeking to put any person in fear of being then and there subjected to force.

The use or threat of force must be done "in order to" steal. Thus, it is not robbery if A, having taken B's property without force, subsequently uses or threatens C with force in order to get away (though A has committed both theft and assault, they are not combined in these circumstances to make robbery). We should note, however, the victim of the theft and of the assault need not be the same person—it is still robbery where A uses or threatens force against B in order to appropriate property from C. Also, with the threat of force, the victim must be placed in fear of immediate ("there and then") force.

The *mens rea* of robbery is:

- dishonesty and an intention to permanently deprive (theft); **and**
- the intention to use force or the threat of force in order to steal.

Burglary

Under **s.9** of the **Theft Act 1968**, there are two forms of burglary—**s.9(1)(a)** and **s.9(1)(b)**. These are subject to a maximum of fourteen years' imprisonment for burglary of a "dwelling", and ten years in other cases. The *actus reus* of **s.9(1)(a) burglary** is:

- entering a building or part of a building as a trespasser—a trespasser is someone who enters the building or part of a building without permission or authority or, if s/he has some limited permission or authority, acts in a manner outside its scope. Thus, a shopper who moves from the shopfloor (public) space of a store into the stockroom (private) space is entering as a trespasser (*R. v Jones and Smith* [1976]; *R. v Walkington* [1979]). The concept of entry is more problematic. In *R. v Collins* [1972], it was held that there must be a "substantial and effective" entry, while in *R. v Brown* [1985], an "effective" entry was held sufficient—it need not be "substantial". However *R. v Ryan* [1996], the defendant was held to be guilty after being found stuck in a downstairs window with only his head and right arm inside the building—hardly either "effective" or "substantial". It may be, therefore, that any degree of physical presence, however slight, is sufficient if accompanied by the requisite *mens rea*.

The *mens rea* is:

- intention or subjective recklessness with regard to the trespass; **and**
- an intention, having entered, to:
  - ➢ steal; or
  - ➢ inflict grievous bodily harm; or
  - ➢ rape; or
  - ➢ commit criminal damage.

The *actus reus* of **s.9(1)(b) burglary** is:

- entry to a building or part of a building as a trespasser; **and**
- the appropriation or attempted appropriation of property belonging to another (theft or attempted theft); **or**
- the inflicting or attempted inflicting of grievous bodily harm.

The *mens rea* is:

- intention or subjective recklessness with regard to the trespass; **and**
- dishonesty and an intention to permanently deprive; **or**
- intention or subjective recklessness with regard to causing some harm, albeit not serious harm.

Finally, a "dwelling" is a building (or vessel or vehicle—for example, a houseboat or caravan) that is used for residential purposes.

NOTES

Obtaining property by deception

Under **s.15** of the **Theft Act 1968**, it is an offence to dishonestly obtain by deception property belonging to another with an intention to permanently deprive the other of it. The maximum sentence is ten years' imprisonment. Therefore, the *actus reus* of this offence is:

- **obtaining**—a person obtains property where they obtain ownership, possession or control of it. This includes obtaining for another or enabling another to obtain or retain the property. It was thought that the difference between obtaining and appropriating was that obtaining could be done with the consent of the owner whereas appropriating could not. However, as we have seen, since *Gomez* and *Hinks*, this distinction no longer holds.

- **property**—this means all property, including land (unlike theft).

- **belonging to another**—this has the same meaning as for theft.

- **deception**—the obtaining must be as a result of a deception. A deception is a false representation (whether express or implied—*R. v Laverty* [1970]; *Commissioner of Police of the Metropolis v Charles* [1977]; *R. v Lambie* [1981]) by words or conduct as to a question of fact, law or present intention. This must induce the other person to allow or enable the obtaining—where the deception does not influence the decision or actions of the other person, the obtaining cannot be a result of the deception. This also means that, with the exception of money transfers (**s.15A**), machines cannot be deceived. Finally, it follows that the deception must precede the obtaining (*R. v Collis-Smith* [1971]).

The *mens rea* is:

- **deliberate or reckless deception**—a deception is deliberate where the deceiver knows his/her representation is false and that the other person will or may believe it is true, or where the representation is ambiguous and may be understood by the other person in the false sense. Recklessness is used here in the subjective sense (*Large v Mainprize* [1989]; *R. v Goldman* [1997]).

- **dishonesty**—the *Ghosh* test (above) applies. We should note that not every deception is necessarily dishonest.

- **intention to permanently deprive**—see above.

Obtaining services by deception

Under **s.1** of the **Theft Act 1978**, it is an offence to dishonestly obtain services from another by deception. The maximum sentence is five years' imprisonment. Therefore, the *actus reus* of this offence is:

NOTES

- **obtain by deception**—the same principles apply here as for obtaining property by deception (above).

- **services** - this is the conferring of a benefit by doing some act, or causing or permitting some act to be done, on the understanding that the benefit has been or will be paid for. Unlike **s.2** and **s.3** (below), there is no requirement under **s.1** that the payment be legally enforceable.

The *mens rea* is:

- **dishonesty**—the Ghosh test (above) applies.

- **deliberate or reckless deception**—see above.

Evading a liability by deception

Under **s.2** of the **Theft Act 1978**, it is an offence to dishonestly evade a liability by deception. The maximum sentence is five years' imprisonment. Therefore, the *actus reus* of this offence is:

- **evasion**—evasion may take three forms:
  - ➤ securing the **remission** (in whole or in part) of an existing liability to make payment—for example, A owes B £50 and persuades B to release him/her from the debt by falsely pretending to have lost his job.
  - ➤ inducing a creditor to **wait for or forgo** payment with an intention to make permanent default (in whole or in part) of an existing liability to make payment. Forgoing means not claiming a debt because you do not know it exists—for example, in *R. v Holt* [1981], the defendant induced a waiter in a restaurant to forgo payment by falsely claiming to have already paid another waiter.
  - ➤ obtaining an **exemption** from or **abatement** (reduction) of a liability to make payment—for example, where A falsely claims to be a student in order to claim a discount to which s/he is not entitled.

- **liability**—unlike **s.1**, this must be a legally enforceable liability.

- **deception**—see above.

The *mens rea* is:

- **dishonesty**—see above.

- **deliberate or reckless deception**—see above.

NOTES

- **intention to make permanent default**—regarding inducing a creditor to wait for or forgo payment, this must be done with an intention to make permanent default—for example, if A gives B a dud cheque (here, B waits for payment), this will not be an offence if A does this only in order to overcome a short term cash flow problem.

The main criticism that can be made of these various deception offences is that they make the law in this area unnecessarily complex and difficult for prosecutors, judges and juries to apply. Consequently, the Law Commission, in its Report on Fraud (2002), recommends replacing the present offences with a single general offence of fraud. The Commission argues that this would have a number of advantages:

- it will make the law more comprehensible to juries;

- it will be a useful tool for the effective prosecution of fraud from investigation through to trial;

- replacing the current patchwork of crimes with a single, properly defined crime of fraud will dramatically simplify the law;

- a single, comprehensive offence of fraud will encompass fraud in its many unpredictable forms. Thus the law will be better able to keep pace with developing technology.

In fact, the Report recommends the creation of two new offences—one of fraud and one of obtaining services dishonestly. The offence of fraud would be committed where a person dishonestly:

- makes a false representation; *or*

- wrongfully fails to disclose information; *or*

- secretly abuses a position of trust, with intent to make a gain or cause loss or expose another to the risk of loss.

Regarding the secret abuse of trust, it is interesting to note that such an offence might well have offered an alternative prosecution to that of theft in the case of *Hinks* (see above). The Commission state that a position of trust may arise within a family, or in the context of voluntary work, or in any context where the parties are not at arm's length. It could be argued that Hinks, who described herself as the victim's "primary carer", could properly be regarded as being in such a position. More problematic would be the requirement that the abuse of trust be not only dishonest but secret. The Commission observes that if the defendant lets the victim know what is happening, then in their view the defendant's conduct cannot properly be regarded as fraud, and the Commission's draft Bill states that a person abuses his position secretly only if he believes that the victim and any person acting on the victim's behalf are

NOTES

ignorant of the abuse. However, it could be argued that the victim in *Hinks*, due to his limited intelligence, was ignorant of the abuse—he knew he was transferring the money, but could not appreciate that advantage was being taken of him. Furthermore, in view of the state of the law of theft following *Hinks*, it is interesting to note that in the same report the Commission comes out strongly against any general offence of dishonesty.

The offence of obtaining services dishonestly is intended to be a "theft-like" offence, which would make it unlawful to "steal" services by simply helping oneself to them. The offence would not require proof of deception or fraud. It would be committed where a person obtains services by any dishonest act with intent to avoid payment when payment is required. It would therefore extend to those who obtain services by providing false information to computers and machines.

Making off without payment

Under **s.3** of the **Theft Act 1978**, it is an offence to dishonestly make off without payment for goods supplied or service done with an intention to avoid payment. The maximum sentence is two years' imprisonment. Therefore, the *actus reus* of this offence is:

- **making off**—this simply means leaving the place at which payment is expected or required (*R. v Brooks and Brooks* [1982]).

- **without payment for goods supplied or service done**—this offence only applies to situations where payment is required or expected **"on the spot"**—for example, one is expected/required to pay for a meal before leaving a restaurant or a haircut before leaving the barber's shop. This requirement has caused some difficulties. In *R. v Vincent* [2001], the defendant had left two hotels without paying his bill. His subsequent convictions were quashed because, as he had reached an agreement with the hotel owners to pay *after* he had departed, then payment on the spot was *not* required or expected. The fact that the agreement had been obtained dishonestly did not reinstate this expectation. It is interesting to note that the Court of Appeal also pointed out that in such circumstances, while the customer would be liable to be charged with obtaining services by deception, if he continued to stay at the hotel with that dishonest intention, he would not infringe **s.3**. In thus pointing out the alternative and correct charge, without, at the same time, doing violence to the wording of **s.3**, it could be argued that the Court of Appeal in *Vincent* has followed a preferable path to that taken by the House of Lords in *Hinks* (see above). Finally, as with **s.2**, this offence only applies to payments that may be legally enforced.

The *mens rea* is:

NOTES

- **dishonesty**—see above.

- **knowledge that payment on the spot is required or expected** (either through specific notice or custom and practice).

- **intention to avoid payment**—this means an intention to permanently avoid payment (*R. v Allen* [1985]).

Criminal Damage

Basic criminal damage

Under **s.1(1)** of the **Criminal Damage Act 1971**, it is an offence, without lawful excuse, to intentionally or recklessly destroy or damage property belonging to another. The maximum sentence is ten years' imprisonment (fourteen years' if racially aggravated—**Crime & Disorder Act 1998, s.30**). Therefore, the *actus reus* of this offence is:

- **destroy or damage**—property is damaged if it suffers some physical harm, impairment or deterioration which requires expense or (more than minimal) effort to remedy (*A (a juvenile) v R.* [1978]; *Hardman v Chief Constable of Avon and Somerset* [1986]; *Morphitis v Salmon* [1990]).

- **property**—this includes all tangible property, including land.

- **belonging to another**—by **s.10**, property belongs to those having custody or control of it or any proprietary right or interest in it.

The *mens rea* is:

- **intention or recklessness**—recklessness is used here in its objective sense (*R. v Caldwell* [1981]). This is the major issue in relation to criminal damage and the criticisms of objective recklessness are dealt with above (see **Chapter 14).**

- **without lawful excuse**—this obviously allows for an appropriate general defence. Furthermore, under **s.5(2)**, a person will also have lawful excuse where:
  - ➢ s/he believes that the person s/he believes to be entitled to consent to the destruction or damage has consented or would have consented had they known of the destruction or damage and its circumstances.
  - ➢ s/he destroyed or damaged the property in order to protect property belonging to him/herself or another, believing that the property was an immediate need of protection and that the means of protection adopted or proposed were reasonable

NOTES

in the circumstances. By **s.5(3)**, this belief need only be honest—it need not be reasonable.

Aggravated criminal damage

Under **s.1(2)** of the **Criminal Damage Act 1971**, it is an offence for a person to, without lawful excuse, intentionally or recklessly destroy or damage property, whether belonging to him/ herself or another intending thereby to endanger the life of another or being reckless as to whether the life of another would be endangered. The maximum sentence is life imprisonment.

The *actus reus* is essentially the same as for **s.1(1)** with the exception that it may also include damage to one's own property. The *mens rea* requires, in addition to that for **s.1(1)**, the defendant must intend or be objectively reckless to a risk that the destruction or damage will endanger life. Furthermore, while lawful excuse may be a defence here, the specific defences under **s.5(3)** do **not** apply.

Arson

Under **s.1(3)** of the **Criminal Damage Act 1971**, criminal damage or aggravated criminal damage caused by fire is regarded as arson. The defendant must either intend or be objectively reckless as to damage by fire. The maximum sentence is life imprisonment.

Revision Notes

You should now write your revision notes for this topic. Here is an example for you and some suggested headings:

Making Off (1978, s.3)

- ar = making off (leaving spot where payment required/expected—*R. v Brooks & Brooks*) without payment for goods/services (only where payment on the spot required/expected (*R. v Vincent*)—payment must be legally enforceable)

- mr = dishonesty (*Ghosh* test); knowledge that payment on the spot required/ expected; intention to permanently avoid payment (*R. v Allen*)

- Theft (1968, s.1)—Appropriation
- Theft (1968, s.1)—Property

NOTES

- Theft (1968, s.1)—Belonging to another
- Theft (1968, s.1)—Dishonesty
- Theft (1968, s.1)—Intention to permanently deprive
- Robbery (1968, s.8)
- Burglary (1968, s.9(1)(a))
- Burglary (1968, s.9(1)(b))
- Obtaining Property by Deception (1968, s.15)—ar
- Obtaining Property by Deception (1968, s.15)—mr
- Obtaining Services by Deception (1978, s.1)
- Evasion of a Liability by Deception (1978, s.2)
- Criminal Damage (1971, s.1(1))
- Aggravated Criminal Damage (1971, s.1(2))
- Arson (1971, s.1(3))

Using your cards, you should now be able to write a short paragraph in response to each of the following questions:

1. Explain and discuss the meaning of "appropriation".

2. What property can be stolen?

3. When is property regarded as belonging to another?

4. Explain and discuss the meaning of dishonesty?

5. Explain the meaning of "intention to permanently deprive".

6. Explain and discuss the elements of the following offences:
    (a) Robbery.
    (b) Burglary.
    (c) Obtaining property by deception.
    (d) Obtaining services by deception.
    (e) Evading a Liability by deception.
    (f) Making Off Without Payment.
    (g) Criminal damage.
    (h) Aggravated criminal damage.
    (i) Arson.

NOTES

Useful Websites

- Law Commission Report on Fraud (2002)—**www.lawcom.gov.uk/files/lc276.pdf**, **www.lawcom.gov.uk/files/lc276sum.pdf** and **www.lawcom.gov.uk/files/lc276bill.pdf**

19 Criminal Law—Preliminary Offences and Participation

Key Points

What you need to know and discuss:

- Whether and why preliminary behaviour should be criminalised.
- The *actus reus* and *mens rea* of attempt.
- The *actus reus* and *mens rea* of incitement.
- The *actus reus* and *mens rea* of conspiracy.
- Whether and why secondary participation should be criminalised.
- Discuss principal and secondary offenders.

Introduction

The preliminary offences (sometimes called inchoate offences) concern criminal liability for the preparation or instigation of criminal acts. It is obviously necessary and desirable that the law enables the police to intervene to prevent planned criminal activity and the courts to punish those involved without having to wait for the full offence to be committed.

Attempt

Under **s.1(1)** of the **Criminal Attempts Act 1981**, a person will be guilty of attempting to commit an offence to which the Act applies where, with intent to commit the full offence, they do an act that is "more than merely preparatory" to the commission of that offence. Summary-only offences and secondary offences (see below) are not covered by the Act. The maximum sentence is the same as the maximum possible for the full offence.

As noted above, criminalising attempts enables effective police intervention before commission of the full offence. Also a person who makes an unsuccessful attempt may seek to make a further attempt. However, we should not criminalise people simply for having wicked thoughts or criminal fantasies. They must have *done* something to put those thoughts or fantasies into effect. Precisely *what* they must have done is the central issue/problem in relation to attempts—*i.e.* what is the *actus reus* of attempt? The **1981 Act** requires an act that is "more than merely preparatory" to the commission of the full offence—but what does this mean? In *R. v Eagleton* [1855] the court took the view that the defendant must have done the last act required prior to commission of the full offence. This "last act" approach was supported by Lord Diplock in *DPP v Stonehouse* [1977], where he stated that "the offender must have crossed the Rubicon and burnt his boats". However, such an interpretation can be seen as too restrictive, thereby making effective early intervention very difficult. By contrast, in *Stephen's Digest* [1894] it was argued that any act forming part of series of acts which, if uninterrupted, would constitute the full offence could be regarded as an attempt. This approach can be equally criticised as being too broad. In *R. v Gullefer* [1990], the Court of Appeal took a middle road between these two positions in interpreting the **1981 Act**. According to Lord Lane, this means that the defendant must have moved beyond mere preparation and embarked upon the crime proper. Ultimately, whether the defendant has in fact done so is a question of fact for the jury to decide. It can be argued that this test remains rather vague and unpredictable (contrast, for example, *R. v Geddes* [1996] with *R. v Tosti* [1997]). However, in this regard we should note that the Law Commission report that preceded the Act accepted there was no "magic formula" and that there was bound to be some uncertainty. It may also be argued that this approach is still rather restrictive (contrast, for example, *R. v Jones* [1990] with *R. v Campbell* [1991]). In this respect, it is interesting to note the proposed offence in the **Sexual Offences Bill 2003** of meeting or travelling with the intention of meeting a child following sexual grooming. The White Paper that preceded the Bill stated that this "will enable action to be taken before any sexual activity takes place where it is clear that this is what the offender intends". As such, this offence must be broader than the existing law on attempts and may well constitute an offence of "mere preparation".

The Act also makes it clear a person can be convicted of attempt in circumstances where the facts are such that the commission of the full offence is impossible—for example, a pickpocket will be guilty of attempted theft if s/he slips his/her hand into someone's pocket, intending to steal whatever is there, but finds the pocket empty. Somewhat bizarrely, the House of Lords in *Anderton v Ryan* [1985] held the impossible could not be attempted, but rapidly reversed this error in *R. v Shivpuri* [1986]. We should note that this only applies to factual impossibility. If the intended "offence" is not actually a crime (legal impossibility), then there can be no criminal attempt—it is not a crime to attempt to do an act which is not itself a crime, even where the defendant mistakenly believes that it is (*R. v Taafe* [1983]).

The *mens rea* of attempt is an intention to commit the full offence. Therefore, the *mens rea* of the attempt can be more restricted than that of the full offence—for example, attempted

NOTES

murder requires an intention to kill, whereas murder requires either an intention to kill or cause GBH. Also, attempted criminal damage requires an intention to cause criminal damage, whereas the full offence can be committed recklessly. This applies to an intention to bring about the unlawful result—where recklessness as to the surrounding circumstances is sufficient for the full offence, then it will also be sufficient for an attempt to commit that offence (*R. v Khan* [1990]).

Incitement

Incitement is an offence at common law. To incite means to instigate the commission of a crime through advice, encouragement, persuasion or compulsion. The *actus reus* of the offence is the act of incitement, whether this is in writing, speech or by conduct, and may be explicit or implicit (*Invicta Plastics Ltd v Clare* [1976]). As with attempts, a person may be liable for incitement even where commission of the offence is factually impossible (*R. v McDonough* [1962])—impossibility is only a defence where the act incited is not, in fact, a crime (*R. v Whitehouse* [1977]). The *mens rea* is an intention that the offence will be carried out.

Do we need an offence of incitement? There are clear overlaps with conspiracy and with aiding, abetting, counselling and procuring (see below). For example, if the person incited agrees to carry out the offence, there will be a conspiracy. Also, if the offence is carried out, then the inciter may be liable as a secondary party. However, if the incitement is through compulsion, then the existence of a conspiracy is questionable. Furthermore, as in *Invicta Plastics*, can a company that places an advertisement in a magazine really be said to enter into a conspiracy with every person who responds to that advertisement? Also, secondary participation only arises where the offence is carried out, whereas incitement allows early intervention and provides for liability where the offence is not in fact carried out. Therefore, it would seem that incitement is a necessary element in the patchwork of preliminary (inchoate) and secondary offences.

Conspiracy

While certain common law conspiracies may still arise (for example, conspiracy to outrage public decency), we are concerned here with statutory conspiracies under the **Criminal Law Act 1977**. Under **s.1**, a conspiracy is an agreement between two or more persons to pursue a course of conduct that, if carried out in accordance with their intentions, would result in the commission of an offence by one of the parties to the agreement. Thus, the *actus reus* is the fact of agreement. It is not necessary to show that each conspirator knew all the other conspirators, so long as each had reached agreement with at least one other (*i.e.* liability will still arise in both "wheel" and "chain" conspiracies). By **s.2**, it will not be a conspiracy where the only other person involved is the intended victim, the defendant's spouse, or a person under the age of criminal responsibility (though in this case, D may be liable under the principle of innocent agency if the young person carries out the offence). By **s.1**, as with both attempts and incitement, liability may arise for a conspiracy to commit the factually impossible. While there is no authority on the point, we can also presume that, consistent with the position on attempt and incitement, there can be no criminal conspiracy to commit and act which is not itself an offence (*i.e.* legal impossibility). The *mens rea* is an intention that the agreement be carried out and that the offence be committed by one of the conspirators (*R. v Edwards* [1991]). However, contrary the position on attempt (and probably incitement), mere recklessness as to surrounding circumstances is *not* sufficient to ground a charge of conspiracy—D must know or intend that those circumstances exist or will exist (**s.1**). The maximum sentence is the maximum for the offence conspired at.

Do we need an offence of conspiracy? First of all, it allows earlier intervention than the law on attempts. For example, in *R. v Campbell* [1991], there was no attempt as C had not entered the Post Office. However, if C had an accomplice such as a getaway driver (A), then both C and A could have been guilty of conspiracy to rob the Post Office. Secondly, conspiracy can bring the "criminal mastermind" or "Mr Big" within the scope of the criminal law where they would otherwise be insulated from liability on the basis of attempt, incitement or secondary participation. Therefore, again, conspiracy seems a necessary element in the patchwork of preliminary (inchoate) and secondary offences.

Participation

Those who commit the *actus reus* of an offence are referred to as the **principal offenders**. However, others may participate in the commission of the offence without making a direct contribution to the *actus reus*—for example, the person who supplies a gun to be used in an armed robbery—these are known as **secondary offenders**. Under **s.8** of the **Accessories and Abettors Act 1861** (as amended by the **Criminal Law Act 1977**) any person who aids, abets, counsels or procures the commission of an indictable offence is liable to tried and punished as a principal offender. Unlike the preliminary offences above, here the principal offence must have been committed—*i.e.* the principal offender must have committed the *actus reus* of the principal offence with the requisite *mens rea*. The one exception relates to procuring, where it need only be shown that the *actus reus* of the principal offence has been committed (*R. v Millward* [1994]).

Therefore, the *actus reus* of secondary participation is:

- **aiding**—the provision of material assistance to the principal at the time the offence is committed. It is not necessary to show the principal was aware of this assistance—for example, A, unknown to B, trips a police officer who is about to intervene in a robbery being committed by B.

- **abetting**—the provision of encouragement to the principal at the time the offence is committed—for example, A shouts words of encouragement to B while B is assaulting C.

- **counselling**—the provision of assistance, advice or encouragement to the principal prior to the commission of the offence.

- **procuring**—means to "produce by endeavour"—*i.e.* the commission of an act which causes or brings about the commission of the principal offence. Again, it is not necessary to show the principal was aware of this act—for example, A spikes B's drink which results in B driving with excess alcohol (**Attorney-General's Reference (No.1)** [1975]).

The *mens rea* is an intention to do the acts that the defendant knows are capable of assisting, encouraging or procuring the commission of the principal offence. It follows that s/he must also know or be subjectively reckless to the existence of the facts and circumstances that constitute the principal offence. It is not necessary to show D intended the commission of the principal offence (*DPP for Northern Ireland v Lynch* [1975]; *R. v J.F. Alford Transport Ltd* [1997]).

We should note two further points regarding participation:

- **joint enterprise**—where the defendant is aiding or abetting the principal in the commission of the principal offence, they are engaged in a joint enterprise. The defendant will be liable for aiding and/or abetting any offence falling within their common purpose, but not for those that are fundamentally different and that were outside the range of offences contemplated by the defendant—for example, A aids B in a burglary by keeping look-out. B is disturbed by C and is killed by B. A will only be liable as a secondary party to murder if it can be shown that s/he knew or contemplated that B might kill in the course of the burglary (*R. v Powell, R. v English* [1997]). Even where A knows or contemplates that B may use violence, it must be shown that this was of a type and degree contemplated by A (*R. v Uddin* [1998]; *R. v Greatrex* [1999]).

- **withdrawal**—it may be possible for a secondary party to avoid liability by withdrawing his assistance or encouragement prior to the commission of the principal offence. Any such withdrawal must be clear and unequivocal and the defendant must do all that is reasonably possible to neutralise the effects of any aid or encouragement already given (*R. v Rook* [1993]).

NOTES

Is the present law on secondary participation satisfactory?

- A Law Commission consultation paper (1993) proposed to replace the present complex law on secondary participation with offences of assisting the commission of crime and encouraging the commission of crime.

- These would be preliminary (inchoate) offences, thereby removing the present requirement that the principal offence actually be committed. This has the advantage of consistency with the related law on attempts, incitement and conspiracy, and as Professor Sir John Smith has pointed out, D's "moral culpability is determined at the moment he does [the act of assistance or encouragement], whether or not the contemplated offence is committed."

- However, would "assisting or encouraging" cover the "spiked drink" situation? Here, D cannot be said to have "assisted" the commission of the offence, as the principal lacks the *mens rea* for that offence. Also, the principal cannot be "encouraged" by something of which he is unaware.

- More modern statutes use alternative terminology. For example, the **Sexual Offences Act 1956** talks of "causing or encouraging", while the **Misuse of Drugs Act 1971** speaks of "assisting or inducing". Here, "causing" and "inducing" would seem to share the same meaning and would appear to cover situations where D commits an act which brings about the commission of the offence by the principal, but of which the principal need not be aware.

- Therefore, it may be that the best solution would be to replace the present law on secondary participation with preliminary (inchoate) offences of assisting, encouraging or causing (inducing) the commission of crime.

Revision Notes

You should now write your revision notes for this topic. Here is an example for you and some suggested headings:

NOTES

POP②—Incitement

- common law offence
- ar = instigate (writing, speech, conduct) crime through advice, encouragement, persuasion or compulsion
- mr = intention that offence carried out
- can incite the factually impossible (*R. v McDonough*)
- cannot criminally incite conduct which is not itself a crime (*R. v Whitehouse*)

POP①—Attempts

POP②—Incitement

POP③—Conspiracy

POP④—Participation

POP⑤—Joint Enterprise & Withdrawal

Using your cards, you should now be able to write a short paragraph in response to each of the following questions:

1. Explain and discuss the *actus reus* and *mens rea* of attempt.
2. Explain and discuss what is meant by "incitement".
3. Explain and discuss liability for statutory conspiracies.
4. Explain and discuss how a person can be a secondary offender.
5. Explain and discuss the law relating to joint enterprises.

NOTES

20 Sentencing

Key Points

What you need to know and discuss:

- The need for a criminal justice system.
- The main aims of punishment.
- Key concepts in effective punishment.
- The current approach to sentencing of adult offenders.
- The current approach to sentencing of young offenders.
- The effectiveness of the system in achieving its aims

Introduction

There are two main reasons for the existence of a criminal justice system:

- to discourage anti-social conduct;
- to satisfy a general moral sense that those who engage in such conduct deserve to be punished. Punishment is seen as the correct moral outcome of criminal activity.

The aims of punishment

The **Criminal Justice Bill 2003** provides for the first time a statutory statement of the aims of sentencing:

- Punishment (**retribution**).
- Crime reduction through **deterrence**.

- Crime reduction through reform and **rehabilitation**.
- Public protection (**incapacitation**).
- **Reparation** by offenders to persons affected by their offences.

We need to consider some of these aims in more detail. We should also note that the different sentencing options available to the courts relate differently to the various aims (for example, custodial sentences serving the aims of retribution, deterrence, incapacitation and, hopefully, rehabilitation, while Community Punishment Orders (formerly Community Service) are more concerned with rehabilitation and reparation).

Retribution

This is where punishment is seen as the way in which society gains revenge on the criminal. It is based on the idea that the criminal deserves to be punished and society gains a cathartic benefit from this. While the importance of this retributive element has declined, it can still be seen in the response to particularly horrifying crimes (for example, offences against children).

Deterrence

This is where punishment is intended to discourage further crime. This has two aspects:

- **individual deterrence**—it is hoped that punishment will deter the individual criminal from re-offending.
- **general deterrence**—it is hoped that punishment of the criminal will act as an example to deter others from committing crimes.

However, as many crimes are committed in the heat of the moment, while intoxicated, or are opportunistic rather than considered, we should not over-emphasise the deterrent quality of punishment. Many offenders simply do not stop to consider the possible consequences of their actions. Others view the likelihood of being caught as so small that the risk is worth taking.

Rehabilitation

This is where punishment is designed to discourage re-offending by rehabilitating the offender into the law-abiding mainstream of society, by reforming his/her character. It is based on the view that people are not born criminals but commit crimes for identifiable reasons. It follows that if the punishment regime addresses these reasons successfully, the criminal behaviour should stop.

NOTES

Key concepts in effective punishment

Whichever balance of these three elements is used, there are four key concepts which must be incorporated into any successful criminal justice system.

Proportionality

The severity of the punishment should be proportionate to the gravity of the offence because:

- punishment is justified by the fault of the offender. It follows that the degree of punishment should therefore reflect the degree of fault.
- if the punishment is perceived as excessively harsh, there will be a reluctance to prosecute and convict, creating the danger of the law falling into disrepute.
- without proportionality, there is no reason to commit minor rather than serious offences.
- without proportionality, there is nothing to deter the criminal from committing a further offence to avoid punishment for an earlier one.

Therefore, proportionality is essential to deterrence and to maintaining public confidence in the justice of the system. It is even implicit in the just desserts policy of retribution.

Certainty

The more certain the prospect of punishment, the stronger its deterrent effect. The threat of even a very severe punishment is unlikely to deter if the chances of being caught are small. Therefore, we can argue that investment in policing and other crime prevention strategies is likely to be more effective than investing in more prisons.

Publicity

Informing people (through the education system and by other means) about the criminal justice system and the consequences of crime is vital to the success of the system. This again enhances the deterrent quality of punishment. People cannot be deterred by something they do not know.

Promptness

It is important the system is efficient in the detection and punishment of crime. The more prompt the punishment, the clearer and more effective its association with the crime, both in the mind of the individual offender and amongst society at large.

NOTES

The present approach to sentencing in the English courts

This is governed primarily by the **Powers of Criminal Courts (Sentencing) Act 2000**. Regarding adult offenders, the Act refers to three main forms of punishment:

- Custodial sentences—the court can only pass a custodial sentence where either (**s.79(2)**):

  ➢ the offence was so serious that only a custodial sentence can be justified; or
  ➢ in the case of a violent or sexual offence, a custodial sentence is necessary to protect the public from serious harm.

  In making this assessment, the court must take into account any aggravating or mitigating factors and any previous convictions.
  The court must also (except where the sentence is fixed by law—for example, for murder) decide the length of any custodial sentence. **S.80(2)** provides that the length of the sentence shall be either:

  ➢ commensurate with the seriousness of the offence; or
  ➢ in the case of a violent or sexual offence, for such longer term as is necessary to protect the public from serious harm.

  In *R. v Cunningham* [1992], Lord Taylor stated "the purpose of a custodial sentence must primarily be to punish and deter. Accordingly, the phrase 'commensurate with the seriousness of the offence' must mean commensurate with the punishment and deterrence which the seriousness of the offence requires". This emphasises that notions of deterrence and proportionality are central to current practice.

- **Community sentences**—where a custodial sentence is not justified, the court may consider a community sentence, for example, a **community rehabilitation order** (formerly probation) or a **community punishment order** (formerly community service). Again, a community sentence can only be passed where it is justified by the seriousness of the offence (**s.35(1)**) and any restriction on liberty must be commensurate with the seriousness of the offence (**s.35(3)**).

- Fines—alternatively, or in addition to, the above sentences, the court may impose a fine. The amount of the fine must reflect the seriousness of the offence (**s.128(2)**) and take into account the offender's financial circumstances (**s.128(3)**). It is, however, worth noting that recent statistics show that approximately 40 per cent of fines are never paid.

NOTES

- Miscellaneous sanctions:

  - ➤ **Compensation orders**—the court may order the offender to compensate the victim of the crime.
  - ➤ **Confiscation orders**—the court may in some cases (for example, drugs offences) confiscate any assets gained as a result of the crime. The **Proceeds of Crime Act 2002** has extended the scope of confiscation proceedings and established an Assets Recovery Agency.
  - ➤ **Curfew orders**—these involve the electronic tagging of offenders in order to monitor their movements.
  - ➤ **Drug treatment and testing orders**—these can be made for a period of between six months and three years. Given the clear relationship between drug use and criminality, these orders are seen by many, including Lord Woolf, as a valuable attempt seriously to address the causes of offending behaviour and assist in the rehabilitation of offenders.

- **Mentally Ill Offenders**—the court must obtain a medical report before sentencing and must take into account the likely effect of the sentence on the offender's illness and any treatment regime (**s.82**).

- **Youth Offfenders**—special rules apply to young offenders. These operate within an overall youth justice context that places a priority on welfare, reform and rehabilitation. For example, regarding custodial sanctions, young offenders are subject to **Detention and Training Orders** in special institutions rather than detention in adult prison. There are also a variety of community sentences specifically designed to respond to young offending:

  - ➤ **Referral orders**—whereby the young offender is referred to the local Youth Offending Team in order to address the causes and consequences of his/her offending behaviour. This is a multi-agency approach involving the court, educationalists and social workers, etc.
  - ➤ **Supervision orders**—these are the youth version of community rehabilitation orders.
  - ➤ **Reparation orders**—these require the young offender to make reparation to the victim of the offence or to the community at large—for example, a letter of apology, repairing damage done, cleaning graffiti, collecting litter, etc.
  - ➤ **Action Plan orders**—these require the young offender to take steps to address the causes of the offending behaviour—for example, by attending an anger management course, a drug misuse programme or motor education project.
  - ➤ **Parenting orders**—where a young person has been convicted of an offence or is subject to an anti-social behaviour order, his/her parents may be required to attend parental guidance or counselling sessions.

NOTES

- **Minimum and Mandatory Sentences—s.109** provides for a mandatory life sentence following a second conviction for a serious offence (*e.g.* murder, manslaughter, and rape). **S.110** provides for a minimum sentence of seven years' imprisonment following a third conviction for trafficking in Class A drugs (for example, heroin). **S.111** provides for a minimum three years' imprisonment following a third conviction for domestic burglary. The courts may only depart from these sentences in exceptional circumstances. This approach has been criticised as interfering with the judge's discretion to impose the sentence s/he believes the offence demands, having heard all the evidence, and as being contrary to the principle of proportionality. However, in *R. v Offen and others* [2000], the Court of Appeal held that where the defendant does not represent a significant risk to the public, this is an "exceptional circumstance" that justifies the court in not imposing the mandatory sentence. This highlights the potential for conflict between the pursuit of policy by the Government and application of principle by the judiciary.

The effectiveness of the criminal justice system

Doubts have been expressed regarding the effectiveness of the present range of sanctions, particularly custodial sentences. Official statistics reveal that approximately 56 per cent of offenders are re-convicted within two years of release. We can argue this is due to prison overcrowding (described by Lord Woolf as a "cancer eating at the ability of the prison service to deliver"), consequent weaknesses in rehabilitation programmes and lack of support following release. We should also note that the cost to the criminal justice system of recorded crime alone committed by ex-prisoners has been estimated to be at least £11 billion per year. Until recently, community sentences thought to be only marginally more effective (less than 1 per cent) than custodial, but the latest Home Office research (February 2003) show a reconviction rate of only 44 per cent. Also, community sentences are much cheaper and have lower social costs (for example, family breakdown—43 per cent of convicted prisoners and 48 per cent of those held on remand lose contact with their families; 125,000 children each year have a parent imprisoned). Community sentences are also considerably cheaper to implement. The financial and social costs of custody are in many cases not justified by its results.

We can also argue the present system pays too much attention to the consequences of crime, and not enough to its causes or prevention. While acknowledging that social and economic factors do not excuse criminal behaviour, causative elements must be addressed if effective crime prevention strategies are to be developed. As Lord Scarman observed in his report on the Brixton disorders of 1981, "the social conditions in Brixton do not provide an excuse for disorder. But the disorders cannot be fully understood unless they are seen in the context of complex political, social and economic factors which together create a predisposition towards violent protest." There are also significant links between offending and factors

NOTES

such as education, employment, mental health, and housing—in this respect, the report by the Social Exclusion Unit (see "Useful Websites" below) makes interesting reading. It may also be argued that increasing clear-up rates would have a stronger deterrent effect than heavier sentences (*i.e.* it is certainty of punishment, rather than severity that deters). Currently, the so-called "Justice Gap" means that only 20 per cent of reported crimes result in a successful prosecution.

The Halliday Report—*Making Punishments Work: Review of the Sentencing Framework for England and Wales*

In July 2001, John Halliday published his review of the sentencing framework in England and Wales. The review was established in response to concerns that the present framework suffers from serious deficiencies that reduce its contributions to crime reduction and public confidence. The review found those concerns to be well founded, although identified some strengths within the present system on which to build. In arguing the case for change, the review identified an unclear and unpredictable approach to persistent offenders, who commit a disproportionate amount of crime, and the inability of short prison sentences (those of less than twelve months) to make any meaningful intervention in the criminal careers of those who receive them. The review noted that sentencing serves the purposes of crime reduction and reparation as well as punishment, commenting that the available evidence suggests that greater support for reform and rehabilitation, within the appropriate "punitive envelope" of the sentence, to reduce risks of re-offending, offers the best prospects for improved outcomes. It also noted that there remains a need for wider crime reduction strategies, outside sentencing, aimed at preventing offending in the first place, and increasing the likelihood that those who do commit crime will be caught and brought to justice speedily. Among the review's main recommendations were:

- A new framework should do more to support crime reduction and reparation, while meeting the needs of punishment. In support of crime reduction, the framework should in particular do more to target persistent offenders and support the work of the prison and probation services to reduce re-offending.

- The existing "just desserts" philosophy should be modified by incorporating a new presumption that severity of sentence should increase when an offender has sufficiently recent and relevant previous convictions.

- The principles governing severity of sentence should be as follows:
    - ➢ severity of punishment should reflect the seriousness of the offence (or offences as a whole) and the offender's relevant criminal history;

NOTES

> the seriousness of the offence should reflect its degree of harmfulness, or risked harmfulness, and the offender's culpability in committing the offence;
> in considering criminal history, the severity of the sentence should increase to reflect a persistent course of criminal conduct, as shown by previous convictions and sentences.

- Imprisonment should be used when no other sentence would be adequate to meet the seriousness of the offence (or offences), having taken into account the offender's criminal history.

- Courts should be free to choose from the full range of non-custodial sentences, while being required to match the punitive weight of such a sentence with the seriousness of the offence (or offences), having taken into account the offender's criminal history.

- Unless only a prison sentence of 12 months or more would meet the needs for punishment, sentencers should consider the scope for a community sentence to meet the needs of punishment, crime reduction and reparation.

- Prison sentences of less than 12 months need to be substantially reformed to make them more effective in reducing crime and protecting the public.

- All such sentences should normally consist of a period in prison (maximum 3 months) and a period (minimum 6 months) of compulsory supervision in the community, subject to conditions and requirements whose breach may lead to a return to prison— so-called "custody plus".

- Prison sentences of more than 12 months should continue to be served partly in prison and partly in the community, but conditions of release, and supervision, should continue to the end of the sentence, with liability to recall to prison if conditions are breached. For most offenders (excluding violent or sexual offenders), release would be at the half-way point of the sentence.

- Existing community sentences should be replaced by a new generic community punishment order, whose punitive weight would be proportionate to the current offence and any additional severity for previous convictions. The sentence would consist of ingredients best suited to meeting the needs of crime reduction, and exploiting opportunities for reparation, within the appropriately punitive "envelope".

- More should be done to improve public knowledge and understanding of the sentencing framework.

The report was welcomed by the Government and many of its recommendations are taken up in the **Criminal Justice Bill 2003**. The main proposals in the Bill regarding sentences are:

- Relevant previous convictions, the fact that the offence was committed while on bail, and either racial or religious motivation are all to be regarded as aggravating factors.

NOTES

- Magistrates' sentencing powers are to be increased from 6 months' to 12 months' imprisonment.

- A new Sentencing Guidelines Council.

- A rationalisation of community sentences for adult offenders allowing courts to mix and match different elements (for example, unpaid work, curfews, drug treatment) within a new generic Community Order.

- The replacement of short prison sentences (less than 12 months) with Custody Plus sentences—a maximum of 3 months in prison followed by a minimum of 6 months' community supervision. This should enhance potential for rehabilitation.

- The introduction of Intermittent Custody—a minimum 6 months (maximum 12 months) with a minimum of 14 days (maximum 90 days) in custody, the intervals between custodial days to be subject to community supervision. This should enable offenders to maintain family, community and work links, and enhance potential for rehabilitation.

- A new sentence of imprisonment for public protection—this would apply to those convicted of specified violent (for example, manslaughter, assault occasioning actual bodily harm, robbery) or sexual offences (for example, rape, unlawful sexual intercourse, indecent assault) and the court is satisfied that no other available sentence would be adequate to protect the public from serious harm. This would be a sentence of detention for an indeterminate period. This is likely to be the most controversial of the Bill's proposals relating to sentencing.

Conclusion

The sentencing process, both in the choice and severity of sentence, is closely related to fault and the degree of fault on the part of the offender. The criminal justice system must continue to develop in such a way as to maintain public confidence while at the same time developing and implementing a range of punishment strategies appropriate to the individual circumstances of each case. It is in this context that concerns over the desirability of mandatory and minimum sentencing have been expressed. Furthermore, while acknowledging that custody is in some cases the only acceptable and effective option, both the cost and effectiveness of the various strategies available indicate custody should only be used where absolutely necessary, and greater and more effective use should be made of non-custodial alternatives—as recommended by the Home Affairs Select Committee in 1998 (**3rd Report: Alternatives to Prison Sentences**—available at **www.publications.parliament.uk/pa/cm199798/cmselect/ cmhaff/486/48602.htm**).

NOTES

Revision Notes

You should now write your revision notes for this topic. Here is an example for you and some suggested headings:

C&P④Custodial Sentences

- PCC(S)A 2000

- s.79(2)—only pass custodial where (a) only custodial can be justified or (b) if violent/sexual custody, necessary to protect public

- s.80(2)—length of sentence must be (a) commensurate with seriousness of offence or (b) if violent sexual, for such longer term as necessary to protect public

- "commensurate" = proportionate to punishment and deterrence seriousness of offence requires (_R. v Cunningham_ [1992])

C&P①—Intro (need for system)

C&P②—Aims of Punishment

C&P③—Key Concepts

C&P④—Custodial Sentences

C&P⑤—Other Sentences

C&P⑥—Young Offenders

C&P⑦—Minimum and Mandatory Sentences

C&P⑧—Effectiveness of System

C&P⑨—Conclusion

Using your cards, you should now be able to write a short paragraph in response to each of the following questions:

1. Why do we need a criminal justice system?
2. What aims and objectives may a judge be pursuing when sentencing an offender?
3. What elements should be present in an effective system of punishment?
4. Describe the approach to sentencing under the Powers of Criminal Courts (Sentencing) Act 2000.

NOTES

5. Discuss the special provision made for young offenders.

6. Discuss the use of minimum and mandatory sentences.

7. How effective is the system in achieving its aims?

Useful Websites

For more information and statistics on the criminal justice system, visit:

- www.criminal_justice_system.gov.uk (a portal site with links to other relevant sites)
- www.homeoffice.gov.uk
- www.hmprisonservice.gov.uk
- www.homeoffice.gov.uk/rds/pdfs/hosb1800.pdf (British Crime Survey 2000)
- The Halliday Report: *Making Punishments Work: Review of the Sentencing Framework for England and Wales*—www.homeoffice.gov.uk/docs/halliday.html
- Reducing re-offending by ex-prisoners: Summary of the Social Exclusion Unit report—www.socialexclusionunit.gov.uk/reduce—reoff/rr—summary.pdf
- Narrowing the Justice Gap Framework Document—www.cjsonline.gov.uk/njg/documents/njg-framework.pdf
- Lord Woolf, "A New Approach to Sentencing"—www.lcd.gov.uk/judicial/speeches/lcj090403.htm

NOTES

SECTION FOUR:
CONTRACT LAW AND CONSUMER PROTECTION

21 Contract Law—Formation of Contract

Key Points

What you need to know and discuss:

- The rules of law relating to contractual offers (including invitations to treat).
- The rules of law relating to contractual acceptance.
- The rules of law relating to consideration.
- The rules of law relating to contractual intention.
- The rules of law relating to contractual capacity.

Introduction

Put simply, a contract is an agreement enforceable at law. However, while all contracts are agreements, not all agreements are contracts. Therefore, a contract is a particular type of agreement that can be identified by certain characteristics:

OFFER	}		
	} AGREEMENT	}	
ACCEPTANCE	}	}	
		} BARGAIN	}
CONSIDERATION		}	}
			}
INTENTION			} CONTRACT
			}
CAPACITY			}

NOTES

Offer

An offer is a proposition put by one person (offeror) to another (offeree) with an indication that he is willing to be bound by its terms should the other person accept. The proposition can be made orally, in writing or by conduct, and made to a specific individual, group or the world at large. To be regarded as an offer it must be clear, precise and capable of acceptance as it stands (*Harvey v Facey* [1893]; *Gibson v Manchester City Council* [1979]).

Invitations to treat

An invitation to treat is a proposition indicating a willingness to consider offers made by others or to enter into negotiations. It is important to distinguish between offers and invitations to treat, as while an offer is binding once accepted, an invitation to treat is not. However, this is not always an easy distinction to make, as some propositions commonly regarded as offers are, in legal terms, only invitations to treat. Common forms of invitation to treat are:

- **displays of goods for sale**, either in-store (*Pharmaceutical Society of Great Britain v Boots Cash Chemists (Southern) Ltd* [1952]) or in a shop window (*Fisher v Bell* [1961]). The shop is not offering to sell the goods but is inviting customers to make offers to buy.

- **advertisements** (*Partridge v Crittenden* [1968]). Again, the general position is that the advertiser is not offering to sell but is inviting offers to buy. However, an advertisement may be regarded as an offer where it forms the basis of a unilateral contract (see below).

- **auctions**—the auctioneer's request for bids is an invitation to treat, with the buyer's bid forming the offer (**Sale of Goods Act 1979, s.57**). Therefore, it is open to the auctioneer to decide not to sell to the highest bidder provided any reserve price has not been reached. If, however, the sale advertised as without reserve, then the auctioneer is bound to accept the highest bid (*Warlow v Harrison* [1859]; *Barry v Davies* [2000]).

- **tenders**—generally, an invitation to tender is regarded as an invitation to treat (*Spencer v Harding* [1870]). If, however, the tender invitation states that the lowest tender will be accepted, then this will be binding (*Harvela Investments Ltd v Royal Trust Co of Canada Ltd* [1985]). It may also be the case that the tender invitation is binding to the extent that the party issuing the tender is bound to give proper consideration to any tender properly submitted (*Blackpool and Fylde Aero Club Ltd v Blackpool Borough Council* [1990]).

Once an offer has been made it will either be accepted or terminated. No offer remains open indefinitely.

NOTES

Termination of offer

- **revocation**—an offer may be revoked at any time prior to acceptance, even where stated to be open for a certain period of time (*Payne v Cave* [1789]). A promise to keep the offer open for a certain period is not binding unless supported by consideration—*i.e.* it is an option purchased under a separate contract (*Routledge v Grant* [1828]). For revocation to be effective, it must be communicated to the offeree. We should note that the postal rule (see below) does not apply to letters of revocation (*Byrne & Co v Leon Van Tienhoven & Co* [1880]). However, communication does not have to be made by the offeror him/herself—communication via a reliable third party is effective (*Dickinson v Dodds* [1876]).

- **rejection**—rejection by the offeree immediately terminates the offer (*Hyde v Wrench* [1840]). This includes not only straightforward refusals, but also counter-offers. These are responses that seek to vary or amend the original offer and, therefore, reject it and establish a new offer in its place. However, it is important to distinguish counter-offers from mere enquiries or requests for further information (for example, whether payment on credit terms is available). These sorts of enquiries do not terminate the offer (*Stevenson, Jacques & Co v McLean* [1880]).

- **lapse of time**—where the offer is stated to be open for a certain period of time, it will lapse once that time has expired. Where no time limit for acceptance is specified, the offer will lapse after a reasonable time (*Ramsgate Victoria Hotel Co v Montefiore* [1866]).

- **failure of condition**—where the offer is made subject to a condition, then it will lapse if that condition is not fulfilled (*Financings Ltd v Stimson* [1962]).

- **death of one of the parties**—death of the offeree terminates the offer. Death of the offeror will terminate the offer where the offeree has notice of the death prior to acceptance (*Re Whelan* [1897]). However, where the offeree is unaware of the death, the offer will only be terminated where the contract could not be fulfilled by the offeror's personal representatives (for example, where it is one for personal services) (*Bradbury v Morgan* [1862]).

Acceptance

The general rule is that acceptance must exactly match the terms of the offer. As has been seen, a response that seeks to vary or amend the terms of the offer is a counter-offer, not an acceptance. Generally, to be effective, acceptance must be communicated to the offeror—*i.e.* actually brought to his attention (*Entores Ltd v Miles Far East Corporation* [1955]). Where the offer specifies a particular method of communication, acceptance is only effective if this method is used. Where the offer indicates a preferred (but not compulsory) method, then communication by any method which is at least as advantageous to the offeror will be effective (*Tinn v Hoffman & Co* [1873]; *Manchester Diocesan Council for Education v Commercial and General Investments Ltd* [1969]).

The postal rule

The postal rule is the one significant exception to this general rule regarding communication of acceptance. Acceptance by post is effective (and therefore binding) as soon as it is posted (*Adams v Lindsell* [1818]) even where the letter is delayed or lost in the post (*Household Fire and Carriage Accident Insurance Co v Grant* [1879]) provided it was capable of delivery (*i.e.* correctly addressed and stamped) (*Re London and Northern Bank Ex p. Jones* [1900]). However, the rule will only apply where:

- postal acceptance is specified by the offeror; *or*

- postal communication is reasonable in the circumstances.

Furthermore, the offeror can exclude the rule by stating in the offer that postal acceptance will only be effective upon receipt (*Holwell Securities Ltd v Hughes* [1974]). The postal rule also applies to analogous forms of non-instantaneous communication (*e.g.* cables and inland telemessages), but not to written communication transmitted instantaneously (for example, telex and fax) (*Brinkibon Ltd v Stahag Stahl GmbH* [1983]). This emphasises that it is the delay between despatch and receipt which is relevant, not the written nature of the communication. Regarding e-commerce over the internet, the **Electronic Commerce (EC Directive) Regulations 2002** place a number of obligations on sellers, including giving the buyer the opportunity to review and amend the order. This would seem to indicate that both the internet site and the buyer's initial communication are invitations to treat. The seller's communication of the details of the order placed would then be the offer, and the buyer's confirmation would be the acceptance.

Uncertainty

There may be rare cases where the parties believe they have reached agreement but the courts decide that it is too vague or uncertain to be enforced (*Scammell (G) and Nephew Ltd v Ouston* [1941]). However, the courts attempt to remove apparent uncertainty by reference to previous dealings between the parties and to relevant commercial custom and practice (*Hillas & Co Ltd v Arcos Ltd* [1932]).

NOTES

Consideration

As noted above, an agreement must be supported by consideration if it is to be a contract. Consideration transforms the agreement into a bargain. It is what one person does (executed consideration) or promises to do (executory consideration) in return for the act or promise of the other.

There are four main rules regarding consideration:

- It must be either a detriment to the promisee or a benefit to the promisor (though usually it is both), incurred by the promisee at the promisor's request—for example, A agrees to sell his car to B for £1,000. A's consideration for B's promise to pay £1,000 is his promise to transfer ownership of the car. This is a detriment to A (he no longer owns the car) and also a benefit to B (who now owns the car).

- Consideration must move from the promisee but need not move to the promisor (*Tweddle v Atkinson* [1861])—for example, A's promise to give C £100 is valid consideration for B's promise to do the same. The consideration (£100) moves from the promisee (A) at the request of the promisor (B). The fact that it moves to C rather than B is irrelevant. Therefore A can enforce B's promise and vice versa. In the past, C could not enforce either promise as he was not a party to the bargain—under the doctrine of **privity of contract**, a person who was not a party to the contract could not accrue rights or incur obligations under it. This was sometimes explained by saying that C was a stranger to the consideration. However, following the **Contracts (Rights of Third Parties) Act 1999, s.1**, a third party will be able to bring a claim where:
  - ➤ the contract expressly provides for this; or
  - ➤ the contract purports to confer a benefit on him/her (unless it is clear from the contract that the parties did not intend it to be enforceable by the third party).

- consideration must be sufficient but need not be adequate. "Sufficient" means something of value, however small or trivial. There is no requirement it be of equal value to that which is being given in return. The law is generally only concerned with the existence of the bargain, not its quality (*Thomas v Thomas* [1842]; *Chappell & Co Ltd v Nestle Co Ltd* [1960]).

- Consideration must not be past—past consideration is no consideration (*Roscorla v Thomas* [1842]; *Re McArdle* [1951])—for example, A cleans B's windows and B later promises to pay A £10 for doing so. A cannot enforce B's promise to pay because his consideration (the window cleaning) was already past when B made the promise.

There are two difficult areas regarding consideration:

NOTES

- Can performance of an existing duty be valid consideration for a later agreement? This depends on the origin of the existing duty:
  - where the duty is one imposed by the general law, performance of that duty can only be valid consideration where performance exceeds that required by law. It is this additional element that forms the consideration for the later agreement (*Collins v Godefroy* [1831]; *Glasbrook Bros Ltd v Glamorgan County Council* [1925]);
  - where the duty is imposed by an earlier contract with the same party, performance of that duty will again be valid consideration for the later agreement where it exceeds that required by the earlier one (*Stilk v Myrick* [1809]; *Hartley v Ponsonby* [1857]). However, it has been held that mere re-affirmation of an earlier promise may be valid consideration where the re-affirmation is a benefit to the promisee, provided the later agreement was not the result of fraud or economic duress (*Williams v Roffey Bros & Nicholls (Contractors) Ltd* [1991]);
  - where the duty is imposed by an earlier contract with a different party, performance of that duty may be valid consideration for a later agreement (*Scotson v Pegg* [1861]; *New Zealand Shipping Co Ltd v A M Satterthwaite & Co Ltd (The Eurymedon)* [1975]).
- Can a promise to pay part of a debt be valid consideration for a promise to release from the remainder? Under the rule in **Pinnel's Case [1602]** this is not valid consideration. However, there are a number of exceptions:
  - part-payment at the creditor's request before the date the debt is due is valid consideration. The early payment provides additional and fresh consideration;
  - part-payment at the creditor's request at a different place is similarly valid;
  - part-payment at the creditor's request together with some goods, or settlement by goods alone is similarly valid;
  - the rule does not apply where the amount is disputed. The consideration is the risk of paying more than is in fact due;
  - the rule does not apply where the smaller sum is paid by a third party. To allow the creditor to go back on his/her promise would be a fraud on that third party (*Hirachand Punamchand v Temple* [1911]);
  - the rule does not apply where the debtor has entered into a composition agreement with his/her creditors. Under this, all creditors agree to accept a dividend (so much in the £) in full settlement of their claims. Again, to allow one creditor to go back on this agreement would amount to a fraud on the others (*Wood v Robarts* [1818]).

Promissory estoppel

Despite these limitations on the rule in *Pinnel's Case*, there may still be circumstances where the common law rule applies yet it would be unjust to allow the creditor to go back on his promise. In such circumstances, the debtor may be able to rely on the equitable doctrine of promissory estoppel: where the debtor has acted in reliance on the creditor's promise, the court may exercise its discretion to estop (prevent) the creditor going back on that promise, even though the debtor has provided no consideration (*Central London Property Trust Ltd v High Trees House Ltd* [1947]).

The requirement of consideration has been subject to a number of criticisms over the years, together with the allied principle of **privity of contract**. In response to a number of difficulties, the courts have found it necessary to develop a number of complex and arguably artificial mechanisms, such as the exceptions the rule in *Pinnel's Case*, promissory estoppel, the ruling in **Williams v Roffey**, and the notion of collateral contracts (*Shanklin Pier Ltd v Detel Products Ltd* [1951]). The potential difficulties regarding privity have been largely removed by the **Contracts (Rights of Third Parties) Act 1999**. It is also important to remember that the law of contract, quite rightly, is a law of bargains or exchange, not a general law of promises. If a person regards a gratuitous promise as sufficiently important to warrant it being legally binding, s/he may always make it in writing in a deed under seal. Furthermore, while the law relating to consideration is somewhat complex, it is unlikely that any general law of promises or obligations would be any less so (and might well be more).

Unilateral contracts

As indicated above, slightly different rules regarding offer, acceptance and consideration apply in relation to unilateral contracts. A unilateral contract arises where one party has made a conditional offer—for example, an offer of reward. If A offers a £50 reward to anyone who finds and returns his lost dog (the condition), then he is bound to pay that reward to anyone who fulfils that condition. Therefore, while advertisements are generally regarded as invitations to treat, an advertisement of reward will usually be held to be a conditional offer (*Carlill v Carbolic Smoke Ball Co* [1893]). However, unilateral contracts are rare, and largely limited to contracts of reward and analogous circumstances.

Once a conditional offer has been made, acceptance is effective (in that the offer cannot be revoked) as soon as someone begins to perform the condition (*Errington v Errington and Woods* [1952]), and the offeror is held to have waived the requirement of communication (*Carlill*). However, the offeror will be released from his/her obligations if performance of the condition is begun but not completed. While partial performance is sufficient acceptance to prevent revocation, only full performance will amount to consideration.

Intention

For the bargain to be a contract, the parties must have intended it to give rise to legal obligations. In deciding this, the courts are guided by two presumptions:

Notes

- social and domestic agreements—here no contractual intention is presumed (for example, agreements between husband and wife—*Balfour v Balfour* [1919]). However, this presumption may be rebutted by clear evidence to the contrary (for example, where the husband and wife have separated—*Merritt v Merritt* [1970]);

- business and commercial agreements—here a contractual intention is presumed, though this may again be rebutted by clear evidence to the contrary (for example, through the use of honour clauses—*Rose & Frank Co v J. R. Crompton & Bros Ltd* [1923]).

Capacity

The parties must have the legal capacity to enter into contractual relations. While most people have full contractual capacity, the law places restrictions on the capacity of certain groups to protect them from exploitation:

- **The mentally disordered**—where a person, at the time of making a contract, is suffering from a mental disorder that prevents him/her understanding the nature or significance of the arrangement, then s/he may subsequently avoid the contract, provided the other party was or ought to have been aware of the disorder at the time the contract was made (*Molton v Camroux* [1848]). This applies to all contracts except contracts for necessary services (*Re Rhodes* [1890]) and goods (**Sale of Goods Act 1979, s.3**), where the disordered party may be required to pay a reasonable price for them. A reasonable price is not necessarily the same as the contract price, thus still providing protection against exploitation.

- **Drunkards**—drunkards are given the same protection and are in the same position as the mentally disordered (*Gore v Gibson* [1845]; **Sale of Goods Act 1979, s.3**).

- **Minors**—minors' (those under 18) contracts fall into three categories:

  ➤ **valid**—a minor is bound by contracts for necessary services (*Chapple v Cooper* [1844]) and goods (*Nash v Inman* [1908]; **Sale of Goods Act 1979, s.3**) to pay a reasonable price for them. "Necessaries" are goods and services that are suitable both to the condition in life of the minor and his actual requirements at the time the contract was made. Therefore, a minor will only be bound where the contract is for goods or services that not only might be regarded as necessary (given his/her status and lifestyle) but also that he actually needed at the time. A minor is also bound by beneficial contracts of employment (*Doyle v White City Stadium* [1935])—for example, contracts of apprenticeship;

NOTES

➢ **voidable**—a minor can subsequently avoid contracts concerning interests in land (for example, a lease), contracts to purchase shares or contracts of partnership;

➢ **void**—these are contracts which can neither be enforced by the minor nor enforced against him/her, and include contracts for non-necessary goods and services and contracts of loan. The position here is regulated by the **Minors' Contracts Act 1987**:

"any guarantee of a loan made by an adult guarantor can be enforced notwithstanding that the contract of loan itself is void (**s.2**).

"the courts may order the return of non-necessary goods or any identifiable proceeds of their sale" (**s.3**).

The contractual position of minors has been criticised as being complex and out-of-date in a modern society when many young people start working and earning at the age of 16. In 1982, the Law Commission recommended that the position of minors aged 16 or over should be the same as for adults, and that for minors under the age of 16 that all contracts should enforceable by the minor but not against him/her (*i.e.* voidable at the instance of the minor). This would represent a sensible modernisation and simplification of the law.

Revision Notes

You should now write your revision notes for this topic. Here is an example for you and some suggested headings:

Formation⑨—Intention

● ptys must have intended to create legal relations

● two presumptions:

➢ social/domestic—not binding (*Balfour v Balfour*) unless evidence to contrary (*Merritt v Merritt*)

➢ business/commercial—binding unless evidence to contrary (*e.g.* honour clauses—*Rose & Frank v Crompton*)

Formation①—Offers

Formation②—Invitations to Treat

Formation③—Termination of Offer

Formation④—Acceptance

Formation⑤—Postal Rule

Formation⑥—Uncertainty

Formation⑦—Consideration

Formation⑧—Unilateral Contracts

Formation⑨—Intention

Formation⑩—Capacity

Using your cards, you should now be able to write a short paragraph in response to each of the following questions:

Explain and discuss the rules of law relating to each of the following:

1. Contractual offers.
2. Invitations to treat.
3. Termination of offer.
4. Contractual acceptance.
5. The postal rule.
6. Agreement and uncertainty.
7. Consideration.
8. Unilateral contracts.
9. Contractual intention.
10. Contractual capacity.

Notes

22 | Contract Law—Vitiating Factors

Key Points

What you need to know and discuss:

- The difference between void and voidable contracts.
- The various vitiating factors that may make a contract void or voidable.

Void and voidable contracts

While the presence of the five characteristics outlined above give rise to a prima facie valid contract, there may be other factors at work which either undermine that validity (making it voidable) or destroy it entirely (making it void).

Void contracts

Where a contract is void the general rule is that the parties must be returned to their pre-contractual positions. This is known as **restitution**. Therefore, any money or goods that have changed hands must be returned. Where this is not possible (for example, where goods have been consumed or service performed), the court may order payment in quasi-contract on a *quantum meruit* (as much as it is worth) basis.

Voidable contracts

Where the contract is voidable, the party wishing to avoid it can apply for the equitable remedy of **rescission**. Again, the aim is to return the parties to their pre-contractual position. As with all equitable remedies, rescission is discretionary and the courts will **not** grant it where:

- the party seeking to rescind the contract has previously affirmed it—*i.e.* has continued to perform the contract in the knowledge that it was voidable. Delay in seeking rescission does not, in itself, amount to affirmation but may be regarded as such where rescission would be unreasonable after such a lapse of time (this would be an example of the application of the maxim "delay defeats Equity");

- restitution (or *restitutio in integrum*) is not possible. The courts to do not insist on precise restitution—it is sufficient that goods can be returned in **substantially** the same state as that in which they were received;

- a third party has acquired rights in the subject matter of the contract in good faith and for value.

Vitiating factors

Lack of required formality

Most contracts are simple contracts, meaning that there are no formal requirements to be met in creating one. However, some contracts (for example, those concerning interests in land or shares) must be made in writing or evidenced in writing in order to be valid.

Duress and undue influence

Where a person has been pressurised to enter into a contract, it will be voidable (*Pao On v Lau Yiu Long* [1980]). There are two forms of pressure recognised by law:

- **duress**—originally, the common law notion of duress only applied where the pressure took the form of physical violence to the person or the threat of such violence. More recently, it has been expanded to include commercial pressure (or "economic duress"—**Universe Tankships Inc of Monrovia v International Transport Workers Federation, The Universe Sentinel** [1983]).

- **undue influence**—the equitable doctrine of undue influence recognises more subtle forms of pressure and the abuse of privileged positions of influence. A presumption of undue influence arises where the parties were in a special fiduciary relationship (or relationship of trust)—for example, doctor and patient, solicitor and client.

Illegality

A contract is void if it is illegal either in its objective or manner of performance—for example, contracts to commit a crime, tort or fraud, promote sexual immorality or corruption in public life, contracts of trade with an enemy in wartime. Where a contract is void for illegality, the

NOTES

general position is that any goods or money transferred is not recoverable (*Parkinson v College of Ambulance Ltd and Harrison* [1925]).

Contrary to public policy

Contracts contrary to public policy are void—for example, contracts prejudicial to the institution of marriage, contracts in unreasonable restraint of trade, gaming and wagering contracts.

Mistake

There are rare occasions where a mistake by one of the parties will make the contract void:

- **mistake as to the subject matter**—where one party believes the contract to be about one thing and the other believes it to be about something different, there is no real agreement and the contract is void (*Raffles v Wichelhaus* [1864]). However, where the parties believe they are contracting about the same thing and are merely mistaken as to its quality, the contract is valid;

- **mistake as to the existence of the subject matter**—where, unknown to the parties, the subject matter of the contract has ceased to exist prior to the contract being made, that contract is void (*Strickland v Turner* [1852]). Where the subject matter ceases to exist after agreement but before performance, the contract may be frustrated (see below);

- **mistake as to the person**—where one party is mistaken as to the identity of the other party, this will only make the contract void where the precise identity of the person is relevant to the decision to enter the contract (*Cundy v Lindsay* [1878]). This is particularly important where the contract has been induced through fraud, with the fraudster subsequently re-selling the goods to an innocent third party. Here the courts have to try to reconcile which person should bear the loss of the fraud, the party duped in the original contract or the innocent third party. Whether the courts have been successful in doing so is open to doubt (see, for example, *Shogun Finance Ltd v Hudson* [2001]).

Misrepresentation

Where a statement made during contractual negotiations does not become a term of the contract, it remains a pre-contractual representation. If that statement was untrue, it is a misrepresentation, and the misrepresentee may have a remedy against the misrepresentor. Whether this is the case depends upon the:

- **nature of the representation**—it must be a statement of fact, not of law, opinion or intention. Generally, it must be a positive statement. Silence will not amount to misrepresentation (*Fletcher v Krell* [1873]) except in three circumstances:

NOTES

> where the representor fails to inform the representee of a change in circumstance which makes a previously true statement false (*With v O'Flanagan* [1936]);
> where the representation, although literally true, leaves out important information which thereby creates a false impression (*Nottingham Patent Brick & Tile Co v Butler* [1886]);
> where the contract is one of the utmost good faith (for example, an insurance contract).

- **nature of the inducement**—a misrepresentation is only operative where it induces the misrepresentee to enter into the contract. Therefore the representee must show s/he relied on the truth of the statement in making that decision. Where s/he carried out independent investigations into its truth, there is no such reliance (*Attwood v Small* [1838]). Where, however, the representee had the opportunity to carry out such investigations but declined to do so, there is reliance on the statement (*Redgrave v Hurd* [1881]). While the representation must be a factor in the representee's decision, it need not be the sole factor (*Edgington v Fitzmaurice* [1885]).

- **nature of the misrepresentation**—there are three types of misrepresentation:

  > **fraudulent**—where the representor makes the statement knowing it to be false, believing it to be false or being reckless as to its truth (*Derry v Peek* [1889]);
  > **negligent**—where the representor believes the statement to be true but that belief is unreasonable;
  > **innocent**—where the representor believes the statement to be true and that belief is reasonable.

The consequences of misrepresentation

An operative misrepresentation makes the contract voidable. The remedies available to the misrepresentee depend upon the type of misrepresentation:

- **fraudulent**—damages (in the tort of deceit) and rescission.

- **negligent**—damages (under **s.2(1)** of the **Misrepresentation Act 1967**) and rescission (or damages in lieu under **s.2(2)** of the **1967 Act**).

- **innocent**—rescission (or damages in lieu under **s.2(2)** of the **1967 Act**).

Revision Notes

You should now write your revision notes for this topic. Here is an example for you and some suggested headings:

NOTES

VF②—Voidable contracts

- innocent pty may avoid contract and seek rescission (return to pre-contractual position)
- rescission = equitable = discretionary—not granted:
➢ affirmation
➢ restitution not possible (substantial restitution OK)
➢ legitimate 3rd pty rights

VF①—Void contracts

VF②—Voidable contracts

VF③—Lack of Form

VF④—Duress & Undue Influence

VF⑤—Illegality

VF⑥—Public Policy

VF⑦—Mistake

VF⑧—Misrepresentation

Using your cards, you should now be able to write a short paragraph in response to each of the following questions:

Explain and discuss the rules of law relating to each of the following:

1. Void contracts.
2. Voidable contracts.
3. Lack of required formality.
4. Duress and undue influence.
5. Illegality.
6. Public policy.
7. Mistake.
8. Misrepresentation.

NOTES

23 | Contract Law—Terms of the Contract

Key Points

What you need to know and discuss:

- Contractual terms by status.
- Contractual terms by origin.

It is the terms of the contract that define the rights and duties of the parties to it. These may be classified in two ways:

- **by status**—this creates three categories:
  - ➤ **conditions**—the most significant or important terms. They define the principal rights and duties of the parties, and are central to or lie at the heart of the contract;
  - ➤ **warranties**—the less significant or minor terms. They identify the secondary rights and duties of the parties, and lie at the periphery of the contract;
  - ➤ **innominate terms**—terms whose status or importance is unclear and that can only be decided in light of the consequences of the term being breached.

  The significance of these distinctions relates to the question of remedies for breach of contract. Essentially, breach of condition gives the injured party the right to repudiate (reject) the contract as well as claim damages, while a breach of warranty gives rise to a right to damages only. It could be argued that it would be more sensible to treat all terms as innominate, allowing repudiation and damages where the consequences of breach are severe, but damages only where the consequences are slight. However, this could lead to undesirable uncertainty in the law. Furthermore, while the status of any term is ultimately for the courts and not the parties to decide, the existence of conditions and warranties does give the parties an opportunity to signal what they regard to be the relative importance of the terms of their contract.

- **by origin**—this creates two categories:

> **express terms**—terms expressly stated by the parties themselves.
> **implied terms**—terms implied into the contract by law, either common law or statute. At common law, the courts are reluctant to interfere in the nature of the contract as decided by the parties. Therefore, they will only imply a term where it is both reasonable and obvious and necessary to give business efficacy or make commercial sense of the contract (*The Moorcock* [1889]; *Liverpool City Council v Irwin* [1977]). The most obvious source of such implied terms is commercial custom and practice (**Hutton v Warren** [1836]). Regarding statute, a number of Acts of Parliament imply terms into contracts—for example, the **Sale of Goods Act 1979** and the **Supply of Goods and Services Act 1982**.

Revision Notes

You should now write your revision notes for this topic. Here is an example for you and some suggested headings:

Terms①—Status

- conditions—central or primary obligations
- warranties—peripheral or secondary obligations
- innominate terms—status unclear—determined by consequences of breach

---

Terms①—Status

Terms②—Origin (express and implied)

Using your cards, you should now be able to write a short paragraph in response to each of the following questions:

1. Explain and discuss the distinction between conditions, warranties and innominate terms.

2. Explain the difference between express and implied terms

NOTES

24 | Contract Law—Discharge of Contract

Key Points

What you need to know and discuss:

- Discharge by performance and agreement.
- Discharge by frustration.
- Discharge by breach.

Performance

Most contracts are discharged by each party performing his/her obligations. The general rule is that each party must perform his/her obligations exactly and entirely, otherwise s/he will be in breach and will forfeit any rights under the contract. However, this rule may operate very harshly, and there are a number of significant exceptions:

- **severable contracts**—where the contract consists of obligations which can be sub-divided (for example, to carry freight at so much per ton), a party may claim for those elements performed while remaining liable for breach of those not performed (*Ritchie v Atkinson* [1808]; *Atkinson v Ritchie* [1809]);

- **prevention of performance**—where one party is prevented from performing his/her obligations by the other, that failure of performance will not bar that party from bringing an action for breach of contract by the other (*Planche v Colburn* [1831]);

- **acceptance of partial performance**—where one party has partially performed his/her obligations and the other has accepted this, this may be regarded as the abandonment of the original contract and the creation of a new, less extensive one. However, this will only apply where the other party has a genuine choice whether to accept the partial performance (*Sumpter v Hedges* [1898]);

- **substantial performance**—where one party has substantially performed his/her obligations, then s/he may enforce the contract subject to a reduction to compensate for the defect in performance (*Hoenig v Isaacs* [1952]). This only applies where the defect in performance is minor—*i.e.* where the other party has still received a substantial benefit (*Bolton v Mahadeva* [1972]);

- **tender of performance**—where one party tenders performance and this is rejected by the other, the tender is regarded as equivalent to performance. This exception does not apply where the obligation is one to make payment—an unsuccessful tender of payment does not release the person of the obligation to pay.

Agreement

The parties to the contract can agree to vary or discharge it. As such an agreement amounts to a contract to end a contract, it must be supported by fresh consideration.

Frustration

Generally, contractual liability is strict—it is not necessary to show that the party in breach was at fault in their failure to perform. However, the doctrine of frustration is one area of non-performance where fault (or rather the absence of fault) does play a part (for a more general discussion of the issues of fault and liability, see **Chapter 42**). In *Taylor v Caldwell* [1863], it was held that where performance of the contract had become impossible and neither party was at fault, then both parties were discharged from any further obligations. This position has subsequently developed into the modern doctrine of frustration:

The parties to a contract are released from any further obligations where an unforeseen event occurs which makes further performance either:

- **impossible;**
- **illegal;**
- **radically different from that anticipated by both parties at the time the contract was made,**

and the frustrating event was not the fault of either party.

These three variations require further explanation:

- **impossibility**—subsequent impossibility in performance may occur in three ways:

> the subject matter of the contract is destroyed (*Taylor v Caldwell* [1863]);
> the subject matter of the contract becomes unavailable (*Jackson v Union Marine Insurance Co Ltd* [1874]; *Morgan v Manser* [1948]);
> in a contract for personal services, one of the parties dies.

- **illegality**—where a subsequent event (for example, new legislation or the outbreak of war) makes further performance illegal, the contract will be frustrated (*Fibrosa Spolka Akcyjna v Fairburn Lawson Combe Barber Ltd* [1943]).

- **radical difference**—where further performance would produce a result radically different from that anticipated by both parties at the time the contract was made, the contract will be frustrated (*Krell v Henry* [1903]; *Herne Bay Steamboat Co v Hutton* [1903]). To amount to a radical difference, the actual and anticipated results of performance must be almost totally different—for example, events which would lead to a reduction in anticipated profits will not frustrate the contract (*Davis Contractors Ltd v Fareham UDC* [1956]).

A party cannot plead frustration where the frustrating event is due to his/her own fault—*i.e.* the frustration must not be self-induced (*Maritime National Fish Ltd v Ocean Trawlers Ltd* [1935]).

The consequences of frustration

While the question whether a contract has been frustrated remains an issue of common law, the consequences of frustration are regulated by statute—**Law Reform (Frustrated Contracts) Act 1943**:

- frustration immediately discharges the contract and releases the parties from any further obligations (**s.1(1)**).

- money paid prior to the frustrating event can be recovered (**s.1(2)**).

- money due to be paid prior to the frustrating event, but not in fact paid, ceases to be payable (**s.1(2)**).

- expenses incurred under the contract may be recovered up to the amount of sums paid or due to be paid prior to the frustrating event (**s.1(2)**). If no sums had been or were due to be paid, no expenses may be recovered.

- a party that has acquired a valuable benefit under the contract prior to the frustrating event may be ordered to pay a reasonable sum for it, whether or not any sums had been or were due to be paid (**s.1(3)**).

This allows the court to apportion any loss resulting from frustration in as fair a way as possible in the circumstances.

NOTES

Breach

Breach of contract takes two forms:

- **actual breach**—this is where a party fails to perform any or all of his/her obligations (non-performance) or performs them improperly (defective performance).

- **anticipatory breach**—this is where a party gives a clear indication of an intention not to perform his/her obligations. This gives rise to an immediate cause of action (*Hochster v De la Tour* [1853]).

The consequences of breach depend upon the status of the term breached:

- **breach of condition**—this gives the injured party a right to damages and the option to repudiate (treat as discharged) the contract (*Heyman v Darwins Ltd* [1942])—**repudiatory breach**.

- **breach of warranty**—this gives the injured party a right to damages only. S/he remains bound to fulfil his own obligations under the contract—**mere breach**.

- **breach of an innominate term**—here the rights of the injured party depend upon the consequences of the breach (*Cehave NV v Bremer Handelsgesellschaft mbH, The Hansa Nord* [1976]). If the breach substantially deprives the injured party of his anticipated contractual benefits, it is a breach of condition. Where the consequences are less severe, it is a breach of warranty.

Revision Notes

You should now write your revision notes for this topic. Here is an example for you and some suggested headings:

Discharge⑧—Breach

- actual/anticipatory
- condition = repudiatory breach
- warranty = mere breach
- innominate—depends on consequences (*Hansa Nord*)

NOTES

Discharge①—Performance & Agreement

Discharge②—Frustration

Discharge⑧—Breach

Using your cards, you should now be able to write a short paragraph in response to each of the following questions:

Explain and discuss the rules of law relating to:

1. Discharge by performance.

2. Discharge by agreement.

3. Discharge by frustration.

4. Discharge by breach.

25 Contract Law—Remedies for Breach of Contract

Key Points

What you need to know and discuss:

- Damages.
- Specific performance.
- Injunctions.

At common law, the only remedy is damages. In exceptional circumstances, the equitable remedies of specific performance and injunction may also be available for a breach of contract.

Damages

The aim of damages (financial compensation) is to put the injured party, as far as possible, in their anticipated post-contractual position (*Robinson v Harman* [1848]). Put another way, damages are intended to compensate the injured party for any loss (whether this is an expectation loss or a reliance loss) suffered as a result of the breach of contract. A claim for damages may take two forms.

Liquidated damages

This is where the parties have provided for compensation in the contract itself by specifying the amount to be paid or formula for working it out (for example, cancellation charges in a package holiday contract). These clauses are valid provided they are a genuine attempt to pre-estimate the likely loss.

However, a dominant party may misuse these clauses to introduce penalties into the contract to ensure performance by the weaker party. If the courts decide it is a penalty clause, it will be struck out and the claim treated as one for unliquidated damages (see below). The courts will regard it as a penalty clause where (*Dunlop Pneumatic Tyre Co Ltd v New Garage & Motor Co Ltd* [1915]):

- the sum specified is clearly greater than any conceivable or likely loss;
- the breach is a failure to pay sums due and the damages specified exceed that sum;
- the same sum is specified for a number of breaches, some of which are trivial and some serious.

Unliquidated damages

Where there is no liquidated damages clause, the claim will be for unliquidated damages and assessed according to principles established in *Hadley v Baxendale* [1854] (confirmed in *The Heron II* [1969]). The injured party may recover damages for:

- losses that are a natural consequence of the breach (including any consequential loss);
- losses that, though not a natural consequence of the breach, were either known or ought to have been known to be a possibility by both parties at the time the contract was made.

Two further points should be noted:

- **speculation**—that fact that the loss may be difficult to quantify is no bar to recovery. The court may engage in a degree of speculation in estimating the loss (*Chaplin v Hicks* [1911]).
- **mitigation**—the injured party must take reasonable steps to mitigate his/her loss. S/he cannot recover for loss due an unreasonable failure to mitigate (*British Westinghouse Electric & Manufacturing Co Ltd v Underground Electric Railways Co of London Ltd* [1912]).

Specific performance

This is a court order instructing the party in breach to perform their contractual obligations. As with all equitable remedies, specific performance is discretionary and (with the exception of contracts concerning interests in land) is rarely awarded. It will not be awarded where:

- damages are an adequate remedy—for example, in a contract for the sale of goods, specific performance will not be awarded unless the goods are unique (*Cohen v Roche* [1927]);

NOTES

- the contract lacks mutuality—*i.e.* where the remedy would not be available to both parties (for example, contracts with minors) (*Flight v Bolland* [1828]);
- the order would require constant supervision (*Ryan v Mutual Tontine Westminster Chambers Association* [1893]);
- the contract is one for personal services (*Rigby v Connol* [1880]).

Where an application for specific performance is refused, the court may award damages in lieu.

Injunctions

A prohibitory injunction may be granted to prevent breach of an express negative contractual obligation (for example, a valid restraint of trade clause) (*Lumley v Wagner* [1852]; *Warner Bros Pictures Inc v Nelson* [1937]). However, this will not be done where the consequence would be to compel performance of other positive obligations for which specific performance would be unobtainable (*Page One Records v Britton* [1967]). Again, the court may award damages in lieu where an injunction is refused.

Revision Notes

You should now write your revision notes for this topic. Here is an example for you and some suggested headings:

Remedies④Injunctions

- prohibitory to prevent breach of express -ve obligation (*Lumley v Wagner; Warner Bros v Nelson*)
- not if effect to compel performance of other +ve obligations (*Page One Records v Britton*)

Remedies①—Liquidated Damages

Remedies②—Unliquidated Damages

Remedies③—Specific Performance

Remedies④—Injunctions

NOTES

Using your cards, you should now be able to write a short paragraph in response to each of the following questions:

Explain and discuss the rules of law relating to the following:

1. Liquidated damages.

2. Unliquidated damages.

3. Specific performance.

4. Injunctions.

NOTES

26 | Contract Law—Consumer Contracts

Key Points

What you need to know and discuss:

- The limitations on freedom of contract.
- The implied terms in the Sale of Goods Act 1979.
- The implied terms in the Supply of Goods and Services Act 1982.

Introduction

The main developments in English contract law occurred during the nineteenth century. The great expansion in trade that took place was accompanied by significant developments in the law facilitating that trade. The prevailing economic philosophy one of *laissez-faire* or free trade and, consequently, state intervention in and regulation of economic activity was kept to a minimum. For the law of contract, this meant the role of the law was simply to act as agent for the enforcement of individual agreements, freely arrived at. It was not for the law to intervene and dictate the content of bargains.

Hence, the notion of freedom of contract assumed central importance. Necessarily allied to this was the concept of equality of bargaining power. The law assumed the parties approached negotiations from positions of approximately equal bargaining strength. Therefore, if one party displayed less business acumen and skill and agreed to a relatively disadvantageous contract, s/he could not turn to the law to save him/herself from the consequences of his/her own commercial ineptitude.

While this view was, arguably, consistent with the realities of an emerging industrial capitalist economy, it has become increasingly out-dated and unrealistic in a modern, complex, multinational, post-industrial economy. The idea of equality of bargaining power has become, even in many business-to-business transactions, little more than fiction. In many instances today, one party will approach negotiations from a position of strength or dominance over the other. This clearly leaves the weaker party vulnerable to unfair exploitation.

In order to prevent this, it has become increasingly necessary for the law to adopt a more regulatory and interventionist position. Therefore, the development of the law of contract in the twentieth century has represented, particularly with regard to consumer transactions, an orderly and steady retreat from freedom of contract.

We should note, however, that English law never acknowledged absolute freedom of contract. It has always intervened to protect vulnerable groups (for example, through the rules regarding contractual capacity and the operation of duress and undue influence as vitiating factors) and exercised a degree of regulation in the public interest (for example, through the operation of illegality and public policy as vitiating factors). As equality of bargaining power has declined, the law has simply been forced to recognise new vulnerable groups (for example, consumers, employees and tenants) and new areas of public interest (for example, through fair trading and monopolies and mergers legislation). We should also note that, regarding consumer transactions, intervention in freedom of contract is only one method used by the law to protect the weaker party:

- Legislation has been used to ensure consumers are provided with full and accurate information before entering into a contract (**Trade Descriptions Act 1968; Consumer Credit Act 1974; Consumer Protection Act 1987**).

- Legislation has also sought to ensure that consumer products are safe to use (the **Consumer Safety Acts; Consumer Protection Act 1987**).

- A general regulatory framework has been established under the **Fair Trading Act 1973**, and licensing may be used to regulate traders (for example, consumer credit). The role and powers of the Office of Fair Trading have been extended and enhanced under the **Enterprise Act 2002**.

- The **Director General of Fair Trading** has a statutory duty (**Fair Trading Act 1973, s.124(3)**) to encourage business self-regulation through trade association codes of practice.

Therefore, the law has taken significant measures in recent years to redress the growing contractual inequality between trader and consumer and protect the consumer from unfair exploitation.

NOTES

Legislative Intervention in Freedom of Contract

The Sale of Goods Act 1979 (as amended by the Sale and Supply of Goods Act 1994)

This Act applies to all contracts for the sale of goods—*i.e.* where ownership of goods is exchanged for money (**s.2(1)**). The Act implies up to four important terms into such contracts for the protection of the buyer:

- implied condition as to **title** (**s.12**).
- implied condition as to correspondence with **description** (**s.13**).
- implied condition as to **satisfactory quality** (**s.14**).
- implied condition as to correspondence with **sample** (**s.15**).

There are, therefore, a number of issues to be addressed when considering the application of the Act:

- it must be determined whether the contract is one to which the Act applies by applying the definition in **s.2**.
- **s.12** implies into all contracts for the sale of goods a condition that the seller has the right to sell the goods
- where the sale is a sale by description, **s.13** implies a condition that the goods must correspond with that description (for example, if an overcoat is described (by whatever means) as being "100 per cent pure new wool", it must in fact be 100 per cent pure new wool).
- where the seller is selling in the course of a business (*i.e.* the sale is not a private sale), **s.14(2)**:
    - ➢ implies a general requirement that the goods be of satisfactory quality—*i.e.* of the standard a reasonable person would regard as satisfactory (**s.14(2A)**).
    - ➢ this applies to goods of any type. Any description, such as "seconds", "sale goods", "second-hand", and any reduction in price are merely factors to be considered in deciding whether the goods are of satisfactory quality (**s.14(2A)**).
    - ➢ **s.14(2B)** provides that "quality" includes not only functional characteristics (*e.g.* fitness for common purpose, freedom from minor defects, safety and durability) but also cosmetic characteristics (for example, appearance and finish), together with the general state and condition of the goods.

NOTES

➢ however, **s.14(2C)** provides that this general requirement does not apply to:

> "defects that were specifically drawn to the buyer's attention before the contract was made. Defects that a reasonable examination of the goods would have revealed, provided the buyer did in fact examine the goods before the contract was made."

➢ the general requirement refers only to goods being fit for their **common** purpose. **S.14(3)** provides that where the buyer makes known to the seller any **particular** purpose (whether common or not) for which the goods are being bought, then the goods must be fit for that purpose unless the seller can show either:

– the buyer did not rely on the skill and judgement of the seller; or
– if the buyer did so rely, such reliance was unreasonable in the circumstances.

- where the sale is a sale by sample, **s.15** implies a condition that the bulk must correspond in quality to the sample.

Breach, acceptance and the loss of repudiation

The implied terms are expressly stated to be conditions. Therefore, any breach will, prima facie, be a repudiatory breach, entitling the buyer to reject the goods, repudiate the contract and claim damages. We have already been seen that the right to repudiate may be lost (for example, where *restitutio in integrum* is not possible). **S.11** provides that the right to repudiate is also lost where the buyer has "accepted" the goods. **S.35** provides that goods have been accepted where:

- The buyer indicates to the seller s/he has accepted them.

- The buyer does some act in relation to the goods that is inconsistent with the ownership of the seller. However, we should note that using the goods in order to discover whether they conform to the requirements of the contract (*i.e.* that they work) does not amount to acceptance.

- The buyer keeps the goods beyond a reasonable time without indicating to the seller an intention to reject them. Therefore, the buyer should notify the seller promptly of any defect and any intention to reject the goods.

- Simply asking for or agreeing to the repair of the goods does not amount to acceptance. If the goods are still unsatisfactory following repair, the buyer may still be able to reject them.

Exclusion of liability

S.55 provides that liability for breach of the implied terms can be limited or excluded, subject to the provisions of the **Unfair Contract Terms Act 1977** (see **Chapter 27**).

NOTES

The Supply of Goods and Services Act 1982 (as amended by The Sale and Supply Of Goods Act 1994)

This Act applies to three types of contract:

- contracts for the **transfer of goods**—ownership of goods is exchanged for something other than money (**s.1**).

- contracts for the **hire of goods**—possession of goods is transferred for a specified period (**s.6**).

- contracts for the **supply of a service**—a service is provided (other than under a contract of employment) (**s.12**).

Regarding contracts for the transfer of goods, the Act implies terms (similar to those in the **1979 Act**) as to title (**s.2**), correspondence with description (**s.3**), satisfactory quality (**s.4**) and correspondence with sample (**s.5**).

Regarding contracts for the hire of goods, the Act implies terms (again similar to the **1979 Act**) as to the hirer's right to transfer possession of the goods (**s.7**), correspondence with description (**s.8**), satisfactory quality (**s.9**) and correspondence with sample (**s.10**).

Regarding contracts for the supply of a service, the Act implies the following terms:

- where the supplier is acting in the course of a business, the service will be carried out with **reasonable care and skill** (**s.13**).

- where the supplier is acting in the course of a business, and unless otherwise provided for in the contract, the service will be carried out within a **reasonable time** (**s.14**).

- unless otherwise provided for in the contract, the person contracting with the supplier will pay a **reasonable price** for the service (**s.15**).

Finally, **s.11** (regarding the transfer and hire of goods) and **s.16** (regarding the supply of a service) provide that liability for breach of the implied terms may be excluded or restricted subject to the provisions of the **Unfair Contract Terms Act 1977** (**See Chapter 27**).

The European Dimension

We should also note that an increasing amount of consumer protection legislation is being introduced in response to Directives from the European Union, such as the **Consumer**

NOTES

Protection (Distance Selling) Regulations 2000 and the **Sale and Supply of Goods to Consumers Regulations 2002**, which give consumers a right to the repair or replacement of faulty goods and also make guarantees legally enforceable.

Revision Notes

You should now write your revision notes for this topic. Here is an example for you and some suggested headings:

ConsPro①—Freedom of Contract

- 19th C—*laissez-faire*—minimal legal regulation
- decline in equality of bargaining power—increased regulation
- always some (*e.g.* capacity, duress & undue influence, illegality & public policy)
- now more (*e.g.* protect consumers, employees, tenants, fair trading & monopolies)

ConsPro①—Freedom of Contract

ConsPro②—SOGA '79

ConsPro③—SOGSA '82

Using your cards, you should now be able to write a short paragraph in response to each of the following questions:

1. Discuss the decline in freedom of contract since the 19th century.

2. Describe and discuss the implied terms in the Sale of Goods Act 1979.

3. Describe and discuss the implied terms in the Supply of Goods and Services Act 1982.

27 | Contract Law—Exclusion Clauses

Key Points

What you need to know and discuss:

- The judicial control of exclusion clauses.
- The main provisions of the Unfair Contract Terms Act 1977.
- The main provisions of the Unfair Terms in Consumer Contracts Regulations 1999.

Introduction

These are terms of the contract that seek to exclude or limit liability for breach of contract. While these clauses are, in principle, perfectly legitimate, the law has recognised they are open to abuse by parties in a dominant bargaining position. This is particularly so when included in **standard form contracts**, offered on a "take it or leave it" basis. Therefore, they are subject to both judicial and statutory regulation.

Judicial regulation

Incorporation—to be effective, the exclusion clause must have been properly incorporated into the contract. This means the other party must have been given reasonably sufficient notice of the clause (*Parker v South Eastern Railway Co* [1877]) at or before the time the contract was made (*Olley v Marlborough Court Ltd* [1949]; *Thornton v Shoe Lane Parking Ltd* [1971]).

Construction—to be effective, the clause must, upon proper construction (or interpretation), cover the breach that has occurred. In construing exclusion clauses, the courts are guided by two important principles:

- the *contra proferentem* rule—where there is any doubt or ambiguity in the clause, this will be resolved against the party seeking to rely on it—*i.e.* the benefit of any doubt is given to the injured party (*Baldry v Marshall* [1925]; *Andrews v Singer* [1934]). Nevertheless, a sufficiently carefully and comprehensively drafted clause will succeed (*L'Estrange v F Graucob Ltd* [1934]).

- the **main purpose** rule—it is presumed that an exclusion clause is not intended to defeat the main purpose of the contract by excluding liability for failing to fulfil that purpose (*Glynn v Margetson & Co* [1893]). Nevertheless, this presumption may be rebutted by sufficiently strong and clear words (*Suisse Atlantique Société d'Armement Maritime SA v Roterrdamsche Kolen Centrale NV* [1967]; *Photo Production Ltd v Securicor Transport Ltd* [1980]).

Statutory regulation

While the courts are able to place significant restrictions on the use of exclusion clauses, the common law cannot prohibit their use. It was this (among other considerations) which prompted the enactment of the **Unfair Contract Terms Act 1977**. This Act places an absolute prohibition on the effectiveness of some exclusion clauses, and subjects others to a strict test of reasonableness:

- **S.2** regulates attempts to limit or exclude business liability (whether contractual or tortious) for negligence. Such liability for causing death or personal injury cannot be limited or excluded (**s.2(1)**). Negligence liability for causing other forms of loss or damage can be excluded or restricted, but only in so far as the term is reasonable. This applies to attempts to exclude or restrict liability for breach of the implied term in contracts for the supply of a service as to reasonable care and skill under (**Supply of Goods and Services Act 1982, s.13**).

- **S.6** regulates attempts to exclude or restrict liability for breach of the implied terms in contracts for the sale of goods under the **Sale of Goods Act 1979**:
  - ➤ liability for breach of the implied condition as to title (**s.12, 1979**) cannot be excluded or restricted;
  - ➤ as against a **consumer**, liability for breach of the implied terms as to correspondence with description (**s.13, 1979**), satisfactory quality (**s.14, 1979**) and correspondence with sample (**s.15, 1979**) cannot be excluded or restricted;
  - ➤ as against a **non-consumer**, liability for breach of these implied terms can be excluded or restricted, but only in so far as the term is reasonable;

- **S.7** regulates attempts to exclude or restrict liability for breach of the implied terms in contracts for the transfer or hire of goods under the **1982 Act**:

Notes

> liability for breach of the implied term in contracts for the transfer of goods as to title (**s.2, 1982**) cannot be excluded or restricted;

> as against a **consumer**, liability for breach of the implied terms in contracts for the transfer of goods as to correspondence with description (**s.3, 1982**), satisfactory quality (**s.4, 1982**) and correspondence with sample (**s.5, 1982**) cannot be excluded or restricted;

> as against a **non-consumer**, liability for breach of these implied terms can be excluded or restricted, but only in so far as the term is reasonable;

> liability for breach of the implied term in contracts for the hire of goods as to the right to transfer possession (**s.7, 1982**) can be excluded or restricted, but only in so far as the term is reasonable;

> as against a **consumer**, liability for breach of the implied terms in contracts for the hire of goods as to correspondence with description (**s.8, 1982**), satisfactory quality (**s.9, 1982**) and correspondence with sample (**s.10, 1982**) cannot be excluded or restricted;

> as against a **non-consumer**, liability for breach of these implied can be excluded or restricted, but only in so far as the term is reasonable.

- **S.11** provides that a term is reasonable if can be considered fair and reasonable in the circumstances which were, or ought to have been, in the contemplation of both parties at the time the contract was made. Further explanation is given in **Sch.2** to the Act.

- **S.12** defines a **consumer** as being someone who is not dealing in the course of a business who is contracting with someone who is. Where the contract is one for the sale, supply or hire of goods, there is an additional requirement that the goods be of a type usually supplied for private use or consumption.

The Unfair Terms in Consumer Contracts Regulations 1999

These Regulations were introduced to implement the requirements of the **European Directive on Unfair Terms**, and extend beyond the control of exclusion clauses alone:

- The Regulations apply to any consumer contract which has not been individually negotiated (*i.e.* is a standard form contract) (**regs 4 & 5**).

- Any term which is deemed to be unfair will not be binding on the consumer (**reg.8**).

- A term is unfair where it causes a significant imbalance in the parties' rights and obligations under the contract to the detriment of the consumer (**reg.5(1)**).

- Sellers and suppliers must ensure contracts are written in plain, intelligible language, and where there is any doubt regarding the meaning of a term, the interpretation most favourable to the consumer is to be used (**reg.7**).

NOTES

- The OFT and other "qualifying bodies" (for example, utility regulators) have powers to receive complaints, conduct investigations, obtain undertakings and (where appropriate) injunctions to prevent further use of terms deemed unfair (**regs 10–15**).

- Finally, **Sch.2** provides an indicative and non-exhaustive list of terms that may be regarded as unfair (see **www.legislation.hmso.gov.uk/si/si1999/19992083.htm**).

Revision Notes

You should now write your revision notes for this topic. Here is an example for you and some suggested headings:

ExClause ①—Judicial Control (incorp)

- Effective only if incorporated
- Reasonably sufficient notice (*Parker v SE Railway*)
- At/before contract made (*Olley v Marlborough Court; Thornton v Shoe Lane Parking*)

ExClause①—Judicial Control (incorp)

ExClause②—Judicial Control (construct)

ExClause③—UCTA '77

ExClause④—UTCCR '99

Using your cards, you should now be able to write a short paragraph in response to each of the following questions:

1. Describe the judicial controls over the use of exclusion clauses.

2. What are the main provisions of the Unfair Contract Terms Act 1977?

3. Describe the main provisions of the Unfair Terms in Consumer Contract Regulations 1999.

NOTES

28 Consumer Protection—Criminal and Tortious Aspects

Key Points

What you need to know and discuss:

- The main offences in the Trade Descriptions Act 1968.
- The pricing offences in the Consumer Protection Act 1987.
- Liability for defective products under the Consumer Protection Act 1987.

Trade Descriptions Act 1968

This Act protects the interests of consumers by prohibiting false or misleading trade descriptions. There are criminal offences relating to the description of both goods and services. Under **s.26**, local authorities' Trading Standards Departments are under a duty to enforce the Act.

We should note immediately that the Act regulates **trade** descriptions—*i.e.* descriptions applied in the course of a trade or business—this includes not only the primary activities of the business but also any secondary or incidental activities (*Havering LBC v Stevenson* [1970]; *Davies v Sumner* [1984]).

Regarding goods, there are two offences:

- applying a false trade description to goods—**s.1(1)(a)**;
- supplying or offering to supply goods to which a false trade description has been applied—**s.1(1)(b)**.

What is a trade description?

By **s.2(1)**, a trade description is "an indication, direct or indirect, and by whatever means given" of:

- quantity (including length, width, height, area, volume, capacity, weight and number), size or gauge;
- method of manufacture, production, processing or reconditioning;
- composition;
- fitness for purpose, strength, performance, behaviour or accuracy;
- any other physical characteristic;
- testing by any persons and the results thereof;
- approval by any person or conformity with a type approved by any person;
- place or date of manufacture, production, processing or reconditioning;
- person by whom manufactured, produced, processed or reconditioned;
- other history, including previous ownership or use.

Problems could arise where traders apply what seem to be specific descriptions to what are, in fact, generic products—for example, Dover Sole, Eccles Cakes, etc. To avoid these difficulties, the Department of Trade and Industry may, under **s.7**, issue "definition orders" assigning definite meanings to such expressions.

Is the trade description false?

By **s.3(1)**, a trade description is false if it is false to a material degree. This indicates it must be false in a way and to a degree that might matter to the consumer. This "impact on the consumer" approach is carried through into **s.3(2)**—which states that a description that is not false but that is misleading will be regarded as false—and **s.3(3)**—which states that anything that is not a trade description but that is likely to be taken as one will be regarded as a trade description.

Has the false trade description been applied (s.1(1)(a))?

By **s.4(1)**, a trade description is applied to goods where it is fixed or annexed to, marked on or incorporated with the goods themselves or anything in, on or with which the goods are supplied. The description is also applied if used in any manner likely to be taken as referring to the goods. This can include oral statements (**s.4(2)**).

By **s.4(3)**, where goods are supplied in response to a request from the buyer that includes a trade description and it is reasonable to infer that the goods are supplied as goods corresponding to that description, then the description will be regarded as having been applied to the goods.

NOTES

Regarding advertisements, where a trade description is used in relation to a class of goods, it is regarded as being applied to all goods of that class, whether or not they were in existence at the time of the advertisement (**s.5**). Advertisements include catalogues, circulars and price lists (**s.39**).

Have the goods been supplied or offered for supply (s.1(1)(b))?

By **s.6**, a person exposing goods for supply or having them in his possession for supply is regarded (contrary to the position in general contract law) as offering them for supply. It is sufficient that the supplier knows the description had been applied to the goods—s/he need not know it is false (*Cottee v Douglas Seaton (Used Cars) Ltd* [1972]).

What about services?

By **s.14(1)**, it is an offence for any person in the course of any trade or business to knowingly or recklessly make a false statement regarding the:

- provision of any services, accommodation or facilities;
- nature of any services, accommodation or facilities;
- time at which or person by whom such services, accommodation or facilities will be provided;
- examination, approval or evaluation by any person of such services, accommodation or facilities;
- location or amenities of any accommodation.

By **s.14(1)(b)**, a reckless statement is one which is "made regardless of whether it is true or false . . . whether or not the person making it had reasons for believing that it might be false".

What defences are available?

Disclaimers—a disclaimer is a statement that discourages reliance on the trade description. This is not a defence to a charge under **s.1(1)(a)**—*Newman v Hackney LBC* [1982]. It may be a defence to a charge under **s.1(1)(b)** where:

- it was brought to the customer's notice before the supply takes place;
- it is as bold, precise and compelling as the description itself (*Norman v Bennett* [1974]).

The general defence—s.24(1)—it may be a defence to a charge under **s.1(1)(b)** and **s.14(1)**, but not **s.1(1)(a)** where the defendant has applied the description himself (*R. v Southwood* [1987]), to show that:

NOTES

- the offence was due to a mistake, reliance on information supplied by another, the act or default of another, an accident or some other cause beyond his/her control;

- s/he took all reasonable precautions and exercised all due diligence to avoid the commission of the offence by him/herself or any person under his/her control.

The supplier's defence—s.24(3)—it may be a defence to a charge under **s.1(1)(b)** for the defendant to show that s/he did not know, and could not with reasonable diligence have discovered, that either the description had been applied to the goods or that the goods did not conform to that description.

The advertiser's defence—s.25—it may be a defence for an advertiser to show that:

- the advertisement was received and published in the course of a business involving such publication;

- s/he did not know and had no reason to know that the publication would amount to an offence.

The Consumer Protection Act 1987—Part III

This creates two offences relating to the pricing of goods and services:

- By **s.20(1)**, it is an offence for a person, in the course of any business of his/hers, to give (by any means whatever) to any consumers a misleading price indication regarding goods, services, accommodation and facilities.

- By **s.20(2)**, it is an offence to fail to take reasonable steps to correct a price indication that has become misleading where it is reasonable to expect that consumers may still be relying on it.

Who is a consumer?

By **s.20(6)**, a consumer is:

- regarding goods, any person who might wish to be supplied with the goods for his/hers own private use or consumption;

- regarding services or facilities, any person who might wish to supplied with the services or facilities otherwise than for business purposes;

- regarding accommodation, any person who might wish to occupy the accommodation otherwise than for business purposes.

<u>Notes</u>

Is the price indication misleading?

By **s.21(1)**, a price indication is misleading where what is conveyed, or what a consumer might reasonably be expected to infer from it or any omission from it, includes:

- that the price is less than in fact it is;
- that the applicability of the price does not depend on facts or circumstances on which it does in fact depend;
- that the price covers matters for which an additional charge is in fact made;
- that a person who in fact has no such expectation either expects the price to be increased or reduced or expects the price (or price as increased or reduced) to be maintained;
- that the facts or circumstances by which a consumer might reasonably be expected to judge the validity of any comparison made or implied are not what in fact they are.

What defences are available?

By **s.39(1)**, it may be a defence for the defendant to show that s/he took all reasonable steps and exercised all due diligence to avoid committing the offence. There are also four specific defences under **s.24**:

- the acts or omissions were **authorised by DTI regulations**;
- the **editorial comment** defence—where the indication was given in a book, newspaper, film or broadcast, there is no offence if the indication was not in an advertisement;
- the **advertiser's** defence—where the advertiser had no reason to believe the advertisement constituted an offence;
- the **recommended prices** defence—it is a defence for the person making the recommendation to show that the third party providing the goods, services, facilities or accommodation has unexpectedly failed to observe the recommendation.

The Code of Practice

By **s.25(1)**, the Secretary of State for Trade and Industry may issue a Code of Practice:

- to give practical guidance on the requirements of **s.20**;
- to promote desirable practices in price indications.

NOTES

The Code was introduced in November 1988 (available at **www.dti.gov.uk/access/price_indi/contents.htm**). By **s.25(2)**, breach of the Code is evidence (but is not, in itself, conclusive) that an offence has been committed and, similarly, compliance is evidence that no offence has been committed.

Liability for Dangerous Products

Where a person suffers injury or loss caused by defective goods s/he has him/herself purchased, the obvious remedy lies in an action for breach of contract. However, in many cases the ultimate consumer of the product will be someone other than the purchaser and, therefore, will have no remedy in contract. Until the **Consumer Protection Act 1987**, their only remedy lay in negligence, an extremely demanding process. **Part I** of the Act, giving effect to the **European Product Liability Directive**, offers an alternative and, in many respects, more effective remedy. Most significantly, liability under the Act is strict, whereas liability in negligence is dependent upon proof of fault. By **s.2**, where injury or damage is caused wholly or in part by a defective product, those persons identified in the Act will be liable. We should note that a causal link between the defect and damage must be established.

What damage is covered by the Act?

The Act covers three forms of damage: death; personal injury; and damage to private property. Property is regarded as private where:

- it is of a type ordinarily intended for private use, occupation or consumption;

- it is intended by the person suffering the loss or damage mainly for his/her own private use, occupation or consumption.

The Act does not apply to damage to the product itself (or any product supplied with the defective product comprised in it) or to claims for property damage of less than £275.

What is a product?

This covers any goods, including substances, crops, ships, aircraft and vehicles. However, the Act excludes defects in game and agricultural produce where the product has not undergone an industrial process.

Is the product defective?

By **s.3**, a product is defective if it is not reasonably safe. Relevant factors include:

NOTES

- the manner in which and the purposes for which the product has been marketed;

- what might reasonably be expected to be done with or in relation to the product;

- any instructions for or warnings with respect to doing or not doing anything with or in relation to the product. Hence, effective instructions and/or warnings may make a product safe. Conversely, their absence may make the product unsafe;

- the time at which the product was supplied by its producer to another—the **state of the art** factor. The relevant time for assessing a product's safety is the time of its supply. Therefore, the mere fact that safer versions of the product have subsequently been issued does not, in itself, make the earlier product unsafe.

Who can be sued?

By **s.2(2)**, an action may be brought against:

- the producer—*i.e.* the manufacturer, the person who has abstracted the product, or the person who has applied an industrial process to it;

- any person who, by putting his/her name, trade mark or other distinguishing mark on the product, has held him/herself out as the producer;

- any person who has imported the goods into the EU in order, in the course of business, to supply it to another;

- the supplier of the product where:
    - ➤ the injured party has requested the supplier to identify any person in the first three categories; and;
    - ➤ the request is made within a reasonable time after the damage and it is not reasonably practicable for the person making the request to identify those persons; and;
    - ➤ the supplier fails within a reasonable time either to comply with the request or to identify the person who supplied the product to him.

What defences are available?

In addition to **contributory negligence** by the consumer, **s.4** provides for six possible defences:

- the defect is attributable to compliance with any statutory or EU requirement;

- the person proceeded against did not at any time supply the product to another;

Notes

- the only supply was not done in the course of the supplier's business or was not done with a view to profit;

- the defect did not exist at the time the defendant supplied it to another;

- the state of scientific and technological knowledge at the relevant time was not such that a producer might be expected to discover the defect (the **development risks** defence);

- the defect was a defect in a subsequent product in which the product in question (*i.e.* a component) was comprised and was wholly attributable to the design of the subsequent product or to compliance with instructions given by the producer of the subsequent product.

Where a consumer is unable to rely on the Act, they must fall back on the general law of negligence (see **Chapter 30**).

Revision Notes

You should now write your revision notes for this topic. Here is an example for you and some suggested headings:

TDA③—False?

- False = false to a material degree (manner/degree that matters to consumers) s.3(1)

- Impact on consumer approach:

  ➤ descriptions not false but misleading regarded as false (s.3(2))
  ➤ not a description but likely to be taken as one regarded as one (s.3(3))

TDA①—Intro & Offences

TDA②—Description?

TDA③—False?

TDA④—Applied?

TDA⑤—Supplied/Offered?

Notes

TDA⑥—Services

TDA⑥—Defences

CPA①—Pricing Offences

CPA②—Consumer?

CPA③—Misleading?

CPA④—Defences

CPA⑤—Code of Practice

DefProd①—Intro

DefProd②—Damage under CPA

DefProd③—Product? Defective?

DefProd④—Defendants and Defences

Using your cards, you should now be able to write a short paragraph in response to each of the following questions:

1. What offences relating to goods are created by the Trade Descriptions Act 1968?
2. Explain the elements of these offences.
3. What offences relating to services are created by the Trade Descriptions Act 1968?
4. What defences are available?
5. What pricing offences are created by the Consumer Protection Act 1987?
6. Explain the elements of these offences.
7. What defences are available?
8. Explain the background and importance of Part 1 of the Consumer Protection Act 1987.
9. When and for what is a person liable under this Part of the Act?
10. What defences are available?

NOTES

29 | Consumer Protection—Enforcement, Sanctions and Remedies

Key Points

What you need to know and discuss:

- The enforcement of criminal law provisions for consumer protection.
- The informal approaches available to a dissatisfied consumer.
- The sources of advice on consumer rights.
- The appropriate forms of ADR.
- The formal procedures in bringing a civil claim.

Enforcement of criminal law provisions

The responsibility for the enforcement of criminal provisions relating to trade descriptions, pricing and product safety falls to local authorities. This is carried out by **Trading Standards** and **Environmental Health** departments. They carry out their own investigations and inspections and also act in response to complaints from consumers. Where necessary, they instigate prosecutions and liaise with the **Department of Trade Industry** to avoid unnecessary duplication (for example, multiple prosecutions of a national retail chain for the same offence). The sanctions available are fines and imprisonment—for example, regarding trade descriptions offences, the maximum penalty for each summary conviction is £5000. Following conviction on indictment, the maximum penalty is an unlimited fine and/or up to two years' imprisonment. However, the Divisional Court has stated that prison terms should normally be reserved for cases involving dishonesty (*R. v Haesler* [1973]).

Informal solutions for the dissatisfied customer

The obvious thing for a dissatisfied consumer to do is approach the supplier of the goods or services to seek a remedy. In most instances, this will be successful. If, however, it is not, the consumer should consider taking the matter further within that organisation—for example, by contacting the head office or customer services department. Where an informal approach proves unsuccessful, the consumer will need to take further action involving the intervention of a third party.

Sources of advice on consumer rights

The consumer may need advice on his/her rights and how to enforce them. The various sources of legal advice are discussed in detail in **Chapter 13**. Some of these will not only provide advice but will also assist the consumer in enforcing their rights. The internet is also becoming a very useful source of general advice on consumer rights and a number of websites are listed at the end of this chapter.

Appropriate forms of ADR

It may be necessary for the consumer to undertake formal or semi-formal proceedings to enforce his/her rights. The various forms of ADR are discussed in detail in **Chapter 9**. Among the most relevant to consumers are:

- conciliation and arbitration through Trade Associations;
- ombudsmen schemes;
- utility regulators.

Taking formal action through the civil courts

The consumer may have ultimately to pursue a formal claim through the courts—for example, for breach of contract or negligence (defective goods or services) or misrepresentation (false trade descriptions). Most consumer claims will fall within the limit of the small claims track. Details of this and other civil court procedures can be found in Chapter 8. If successful, the most usual remedy is damages (financial compensation)—for the principles regarding the assessment of damages, see Chapter 25).

Revision Notes

You should now write your revision notes for this topic. Here is an example for you and some suggested headings. You should also cross-reference this topic with relevant notes from other chapters (for example, sources of advice, ADR etc):

Notes

ESR②—Informal Solutions

- approach supplier
- usually successful—if not:
- take higher (*e.g.* head office, customer services)—if not:
- take further—need advice? Third party intervention?

ESR①—Criminal Enforcement

ESR②—Informal Solutions

ESR③—Advice on Consumer Rights

ESR④—Appropriate ADR

ESR⑤—Court Action & Remedies

Using your cards, you should now construct a flow chart showing a dissatisfied consumer's progress from complaint to resolution, including all stages and options along the way.

Useful Websites

For advice of consumer rights and related matters, visit:

- www.compactlaw.co.uk
- www.oft.gov.uk
- www.tradingstandards.gov.uk
- www.adviceguide.org.uk
- www.justask.org.uk
- The various ombudsmen schemes may be accessed via **www.bioa.org.uk**
- The public utility regulators may be accessed via **www.open.gov.uk**

NOTES

SECTION FIVE: THE LAW OF TORT

30 Tort—Negligence

Key Points

What you need to know and discuss:

- The notion of a cause of action.
- The rules relating to duty of care.
- The rules relating to negligent statements.
- The rules relating to nervous shock.
- The rules relating to breach of duty.
- The rules relating to causation.
- The rules relating to foreseeability of damage.
- The defences to negligence.

Introduction

A tort is a civil wrong, other than a breach of trust or breach of contract. The law of tort, therefore, provides remedies for the:

- intentional and direct interference with another's person, property or land (**trespass**);
- indirect interference with another's land (**nuisance**);
- unintentional and careless interference with another's person or property (**negligence**);
- slighting of another's reputation (**defamation**).

It also protects more specialised interests (for example, business and economic interests), and has specific rules regarding liability for **premises** and **animals**.

Prior to examining some of these torts in more detail, it is useful to contrast tortious, criminal and contractual liability:

	Criminal	Contract	Tort
Nature of obligations	mandatory	voluntary	Mandatory
Responsibility for enforcement	state	individual	Individual

Thus, criminal law consists of general (or public) obligations, binding on all citizens, enforced by the state. In contrast, contract law consists of private obligations, voluntarily entered into, enforced by the individuals concerned. The law of tort is curious hybrid, consisting of general (or public obligations), which are binding on all citizens, but that are left to individuals to enforce.

Negligence

Negligence is the failure to take reasonable care where a duty to do so exists, and where that failure causes recoverable loss or damage to the person to whom the duty is owed. Therefore, negligence is more precise than simple carelessness, and is only actionable upon proof of damage. Negligence emerged as a distinct tort from the tort of trespass. Its separate existence was established conclusively by the House of Lords in *Donoghue v Stevenson* [1932]. Here, for the first time, the House of Lords sought to identify the general principles underlying negligence, and Lord Atkin advanced his famous **neighbour principle**:

- you are under a duty to take reasonable care to avoid acts or omissions that you can reasonably foresee might injure your neighbour;

- your neighbour is someone so closely and directly affected by your actions that you ought reasonably to have them in mind as being so affected when considering those actions.

These notions of a duty of care and neighbourhood remain the central foundations of the modern tort of negligence. Following various refinements and variations since 1932, five requirements must be met for negligence liability to arise:

- the damage suffered by the claimant must disclose a **cause of action**;

- the defendant must owe the claimant a **duty of care**;

- the defendant must have been in **breach** of that duty;

- the breach of duty must have been a cause in fact of the claimant's **damage**;

- the claimant's damage must have been a **reasonably foreseeable consequence** of the defendant's breach.

NOTES

The cause of action

The forms of damage that are recoverable in negligence are:

- personal injury.

- physical damage to property.

- economic loss consequential on either of the above.

However, pure economic loss is generally not recoverable (*Spartan Steel & Alloys Ltd v Martin & Co (Contractors) Ltd* [1973]; *D & F Estates Ltd v Church Commissioners* [1989]; *Murphy v Brentwood District Council* [1990]). This limitation is not a matter of principle (as pure economic loss is often reasonably foreseeable). Rather, it is a matter of policy to avoid placing the defendant in a position of almost unlimited liability.

There is one important exception to this general position. Pure economic loss is recoverable where there is a **special relationship** between claimant and defendant—*i.e.* where the claimant was relying on the specialist skill and knowledge of the defendant (*Hedley Byrne & Co Ltd v Heller & Partners Ltd* [1964]; *Junior Books Ltd v Veitchi Co Ltd* [1982]; *Simaan General Contracting Co v Pilkington Glass Ltd (No.2)* [1988]).

The duty of care

As noted above, Lord Atkin's original formulation of neighbourhood as the test for duty of care has been subject to a number of refinements (for example, in *Anns v Merton London Borough Council* [1978]; *Yuen Kun Yeu v Attorney-General of Hong Kong* [1988]).

The present test is one of **proximity**—*i.e.* there must be a sufficiently proximate (or close) relationship between claimant and defendant so that it is fair, just and reasonable in the circumstances to impose a duty of care on the defendant (*Caparo Industries plc v Dickman* [1990]; *Davis v Radcliffe* [1990]). For proximity to arise there must be neighbourhood (in the sense of foreseeability of harm). However, neighbourhood alone does not automatically amount to proximity. The court also considers previous cases by way of analogy and, where appropriate, questions of public policy (for example, *Hill v Chief Constable of West Yorkshire* [1988]). Therefore, proximity is a more flexible (and less predictable) notion than that of neighbourhood.

NOTES

There are two particular situations where the courts have imposed additional requirements (over and above mere neighbourhood) in order to satisfy the requirement of proximity and, hence, to give rise to a duty of care:

- **negligent statements**—in *Hedley Byrne & Co Ltd v Heller & Partners Ltd* [1964], the House of Lords held that liability for negligent statements must be treated differently (and in a more restricted way) to liability for negligent acts because:
  - ➣ reasonably careful people tend to be more careful over what they do than what they say;
  - ➣ while negligent acts tend to have a limited range of effect (giving rise to a limited amount of liability), negligent words can have a much wider effect (for example, where they are broadcast) and could give rise to excessive and almost unlimited liability;
  - ➣ negligent words generally cause only pure economic loss which again, as noted above, could involve the defendant in excessive liability;

Therefore, rather than a mere relationship of neighbourhood, a **special relationship** is required to give rise to the necessary proximity in such cases. According to *Caparo Industries plc v Dickman* [1990], a special relationship arises where:

- ➣ the person seeking the information or advice was relying on the other to exercise care and skill in his/her reply;
- ➣ this reliance was reasonable in the circumstances;
- ➣ the maker of the statement knew that his/her statement would be communicated to the inquirer (either as an individual or member of an identifiable class) specifically in connection with a particular transaction or transactions of a particular kind;
- ➣ the maker of the statement knew that the inquirer would be very likely to rely on it for the purpose of deciding whether or not to enter into that transaction or transactions of that kind.

There is no requirement that the maker of the statement be in the business of giving information or advice of the type sought. It is sufficient that s/he holds him/herself out as possessing the required skill or knowledge and the inquirer reasonably relies on this (*Chaudhry v Prabhakar* [1988]).

- **nervous shock**—nervous shock is a precise term meaning a recognised psychiatric illness (for example, Post-Traumatic Stress Disorder) caused by shock. The law does not recognise claims for ordinary grief or sorrow, no matter how keenly or deeply felt. As with negligent statements, it is the potential breadth of liability that is the prompt for limitations here. As **Lord Wilberforce** observed in *McLoughlin v O'Brian* [1982], "just because 'shock' in its nature is capable of affecting so wide a range of people . . .

NOTES

[there is] . . . a very real need for the law to place some limitation on the extent of admissible claims". Therefore, it would seem that a person is owed a duty of care in respect of nervous shock where:

> the shock is consequent upon physical injury to him/herself; **or**
> the shock is consequent upon a reasonably apprehended fear of physical injury to himself, even though no injury in fact occurs (*Dulieu v White* [1901]); **and**
> personal injury to the claimant (whether physical or psychological) is reasonably foreseeable (*Page v Smith* [1995]).

The position is a little more complicated where shock is caused by injury or fear of injury to another person. The House of Lords stated the present position here when considering a series of test cases arising from the Hillsborough Stadium disaster (*Alcock and others v Chief Constable of South Yorkshire Police* [1991])—a person is owed a duty of care in respect of nervous shock where:

> the shock is consequent upon physical injury to another; **and:**

– the claimant sees or hears (or some equivalent thereof) the accident itself or its immediate aftermath; **and**
– the claimant (the secondary victim) has a close relationship of love and affection with the injured person (the primary victim) (*McFarlane v E. E. Caledonia Ltd* [1993]) or the claimant is a rescuer (*Chadwick v British Transport Commission* [1967]), **and**
– psychological injury to the claimant (the secondary victim) is reasonably foreseeable (*Page v Smith* [1995]).

> the shock is consequent upon a reasonably apprehended fear of physical injury to another, even though no injury in fact occurs, and the requirements stated above are met.

The "immediate aftermath" of the accident extends to the hospital to which the injured person is taken and persists for as long as that person remains in the state produced by the accident, up to and including immediate post-accident treatment (*McLoughlin v O'Brian* [1982]).

The breach of duty

The defendant will be in breach of his/her duty of care if s/he fails to show reasonable care. This is essentially an **objective** test, measuring the defendant's conduct against the degree of care a reasonable person would have exercised in the same circumstances:

The reasonable person
The reasonable person is expected to possess a certain amount of basic knowledge (for

example, that acid burns) and to show a basic or ordinary level of skill. Generally, expert skill or knowledge is not expected unless the defendant has claimed such knowledge or skill (*Phillips v William Whitely Ltd* [1938]). Even where expert skill or knowledge is required, the standard expected remains that of the reasonably competent expert in the given field.

It may be evidence of the fact that the defendant has acted reasonably to show s/he acted in accordance with general, accepted or approved practice in the given field. This comparison must be with the accepted practice at the material time, discounting any subsequent developments, alterations or advances (*Roe v Minister of Health* [1954]). However, this comparison will not help the defendant where it would have been clear to a reasonable person that the accepted practice was itself negligent (*Cavanagh v Ulster Weaving Co Ltd* [1960]).

An exclusively objective test would, in some circumstances, lead to injustice. Therefore, there are circumstances where the court will modify the objective standard by taking into account certain subjective characteristics of the defendant:

- Mental or physical incapacity may make it impossible for the defendant to show reasonable care. It would be unjust to hold him/her negligent in failing to show a degree of care it is impossible for him/her to achieve. However, a person may be negligent in placing themselves in a position that requires a degree of care they knows they are unable to achieve.

- Young children are not required to show the same degree of care as adults. An allowance is made as their youth and immaturity may prevent them appreciating fully the risks and consequences of their actions (*Gough v Thorne* [1966]).

- The elderly are not expected to show the same degree of physical or mental agility or speed of reflex as that of a younger adult (*Daly v Liverpool Corporation* [1939]). The allowance made here is less than that for children, as the elderly have the benefit of knowledge and experience that the child does not. The law also requires people to take account of the effects of ageing and a failure to do so may itself amount to negligence.

- The court may take account of illness on the part of the defendant provided it is both sudden and incapacitating and there has been no forewarning (*Ryan v Youngs* [1938]).

Reasonable care

In deciding what amounts to reasonable care in the circumstances, the courts will consider two main factors:

- The **degree of risk** created by the defendant's conduct. This may be so slight that the reasonable person would be entitled to ignore it (*Bolton v Stone* [1951]). Therefore the

Notes

general approach is that the greater the degree of risk created, the greater the degree of care that should be taken to guard against it.

- The **seriousness of the potential harm**. Again, the greater the potential harm, the greater the obligation to take care to prevent it (*Paris v Stepney Borough Council* [1951]).

The court may also take consider the social utility of the defendant's activities and the cost and practicability of taking precautions against the risk.

Proof of breach

The burden of proving breach lies on the claimant. This is the civil burden of showing that, on the balance of probabilities, the defendant was in breach of duty. However, for a variety of practical reasons, it may be extremely difficult (or even impossible) for the claimant to present definite proof of the defendant's breach. In such circumstances, the claimant may be able to rely on the *res ipsa loquitur* maxim. This is a rule of evidence that asks the court to accept that "the facts speak for themselves" and infer breach of duty from the general circumstances of the case. For the maxim to apply, two requirements must be met (*Scott v London & St Katherine Docks Co* [1865]):

- The accident must be of a type that does not normally occur without someone having been negligent.

- The circumstances must not merely indicate negligence by someone, but negligence on the part of the defendant.

The maxim can only be used to establish breach of duty. It cannot be relied on to establish the required causal link between the defendant's breach and claimant's damage.

The causal link

For the defendant to be liable, there must be a clear, unbroken causal link between his/her breach of duty and the damage suffered by the claimant—*i.e.* the breach must be a cause in fact of the damage. This is established by the application of the "**but for**" test—*i.e.* but for the defendant's breach of duty, would the damage to the claimant have occurred? Where, on the balance of probabilities, the damage would not have occurred, the defendant will be held responsible. Where, by contrast, the damage would probably have occurred in any event, the defendant will not be liable (*Barnett v Chelsea & Kensington Hospital Management Committee* [1969]; *Hotson v East Berkshire Health Authority* [1987]; *Wilsher v Essex Area Health Authority* [1988]).

The defendant's breach need not be the sole cause of the damage. It is sufficient that it makes a significant material contribution (*Bonningtons Castings Ltd v Wardlaw* [1956]).

NOTES

However, it must have been a cause—merely increasing the risk of damage is not sufficient (*Wilsher v Essex Area Health Authority* [1988]; *Page v Smith (No.2)* [1996]). In *Fairchild v Glenhaven Funeral Services Ltd* [2002], the House of Lords developed a limited exception to this requirement. Under the principles in *Fairchild*, where the claimant's loss or damage *must* have been caused by the negligence of one of a group of identifiable tortfeasors but it is not possible to establish which in fact caused the loss, then the claimant will be entitled to succeed against all. However, the claimant will still fail where the loss may have been caused by negligence and may also have been due to other natural causes (as was the case in *Wilsher*). Thus limited, the decision in *Fairchild* would seem to be an acceptable modification to the general rule. However, any further extension that would impose liability on the general basis that the defendant's negligence may have caused the claimant's loss, or materially increased the risk of such loss, should be resisted on the ground that it weakens the fault-based nature of negligence liability (for a more general discussion of fault and liability in negligence, and in tort generally, see **Chapter 42**).

Foreseeability of harm and remoteness of damage

In addition to establishing a factual causal link, the claimant must also establish that the breach was a cause in law of the damage. Following the decision of the Privy Council in *The Wagon Mound (No.1)* [1961], the defendant will only be liable for damage that is a **reasonably foreseeable consequence** of his/her breach. Damage which is not reasonably foreseeable is regarded as **too remote** from the breach and, therefore, not recoverable.

In establishing that damage was reasonably foreseeable, the claimant does not have to show the precise nature, extent or manner of occurrence was foreseeable (*Stewart v West African Air Terminals Ltd* [1964]). What must be established is that the damage suffered was a reasonably foreseeable type of damage, occurring in a reasonably foreseeable manner. For example, in *Hughes v Lord Advocate* [1963], burns sustained in a gas explosion (which was itself unforeseeable) were held to be within the general range of injuries which might reasonably foreseeably arise from leaving a paraffin lamp unattended at road works. In *Bradford v Robinson Rentals Ltd* [1967], frostbite (though itself unforeseeable) was held to be within the general range of reasonably foreseeable injuries resulting from exposure to cold. However, in *Doughty v Turner Manufacturing Co Ltd* [1964], injuries sustained when an asbestos cover fell into a vat of chemicals, causing them to erupt, were held to be outside the general range of reasonably foreseeable injuries that might result from being splashed by chemicals. While splashing was reasonably foreseeable, the chemical eruption was not. Therefore, it is sometimes difficult to predict when the courts will regard unusual injuries or manners of occurrence as being unforeseeable or as being merely an unusual variation of reasonably foreseeable consequences (*Jolley (A.P.) v. Sutton London Borough Council* [2000]).

There is no requirement that the extent of the damage be reasonably foreseeable (*Vacwell Engineering Co Ltd v BDH Chemicals Ltd* [1971]). This principle stands alongside the **thin skull**

NOTES

rule, which requires the defendant take his/her victim as they find him. Therefore, the defendant cannot argue s/he is not responsible for damage aggravated by the physical (*Dulieu v White* [1901]) or mental (*Brice v Brown* [1984]) peculiarities of the claimant. That this rule survives the decision in *The Wagon Mound* is clear from that in *Smith v Leech Brain & Co Ltd* [1962], where latent cancer was triggered into activity by a burn.

Defences to negligence

Where the claimant has met these five requirements, the defendant will be liable unless s/he is able to raise a defence. The three main possibilities are as follows:

Contributory negligence

This is where the claimant's damage is due, in part, to his/her own negligence. Under the **Law Reform (Contributory Negligence) Act 1945**, this is a partial defence, allowing the court to apportion responsibility for the damage between the claimant and defendant and reduce the defendant's liability accordingly. The defendant must show that:

- the claimant failed to exercise reasonable care for his/her own safety (*Davies v Swan Motor Co (Swansea) Ltd* [1949]);
- this failure made a material contribution to the claimant's damage (*Jones v Livox Quarries Ltd* [1952]).

In apportioning responsibility, the court considers two factors:

- the extent to which the actions of the claimant and defendant were a cause of the damage (the **causative potency** test);
- the degree to which the claimant and defendant departed from the standards of the reasonable person (the **degree of blameworthiness** test).

For example, failure to wear a seat belt will generally result in a reduction of 25 per cent where wearing the belt would have eliminated the injury completely, and 15 per cent where the injury would have been less severe (*Froom v Butcher* [1976]).

As with the position of the defendant in general negligence, the court may modify the test of reasonableness by taking into account certain subjective characteristics of the claimant. Regarding contributory negligence, in addition to the factors of mental or physical incapacity, youth or old age, the court may also take into account the following:

NOTES

- where contributory negligence is alleged against a worker, consideration may be given to the fact that the worker's appreciation of risk may have lessened through familiarity with the work or the noise and stress of the workplace (*Grant v Sun Shipping Co Ltd* [1948]).

- where the claimant has been placed in a position of danger by the defendant's negligence and, in the agony of the moment, seeks to escape this danger, s/he will not be contributorily negligent should this decision turn out to be mistaken (*Jones v Boyce* [1816]), provided his/her apprehension of danger is reasonable. This remains so even where the claimant has time to reflect upon their situation (*Haynes v Harwood* [1935]). However, while the claimant may not be contributory negligent in his/her decision to attempt escape, s/he may be negligent in their choice of method or its operation (*Sayers v Harlow UDC* [1958]).

Volenti non fit injuria

Volenti (consent to the risk) is a complete defence to negligence. However, the circumstances in which it may be raised are severely limited and it is of little practical application today. This is partly because the courts prefer to find a claimant contributorily negligent (allowing them to apportion responsibility) rather than as being *volens* to the risk—for example, a claimant who accepts a lift from a driver s/he knows has been drinking will generally be regarded as contributorily negligent (*Owens v Brimmell* [1977]). However, *volenti* may apply where the claimant is aware that the driver is so drunk that an accident is a virtual certainty (*Ashton v Turner* [1981]; *Morris v Murray* [1990]). Furthermore, the effectiveness of consent to express exclusions of liability has been significantly restricted by the **Unfair Contract Terms Act 1977** (see below). *Volenti* may nevertheless be inferred from the claimant's conduct where four requirements are met (*ICI Ltd v Shatwell* [1965]):

- the claimant was aware of the defendant's negligent conduct;

- the claimant was aware of the risk to him/herself that this created;

- the claimant continued to participate freely in the activity in the face of this knowledge;

- the damage suffered was a reasonably foreseeable consequence of the risk consented to.

Regarding the position of rescuers, *volenti* cannot be raised against a rescuer provided the decision to attempt rescue was a reasonable one (*Haynes v Harwood* [1935]; *Cutler v United Dairies (London) Ltd* [1933]). This remains so even where the rescuer knows there is a virtual certainty of injury. Furthermore, even where the decision to rescue was unreasonable, or where the rescuer has been negligent in his/her choice of method or its operation, the courts

---

Notes

will generally regard this as contributory negligence rather than *volenti*. This preferential treatment is because the courts do not wish to discourage people from acting as rescuers. They do not make any fundamental distinction here between the layman and professional rescuer (*Ogwo v Taylor* [1987]). The fact that a person's employment is inherently dangerous does not make him *volens* to risks arising from another's negligence. However, the particular skills and knowledge of the professional are relevant in deciding whether they exercised reasonable care for their own safety in assessing contributory negligence.

Exclusion of liability

The defendant may seek to rely on an undertaking by the claimant to accept the risk of negligence in order to exclude or limit his/her liability. However, as noted above, the extent to which s/he can do this is limited by the **Unfair Contract Terms Act 1977**:

- **s.2(1)** provides that a person cannot, by reference to any contractual term or non-contractual notice, exclude or restrict business liability for causing death or personal injury through negligence.

- **s.2(2)** provides that such liability for other forms of loss or damage can only be excluded or restricted in so far as the term or notice is reasonable.

- **s.2(3)** provides that a person's agreement to or awareness of such a term or notice does not, in itself, amount to *volenti*.

Nevertheless, there may still be certain non-business situations where such undertaking would be effective in excluding or restricting the defendant's liability.

Damages

The principal remedy for negligence is an award of damages (financial compensation). The aim of such an award is to compensate the claimant for the loss or damage suffered. This is a relatively straightforward matter where the loss or damage caused is either physical damage to property or economic loss (where recoverable). The position is, however, more problematic in relation to compensation for personal injury. Here, damages may be awarded under two main heads:

- **non-pecuniary loss**—here, the claimant may recover for the injury itself and any associated pain and suffering and/or loss of amenity.

- **pecuniary loss**—here, any loss of earnings up to the date of trial must be specifically pleaded as "special damages". Loss of future earnings may only be claimed speculatively as "general damages". Any claim for loss of future earnings may, in appropriate circumstances, include an amount for the "lost years" due to a reduction in life expectancy (*Pickett v British Rail Engineering* [1980]).

An award of damages may be paid either as a one-off lump-sum or as a smaller lump-sum accompanied by an annuity or pension (what is known as a "structured settlement", the terms of which must be approved by the court).

Revision Notes

You should now write your revision notes for this topic. Here is an example for you and some suggested headings:

Neg③—Cause of Action

- can recover—personal injury, physical damage, consequential economic loss
- cannot recover pure economic loss **unless** special relationship between C and D—*Hedley Byrne*; *Junior Books*; *Simaan*—see notes on negligent statements

---

Neg①—Duty of Care

Neg②—Negligent Statements

Neg③—Cause of Action

Neg④—Nervous Shock

Neg⑤—Breach of Duty

Neg⑥—Causation

Neg⑦—Foreseeability of Damage

Neg⑧—Defences (Contributory Negligence)

Neg⑨—Defences (volenti and exclusion of liability)

Neg⑩—Damages

Using your cards, you should now be able to write a short paragraph in response to each of the following questions:

Notes

Explain and discuss the rules of law relating to the following areas of negligence:

1. Cause of action.
2. Duty of care.
3. Negligent statements.
4. Nervous Shock.
5. Breach of duty.
6. Causation.
7. Foreseeability of damage.
8. Contributory negligence.
9. *Volenti non fit injuria.*
10. Exclusion of liability.

31 Tort—Occupiers' Liability

Key Points

What you need to know and discuss:

- The common duty of care under the Occupiers' Liability Act 1957.
- The limited duty of care under the Occupiers' Liability Act 1984.
- The different categories of lawful and non-lawful visitors.
- What is meant by "occupier" and "premises".
- The defences available to occupiers.

One area where the law has identified a particular duty owed to others is that of the duty owed by occupiers to those who visit their premises. This is regulated by the Occupiers' **Liability Acts 1957** and **1984**:

The Occupiers' Liability Act 1957

This concerns the duty owed by occupiers to lawful visitors.

The common duty of care

Under **s.2**, occupiers owe a common duty of care to all lawful visitors to their premises. This is a duty to take reasonable care to ensure the visitor is reasonably safe when using the premises for all the purposes for which s/he is invited or permitted to be there. This applies to the visitor's physical safety in all circumstances, but only to his/her property in respect of damage caused by structural defects (**s.1**). What amounts to reasonable care is governed by the same principles as the general tort of negligence. However, the Act does make specific provision for two particular categories of visitor:

- **children**—a higher degree of care should be shown to child visitors. In particular, occupiers must take special care in respect of any allurements on the premises (*Glasgow*

Corporation v Taylor [1922]). An allurement is something tempting or attractive to children but that is also potentially dangerous (for example, bonfires, berries, building materials, railway trucks).

- **professionals**—a lower degree of care may be shown to visiting professionals or specialists regarding risks or hazards incidental to their calling or profession (*Roles v Nathan* [1963]).

Lawful Visitors

- **invitees**—someone permitted to enter the premises by the occupier and whose presence is in the interests of the occupier (for example, customers in a shop or pub, guests at a party).

- **licensees**—someone permitted to enter the premises by the occupier but whose presence is of no interest to the occupier (for example, children recovering a lost ball).

- **contractual visitors**—someone permitted to enter the premises under a contract with the occupier (for example, a window cleaner or milkman).

- **statutory visitors**—someone with statutory authority to enter the premises (for example, a police officer or postman).

The common duty of care is not owed to **common law visitors**, other than invitees and licensees (*Greenhalgh v British Railways Board* [1969]). A common law visitor is someone entitled to enter the premises by reason of some private or public right, such as a right of way. However, occupiers are under a common law duty not to do anything positive that might make their entry dangerous. They may also be protected under the **1984 Act**. Also, the common duty is not owed to **trespassers**, though they are owed a common law duty of humanity (*British Railways Board v Herrington* [1972]) and may also be protected under the **1984 Act**.

The occupier

This is anyone in control of the premises (*Wheat v E. Lacon & Co Ltd* [1966]). There is no requirement the occupier has any legal or equitable interest in the premises, nor need s/he be in exclusive possession—for example, both a building owner and a building contractor may be occupiers for the purposes of the Act.

Premises

This includes not only land and buildings, but also any fixed or movable structure, including any vehicle, vessel and aircraft. Thus, the provisions of the Act have been applied to ships, cranes, scaffolding, ladders, piers and sea platforms.

NOTES

Exclusion of liability

The occupier can modify, restrict or exclude his/her liability under the Act by agreement or otherwise. However, the possibility of excluding or restricting business liability for negligence (which includes breach of the common duty under the Act) is severely constrained by the **Unfair Contract Terms Act 1977**.

Defences

There are three main defences available:

- **contributory negligence;**
- **warnings**—where the occupier has given a clear warning of danger that, if observed, would make the visitor safe, the occupier is not liable for damage caused by the visitor's failure to observe the warning. Whether the warning is effective depends in part on the nature of the warning itself and in part upon the likely nature of potential visitors. A warning that may be effective against an adult visitor may not be effective against a child. Equally, a warning will not be regarded as effective where there was clear evidence, known to the defendant, that the warning was being repeatedly ignored (contrast, for example, *Ratcliff v McConnell* [1999] and *Tomlinson v Congleton Borough Council* [2002]);
- *volenti*—this may arise where the visitor was fully aware of the danger or risk on the premises, knew of the risk to him/herself this created and remained on the premises in the face of that knowledge.

The Occupiers' Liability Act 1984

This concerns the duty owed by occupiers to visitors other than lawful visitors (as defined for the purposes of the **1957 Act**).

The limited duty

Unlike the general duty owed to lawful visitors under the **1957 Act**, the **1984 Act** imposes only a limited duty. This is a duty to take reasonable care to ensure the visitor is not injured as a result of **specific dangers** on the premises. A danger is a specific danger where:

- the occupier is aware of the danger or has reasonable grounds to believe it exists;
- the occupier knows or has reasonable grounds to believe that the other person is in the vicinity of the danger or is likely to come into the vicinity;

NOTES

- the danger is one against which, in all the circumstances, the occupier may reasonably be expected to offer the other person protection. Here, the purpose for the other person being on the premises clearly affects whether s/he ought reasonably be offered protection—for example, a burglar would receive less consideration than a child who had strayed onto the premises.

The limited duty only protects the visitor's physical safety. It offers no protection to his/her property.

The occupier, premises and defences

The same principles and definitions apply as for the **1957 Act**.

Implied licensees

A trespasser may become an implied licensee in circumstances where the occupier is aware of his/her presence and does nothing to prevent or discourage it nor expressly forbids it—for example, children who regularly gain access to the premises to play or take a short cut (*Edwards v British Railway Executive* [1952]). In such circumstances, the visitor would then be owed the common duty under the **1957 Act**.

Revision Notes

You should now write your revision notes for this topic. Here is an example for you and some suggested headings:

OL③—Non-lawful visitors

- common law visitor (other than licensee/invitee)—duty not to act positively to make premises dangerous + protected by 1984 Act

- trespassers—owed duty of humanity (*BRB v Herrington*) + protected by 1984 Act

- may become implied licensees (*Edwards v BRE*)

OL①—Common Duty (1957)

OL②—Lawful visitors

Notes

OL③—Non-lawful visitors

OL④—"Occupiers" & "Premises"

OL⑤—Defences

OL⑥—Limited Duty (1984)

Using your cards, you should now be able to write a short paragraph in response to each of the following questions:

1. What is the common duty of care under the OLA "57?

2. Explain the different types of lawful visitor.

3. Who is an "occupier?

4. What are "premises"?

5. Describe the defences available to an occupier.

6. What is the limited duty of care under the OLA '84?

7. Explain the position of common law visitors, trespassers and implied licensees.

NOTES

32 | Tort—Nuisance

Key Points

What you need to know and discuss:

- The rules of law relating to private nuisance.
- The rules of law relating to public nuisance.
- The rules of law relating to statutory nuisance.

Private nuisance

Private nuisance is the indirect and unreasonable interference with the use or enjoyment of neighbouring land (*Sedleigh-Denfield v O'Callaghan* [1940]). This may be caused by many different things—for example, noise, smoke, odours, fumes, water and plant and tree roots. The basis of liability here is the failure to meet the reasonable expectations of one's neighbours. While this has clear similarities with negligence, there are also important differences. In negligence, the question is whether the defendant's conduct was reasonable, while in nuisance the question is whether the effect of that conduct on the defendant's neighbours is reasonable. Therefore, if the defendant's conduct in fact causes an actionable nuisance, it is no defence to show that s/he has taken reasonable care to prevent this. If the defendant cannot carry on a particular activity without causing an actionable nuisance, then s/he should not carry on that activity or, at least, should carry it on somewhere else (*Rapier v London Tramways Co* [1893]). This means that nuisance can, in certain circumstances, take on the appearance of a tort of strict liability.

Proof of damage

This is the essential element. A nuisance is only actionable where it causes damage to the claimant's interests. This requirement is clearly satisfied where the nuisance causes physical damage to the claimant's land, as this is always unreasonable. Where the damage complained of is disturbance to use or enjoyment, this must be more than trivial (*Andreae v Selfridge* [1938])—the law expects a degree of give-and-take between neighbours (*Bamford v Turnley* [1862]).

NOTES

Other relevant factors

While proof of damage is essential to a successful nuisance action, there are a number of other factors the court may consider:

- generally, the nuisance must be of a continuing or regular nature. Isolated or irregular instances will not normally amount to a nuisance (*Bolton v Stone* [1951]). However, where the defendant is responsible for a continuous state of affairs with the potential for nuisance, s/he may be liable immediately should a nuisance in fact occur (*Spicer v Smee* [1946]);

- where the damage complained of is disturbance to use or enjoyment, the court may consider the character of the neighbourhood (*St Helen's Smelting Co v Tipping* [1865]). What may be reasonable in an industrial area may not be in a residential area. Similarly, what may reasonable in a busy city may not be in a quiet village;

- the fact that the claimant may be unusually sensitive is not relevant to the issue of liability—the test remains the expectations of the reasonable neighbour (*Robinson v Kilvert* [1889]). However, once liability has been established, unusual sensitivity may be relevant to the question of remedies (*McKinnon Industries Ltd v Walker* [1951]);

- while malice on the part of the defendant is not an essential requirement, the presence of malice may tip the balance, converting otherwise reasonable conduct into an actionable nuisance (*Christie v Davey* [1893]; *Hollywood Silver Fox Farm Ltd v Emmett* [1936]);

- the defendant may be liable for a nuisance caused by the fault of another or due to natural causes. This is known as "adoption" or "continuance" of nuisance, and arises where the defendant knew or ought to have known of the nuisance and failed to take reasonable steps to stop it (*Leakey v National Trust* [1980]).

The claimant

The claimant must have a legal or equitable interest in the land affected (*Malone v Laskey* [1907]; *Hunter v Canary Wharf Ltd* [1997]). Where the damage complained of is disturbance to use or enjoyment, the claimant must also be in actual possession (occupation) of the land (*Cooper v Crabtree* [1882]). However, where the damage is physical damage, a person with an interest out of possession (for example, a landlord) may sue (*Colwell v St Pancras Borough Council* [1904]).

The defendant

An action for private nuisance may be brought against the occupier of the offending land, the creator of the nuisance or any person authorising the nuisance (for example, a landlord).

Notes

Defences

- **consent of the claimant**—where the claimant has expressly consented to the nuisance, this is a defence provided it is true consent—*i.e.* to both the nature and extent of the nuisance;

- **prescription**—this is a form of implied consent. Where the defendant has been committing the nuisance for more than 20 years and has done so without force, secrecy or permission (*nec vi, nec clam, nec precario*), this is a defence against a claimant who has not complained during this time. However, this defence is of little practical application today as the time starts running from the time the particular claimant became aware of the nuisance (*Sturges v Bridgman* [1879]). Therefore, it is no defence to argue that the claimant "came into" the nuisance—the fact that a previous occupier of the affected land had not complained does not bind a subsequent occupier;

- **statutory authority**—the defendant may have a defence where his/her actions are in pursuance of a statutory power or duty, though s/he must take all reasonable steps to keep any nuisance caused to a minimum.

Remedies

At common law, a successful claimant has a right to **damages**. However, it may well be that the claimant wants the nuisance stopped by an **injunction**. We should remember that an injunction, being an equitable remedy, lies in the discretion of the court and will only be granted where it is just and equitable to do so. A self-help remedy, **abatement**, is also available. The claimant may take all reasonable steps to stop the nuisance though, for a variety of reasons, this is usually not advisable.

Public nuisance

A public nuisance is an act or omission that materially affects the comfort and convenience in life of a class of Her Majesty's subjects (*Attorney-General v PYA Quarries Ltd* [1957]). Therefore, the nuisance must affect an identifiable group of the general public. Accordingly, actions such as obstructing the highway, keeping a brothel and polluting the public water supply have been regarded as public nuisances.

Public nuisance is essentially a crime and is tried on indictment in the Crown Court. Alternatively, either the Attorney-General or the relevant local council may bring a civil **relator** action on behalf of the affected public. Once the criminal or relator action has been proved, any individual who has suffered **special damage** (*i.e.* particular damage over and above that suffered by the public at large) may bring a civil action for damages (*Halsey v Esso Petroleum Co Ltd* [1961]).

NOTES

Statutory nuisance

Many activities have been effectively removed from the sphere of private nuisance as a result of a range of statutory provisions that grant wide powers to local authorities to take steps to prevent environmental damage. Thus, many forms of pollution (notably noise and smoke pollution) are now statutory nuisances under the **Public Health Act 1936**, the **Clean Air Act 1956** and the **Control of Pollution Act 1974**.

Revision Notes

You should now write your revision notes for this topic. Here is an example for you and some suggested headings:

Nuisance③—Claimants and Defendants

- C must have legal/equitable interest in affected land (*Malone v Laskey*; *Hunter v Canary Wharf*)
- use/enjoyment—C must also be in possession (Cooper v Crabtree)
- physical damage—reversioner may sue (Colwell v St Pancras BC)
- D = occupier/creator/authorisor

Nuisance①—Elements of Private Nuisance

Nuisance③—Defences

Nuisance③—Claimants and Defendants

Nuisance④—Remedies

Nuisance⑤—Public Nuisance

Nuisance⑥—Statutory Nuisance

Using your cards, you should now be able to write a short paragraph in response to each of the following questions:

1. Explain and discuss the elements of private nuisance.

2. Who may bring a claim in private nuisance?

NOTES

3. Who may be sued and what defences may they have?

4. Explain the remedies available for private nuisance.

5. Explain and discuss the elements of public nuisance.

6. Explain the scope of statutory nuisance

33 | Tort—Trespass

Key Points

What you need to know and discuss:

- The law relating to **trespass to land**.
- The law relating to **trespass to the person**.

Trespass to land

This is the direct and intentional interference with another's land:

- **land**—this includes not only the land itself but also the ground beneath it, any building on it, and the airspace above to such a height as is necessary for reasonable use and enjoyment;
- **another**—the claimant must be in possession of the land affected. For the purposes of trespass, possession means having the right to exclusive occupation of the land;
- **direct interference**—the defendant must have interfered directly (indirect interference is dealt with through nuisance—see **Chapter 32**) with the rights of the claimant by, for example:
    - ➤ unauthorised entry to the land;
    - ➤ remaining on the land once asked to leave;
    - ➤ placing things on the land;
    - ➤ tunnelling under the land;
    - ➤ invading the airspace above the land;
- **intentional**—this simply means that the defendant's presence on, or conduct in relation to, the land must be intentional. It is not necessary to show the defendant intended to trespass;
- **defences**—there are a number of defences that may be available:

> statutory authority;
> exercise of a public or private right (including a licence to be on the land);
> necessity (for example, where A trespasses on B's land when fleeing an assault by C);
> abatement of nuisance (where A enters B's land to take reasonable steps to stop a nuisance affecting A's land);
> recovery of goods (only where A's goods have been wrongfully taken to B's land or are accidentally there).

Trespass to the person

There are three forms of trespass to the person:

- **assault**—this is an intentional and direct act which causes the claimant to fear immediate and unlawful personal violence.

- **battery**—this is the intentional and direct application of unlawful force to another person.

We have seen earlier (**Chapter 17**) that assault and batteries are also criminal offences. Essentially the same principles and definitions apply in tort (though the burden of proof is less severe, being the civil rather than the criminal burden). We should note that in both cases the force (threatened or actual) must be unlawful. Therefore, a police officer using reasonable force while acting within his/her powers would not be liable. However, where the officer acts outside those powers, civil liability may arise (for more details on police powers, see **Chapter 6**). It may also be that certain defences, such as consent of the victim, have a broader scope in tort than in the criminal law. Unintentional interference may, of course, give rise to liability in negligence.

- **false imprisonment**—this is the intentional and direct restraint on another's freedom of movement:
  > the restraint must be total—there is no imprisonment if the claimant is prevented from moving in some directions but is free to move in others (*Bird v Jones* [1845]). Similarly, there is no imprisonment where the claimant has a reasonable means of escape from the restraint;
  > the claimant, however, need not know of the restraint at the time (*Meering v Grahame-White Aviation Co Ltd* [1920]; *Murray v Ministry of Defence* [1988])— though in such cases damages are likely to be nominal.

It is obviously a defence to show that the restraint was lawful. This again has obvious relevance to the exercise of police powers.

NOTES

Revision Notes

You should now write your revision notes for this topic. Here is an example for you and some suggested headings:

Trespass④—Person (false imprisonment)

- intentional and direct restraint on freedom of movement
- restraint must be total (*Bird v Jones*)
- C need not know of restraint at the time (*Meering v Grahame-White Aviation*)
- Defence of lawful restraint—see police powers

Trespass①—Land (elements)

Trespass②—Land (defences)

Trespass③—Person (assault and battery)

Trespass④—Person (false imprisonment)

Using your cards, you should now be able to write a short paragraph in response to each of the following questions:

1. Explain and discuss the elements of trespass to land.

2. What defences may raised to such an action?

3. Explain and discuss the elements of assault and battery.

4. Explain and discuss the elements of false imprisonment.

34 Tort—Strict & Vicarious Liability

Key Points

What you need to know and discuss:

- The rule in *Rylands v Fletcher*.
- The concept of vicarious liability.
- Liability for independent contractors.

Introduction

Liability in tort is generally dependent upon proof of fault on the part of the defendant. However, there is a limited amount of strict liability, principally concerning liability for certain extra-hazardous activities and justified on grounds of public policy. This liability may be imposed by statute (for example, the **Nuclear Installations Act 1965**, the **Control of Pollution Act 1974**) or under the common law rule established in *Rylands v Fletcher* [1868].

The rule in *Rylands v Fletcher*

Under this rule:

A person who is in occupation of land and brings onto that land something that is not naturally there, and does so for his/her own non-natural use, and that thing is likely to do mischief should it escape, then that person will be liable for the consequences of any such escape, even in the absence of any fault on his/her part.

The various elements of this rule require further explanation.

- The defendant must have been in occupation (*i.e.* in control) of the land from which the thing escapes.

- The thing must not have been naturally present on the land (for example, self-sown trees and plants are naturally present whereas deliberately cultivated ones are not).

- The thing must have been brought onto the land by the defendant for his/her own use, though not necessarily for his/her own benefit.

- The defendant must have been using the land is some non-natural way—*i.e.* s/he must have been engaged in some special use bringing with it an increased danger to others, and not merely the ordinary use of land or that which is for the general benefit of the community (*Rickards v Lothian* [1913]). This considerably limits the scope of the rule in practice.

- The thing must be likely to do mischief should it escape. This does not mean it has to be inherently dangerous, merely that it is potentially dangerous should it escape in an uncontrolled way.

- The thing must escape—*i.e.* leave the confines of the defendant's land (*Read v Lyons (J.) & Co Ltd* [1947]). Where there is no escape, the claimant must rely on the principles of negligence, occupiers' liability or nuisance as appropriate.

Defences

While liability under the rule is strict, it is not absolute, and there are five main defences available:

- the defendant is not liable where the escape is due to an **Act of God**. This applies where the escape is the result of natural causes without any human intervention, and such natural events were not reasonably foreseeable (*Tennent v Earl of Glasgow* [1864]);

- the defendant may be able to avoid liability where s/he was acting under **statutory authority**;

- the defendant will not be liable where the escape is due to the **unforeseeable act of a stranger** (*e.g.* a trespasser);

- the defendant will not be liable where the claimant had, expressly or impliedly, **consented** to the thing being brought onto the land or to its remaining there. Thus, while "coming into" the situation is no defence to an action in nuisance, it may be a defence to an action based on the rule. Consent here means true consent, in the sense that the claimant was aware not only of the presence of the thing but also of its potential for mischief should it escape;

- the defendant will not be liable where the escape is due to the **sole fault of the claimant**. Where the escape is partly due to the fault of the claimant, **contributory negligence** will apply.

Notes

Remedies

The claimant will be able to claim damages in respect of all reasonably foreseeable consequences of the escape (*Cambridge Water Co v Eastern Counties Leather* [1993]). This allows recovery for personal injury, property damage and consequential economic loss, but not pure economic loss (*Cattle v Stockton Waterworks Co* [1875]).

Given the various limitations and restrictions outlined above, it is best to think of the rule as a peculiar variation of the general law of nuisance, rather than a significant form of liability in its own right (*Cambridge Water Co v Eastern Counties Leather* [1993]).

Vicarious liability

This term is used to describe situations where one person is liable for the torts of another by reason of the relationship between them. By far the most common such relationship is that of employer and employee. There are four main justifications for the imposition of strict liability in here:

- the employee's actions are generally at the instigation of the employer;
- the employee's actions are generally for the benefit of the employer;
- vicarious liability generally provides the claimant with a financially secure defendant;
- vicarious liability acts as an incentive on employers to select competent employees, train them adequately and establish safe working practices.

It follows that employers vicarious liability is a form of enterprise liability, limited to liability resulting from the conduct of the business. Therefore, for such liability to arise, two requirements must be met:

- There must be a **relationship of employment** between the "employee" committing the tort and the "employer". The most obvious evidence of this would be a contract of employment. However, the relationship remains one for the courts, not the parties, to define. Therefore an express contractual provision that the relationship is not one of employment will not prevail over a preponderance of other terms and factors that indicate that it is (*Mersey Docks and Harbour Board v Coggins and Griffiths (Liverpool) Ltd* [1947]). In assessing whether, on balance, the relationship is one of employment, the courts take into account a number of factors:

<u>Notes</u>

> the **issue of control**. Where the "employer" controls the type and manner of performance of the work of the "employee", the relationship is likely to be one of employment;

> the **issue of integration**. A person whose activities are integral to the enterprise (e.g. a ship's master or company chauffeur) is more likely to be regarded as an employee than someone whose activities are ancillary to the enterprise or temporarily attached to it (*e.g.* the harbour pilot or hire car driver) (*Stevenson, Jordan and Harrison Ltd v Macdonald* [1952]);

> the **method of payment** (whether wages or salary or a lump sum), the responsibility for **providing premises, materials and equipment**, and any provisions for **disciplinary measures** and **dismissal** (*Mersey Docks and Harbour Board v Coggins and Griffiths (Liverpool) Ltd* [1947]);

> the claimant does not have to identify the particular employee responsible provided it is clear that the tort must have been committed by one of the defendant's employees (*Grant v Australian Knitting Mills Ltd* [1936]).

- The employee's tort must be "so closely connected with his employment that it would be fair and just to hold the employers vicariously liable" (Lord Steyn in *Lister v Hesley Hall Ltd* [2002]). That this has extended the scope of vicarious liability as compared to the old "course of employment" test is clear. What is far less certain is the precise scope of this new test. In the House of Lords decision in *Dubai Aluminium Co Ltd v Salaam* [2003], Lord Nicholls formulated the test as being that "the wrongful conduct must be so closely connected with acts the . . . employee was authorised to do that, for the purpose of the liability of . . . the employer to third parties, the wrongful conduct may fairly and properly be regarded as done . . . while acting in the ordinary course of the . . . employee's employment", and Lord Millett observed "All depends on the closeness of the connection between the duties which, in broad terms, the employee was engaged to perform and his wrongdoing." While recognising that this test "betoken[s] a value judgment by the court", Lord Nicholls maintained that nevertheless "the conclusion is a conclusion of law, based on primary facts, rather than a simple question of fact." With respect, while the application of clear legal rules to primary facts leads to a conclusion of law, it is difficult to see how the application of a "value judgment" can be anything other than a conclusion of fact or opinion. In this respect, the decision of the House of Lords in *Lister* and *Dubai Aluminium* can be seen as part of a somewhat disturbing trend in the House that may be argued to include the decisions in *Caparo Industries plc v Dickman* [1990] (duty of care in negligence), *R. v Adomako* [1994] (gross negligence manslaughter), *R. v Hinks* [2000] (theft), and *R. v Smith* [2000] (provocation).

- **The position of the independent contractor**—an employer will not normally be liable for the acts of an independent contractor. However, the employer may be liable where

---

NOTES

the contractor is in breach of a non-delegable duty binding on the employer. In such circumstances, while the employer can delegate performance of the duty to a contractor, s/he cannot delegate the duty itself and will remain personally (not vicariously) liable should the contractor breach that duty. Non-delegable duties arise in two main situations:

> where the commissioned work involves exceptional risk to others. Here the employer will be liable for any negligence by the contractor in the performance of that work (*Holliday v National Telephone Co* [1899]) but not any collateral negligence (*Padbury v Holliday and Greenwood Ltd* [1912]);
> where the employer owes the victim a duty of care for their safety and protection (*e.g.* the duty on employers to provide for the health and safety at work of their employees—*Smith v Cammell Laird & Co Ltd* [1940]; the duty on Health Authorities and hospitals for the welfare and safety of patients in their care—*Cassidy v Ministry of Health* [1951]).

Revision Notes

You should now write your revision notes for this topic. Here is an example for you and some suggested headings:

S&VL②—Defences

- Act of God (*Tennent v Earl of Glasgow*)
- Statutory authority
- Unforseeable act of stranger
- Consent of claimant
- Fault of claimant/contributory negligence

S&VL①—Rule in Rylands v Fletcher

S&VL②—Defences

S&VL③—Remedies

S&VL④—Vicarious liability

NOTES

S&VL⑤—Relationship of Employment

S&VL⑥—Close connection test

S&VL⑦—Independent Contractors

Using your cards, you should now be able to write a short paragraph in response to each of the following questions:

1. Explain the rule in *Rylands v Fletcher*.

2. What defences may be raised to an action under the rule?

3. What remedies may be obtained?

4. Explain what is meant by vicarious liability.

5. When does a relationship of employment arise?

6. When is a tort committed in the course of employment?

7. Explain the position regarding independent contractors.

NOTES

35 Tort—Liability for Animals

Key Points

What you need to know and discuss:

- The common law rules on liability for animals.
- Liability for animals under the Animals Act 1971.

Liability for animals at common law

Liability for animals may arise in the ordinary law of tort—for example, in nuisance (*Leeman v Montagu* [1936]) or negligence (*Draper v Hodder* [1972]). The common law also developed a number of special rules relating to animals. These have now been replaced by the provisions of the **Animals Act 1971**, though this is based on and retains many of the principles of the old common law position.

Liability for animals under the Animals Act 1971

Liability for dangerous animals

By **s.2(1)**, a keeper of a dangerous animal is strictly liable for any damage caused by it. By **s.6(2)**, a dangerous animal is:

- one which is not commonly domesticated in the British Islands (even though it may be domesticated overseas—*Tutin v Chipperfield Promotions Ltd* [1980]); and
- whose fully-grown animals normally have such characteristics that they are likely, unless restrained, to cause severe damage or that any damage they may cause is likely to be severe—for example, a tiger is likely to cause severe damage; an elephant, while it may not be likely to cause damage, is likely to cause severe damage if it causes any at all.

A person is regarded as the keeper of the animal if s/he owns it or has it in his/her possession or is the head of a household of which a member under the age of 16 owns the animal or has it in his/her possession (**s.6(3)**). If someone abandons an animal, they are still regarded as the owner unless and until another person assumes ownership. Another person does not assume ownership, and hence become the keeper, merely by taking possession of an animal in order to prevent it causing damage or to return it to its owner.

Liability for other animals

Where damage is caused by an animal other than a dangerous animal, **s.2(2)** provides that the keeper will be strictly liable for that damage where:

- the damage was of a kind that the animal, unless restrained, was likely to cause or that, if caused by the animal, was likely to be severe; and

- the likelihood of the damage or of its being severe was due to characteristics of the animal that are not normally found in animals of the same species (*i.e.* where animals of that species are normally docile but the particular animal in question is not) or are not normally so found except at particular times or in particular circumstances (*i.e.* species of animals which are normally docile but which, in certain circumstances or at particular times, behave differently, even dangerously. For example, dogs are not normally prone to bite all and sundry. But a dog guarding its territory or a bitch with a litter whose pups are being threatened, may well be vicious); and

- those characteristics were known to the keeper (actual knowledge is required—though failure to know what one ought to have known may give rise to liability in negligence).

That the scope of liability under **s.2(2)** is wider than previously thought is clear from the decision of the House of Lords in *Mirvahedy v Henley* [2003]. Here, horses kept by the defendants were seriously frightened by some unascertained cause. They panicked and charged down and flattened the fence of their field. They fled towards the A380 main road where they encountered motor traffic. This aggravated their existing state of panic. In this state of panic, one horse charged into the side of Mr Mirvahedy's car. The roof of the car was peeled off. Mr Mirvahedy suffered serious head and facial injuries. There was no suggestion that the defendants had been negligent in their keeping of the horses or maintenance of the fence. For the majority, Lord Hobhouse stated "Horses are not normally in a mindless state of panic nor do they normally ignore obstacles in their path. These characteristics are normally only found in horses in circumstances where they have been very seriously frightened. It is only in such circumstances that it becomes likely that, due to these characteristics, the horse will cause severe damage. This case clearly comes within the words of s.2(2)(b)." However, whether one can properly regard animals being frightened or "spooked" by some unknown

NOTES

cause as being in the same category as animals in the "territorial" or "parental" examples given above is at least questionable. As Lord Scott (in the minority in **Mirvahedy**) observed, "To impose strict liability on the keeper of an ordinary domesticated animal, or of a non-dangerous wild animal held in captivity, for damage done by the animal when responding normally, as any member of its species would respond, to some external stimulus seems to me inconsistent with the apparent intention of the Act to draw a distinction between dangerous and non-dangerous animals and inconsistent, in particular, with the apparent purpose of paragraph (b) to limit strict liability for non-dangerous animals to damage attributable to abnormal characteristics."

Defences

- contributory negligence (**s.10**);
- sole fault of the claimant (**s.5(1)**)—for example, where A provokes a dog into attacking him (*Nelmes v Chief Constable for of Avon & Somerset* [1993]);
- consent to the risk (**s.5(2)**)—although an employee (for example, a zoo keeper) does not consent to risks incidental to his/her employment (**s.6(5)**).

Liability for injury to livestock by dogs

By **s.3**, the keeper of a dog is strictly liable where the dog causes damage by killing or injuring livestock. Livestock here includes not only the common types of farm animal but also domestic varieties of duck, geese, guinea-fowl, peacock, pigeon and quail, deer not in the wild state, and grouse, pheasants and partridges in captivity. A person may have a defence to an action for killing or injuring a dog to show that, at the material time, the dog was about to, was, or had been worrying livestock (**s.9**).

Liability for straying livestock

By **s.4**, a person to whom livestock (excluding captive grouse, pheasants and partridges) belongs will be strictly liable where that livestock strays onto land owned or occupied by another and causes damage to the land or any property on it that is in the ownership or possession of that other. The owner of the livestock will also be liable for any reasonable expenses incurred in keeping the livestock while the owner is identified or pending its return or (in certain circumstances) sale. The following defences may be available:

- sole fault of the claimant (**s.5(1)**)—**s.5(6)** provides the fact the claimant could have prevented the damage by fencing does not, in itself, make that damage the claimant's fault;

NOTES

- where the straying would not have occurred but for the breach by another person of a duty to fence the land (**s.5(6)**);

- contributory negligence (**s.10**).

Revision Notes

You should now write your revision notes for this topic. Here is an example for you and some suggested headings:

Animals④—1971/Dogs injuring livestock

- K is SL where dog kills/injures livestock (s.3)

- "livestock" = usual farm animals + domestic duck, geese, guinea-fowl, peacock & quail, deer (not wild), captive pheasant, grouse & partridge

- fact that dog was about to/was/had been worrying livestock may be defence to action for killing/injuring dog (s.9)

Animals①—Common Law

Animals②—1971/Dangerous Animals

Animals③—1971/Other Animals

Animals⑤—1971/ Straying Livestock

Using your cards, you should now be able to write a short paragraph in response to each of the following questions:

1. Explain the potential liability for animals at common law.

2. What is the position regarding dangerous animals under the Animals Act 1971?

3. Explain the provisions of the Act relating to other animals.

4. What are the special provisions relating to livestock?

NOTES

SECTION SIX: HUMAN RIGHTS

36 Human Rights—Rights and Freedoms

Key Points

What you need to know:

- The traditional residual approach to freedom in Britain.

What you need to discuss:

- The **background** to the **Human Rights Act 1998**.

Introduction

Until recently, any discussion of the legal protection of human rights in England and Wales has taken place in a context of civil liberties, not civil rights. This distinction was not simply a matter of a choice of words, but had profound consequences for the nature of freedom in this country. To say that a person is at liberty to do something is fundamentally different from saying that a person has a right to do something. Freedom in English law had always been an essentially **residual** concept—one was free to do everything left over once the law had said what one cannot do.

This notion that one is free to do anything except that which is prohibited by law (with its implicit reference to the traditional figure of the "free-born Englishman") was a superficially attractive one. However, its attractions are less clear when we remember that there are no legal constraints on a sovereign Parliament to enact further restrictions on even the most fundamental of freedoms.

Clearly, some restrictions on absolute freedom can be justified either to protect or balance individual interests or the collective interest as represented by the State. Nevertheless, it was the case that, as Geoffrey Robertson put it, "Liberty in Britain is a state of mind rather than a set of legal rules". This approach was increasingly thought to be inadequate to protect our most fundamental freedoms, particularly as an ever more politically, socially, economically and ethnically diverse Britain moved into the twenty-first century. It was this pressure for change that brought about the introduction of more formal protection for human rights under English law with the **Human Rights Act 1998** (the case for change is set out in the White Paper—"Rights Brought Home"—that preceded the Act). We should not underestimate the importance of this legislation. As John Wadham (Director of the civil liberties campaign organisation *Liberty*) stated, it is "a landmark in human rights protection, the most significant human rights reform in the post-war period . . . The Act will make a real difference to individual rights and freedoms such as privacy and family life".

The Convention Rights

The **European Convention on Human Rights** was adopted by the Council of Europe in 1950 and, since 1966, Britain has accepted the right of individual petition to the European Court of Human Rights. The rights protected by the Convention are:

- Art.2—the right to life;
- Art.3—freedom from torture, inhuman or degrading treatment or punishment;
- Art.4—freedom from slavery and forced labour;
- Art.5—freedom of the person;
- Art.6—the right to a fair, public and independent trial;
- Art.7—freedom from retrospective criminal laws;
- Art.8—the right to respect for private and family life, home and correspondence
- Art.9—freedom of thought, conscience and religion;
- Art.10—freedom of expression;
- Art.11—freedom of assembly and association;
- Art.12—the right to marry and found a family;
- Art.13—the right to an effective remedy before a national authority for violation of any rights or freedoms protected under the Convention;
- Art.14—freedom from discrimination.

The First Protocol to the Convention added:

- Art.1—the right to the enjoyment of private property;

NOTES

- Art.2—the right to education;
- Art.3—the right to free elections by secret ballot.

We should note, however, that some of these are **not** absolute rights or freedoms, as the Convention sometimes allows for restrictions to protect national security, public order, health or morals, and the rights and freedoms of others. Nevertheless, there is an important distinction here from the residual approach. The presumption is **against** restrictions, and the validity of any restriction can be tested in the Court.

Revision Notes

You should now write your revision notes for this topic. Here are some suggested headings:

R&F①—Residual Approach

R&F②—Why the HRA?

R&F③—ECHR Rights

Using your cards, you should now be able to write a short paragraph in response to each of the following questions:

1. What was the approach to freedoms under English law prior to the Human Rights Act 1998?

2. What were the main reasons for the enactment of the 1998 Act?

3. What major rights and freedoms are protected by the European Convention on Human Rights?

Useful Websites

- For the Lord Chancellor's Department Human Rights Unit, visit **www.lcd.gov.uk/hract/hramenu.htm**

- For the text of the Human Rights Act 1998, visit **www.hmso.gov.uk/acts/acts1998/19980042.htm**

- For the various guidance documents issued by the Human Rights Unit, visit **www.lcd.gov.uk/hract/guidlist.htm**

NOTES

⊕ For the "Rights Brought Home" White Paper, visit
www.official_documents.co.uk/document/hoffice/rights/rights.htm

⊕ For information on the Human Rights Act issued by *Liberty*, the civil liberties campaign
organisation, visit
www.liberty_human_rights.org.uk/issues/human-rights-act.shtml

NOTES

37 Human Rights—Restrictions and Limitations

Key Points

What you need to know and discuss:

- The position regarding restrictions under the Convention;
- The rule of law in relation to the Convention;
- The principle of proportionality;
- The "margin of appreciation";
- The position under UK law in relation to Art.5;
- The position under UK law in relation to Art.8;
- The position under UK law in relation to Art.10;
- The position under UK law in relation to Art.11.

The position under the Convention

As noted in the previous chapter, not all the Convention rights are absolute. The **absolute** rights include Arts 3, 4 and 7. Others, such as Art.5, are specifically **limited** by the Convention itself. Finally, others, such as Arts 8, 9, 10, and 11, may be **qualified** where:

- the qualification has its basis in law;
- it is necessary in a democratic society—this means it must fulfil a pressing social need in pursuit of a legitimate aim and be proportionate to that aim.

We should consider some of the elements of this principle of qualification in further detail.

The rule of law

As noted in the previous chapter, under a Convention rights approach there is a presumption against restriction or qualification of those rights. Any qualification must be authorised by law. In the absence of precise, specific, and detailed legal authorisation, any interference with a Convention right, however justified, will be a violation of that right.

The principle of proportionality

Under English law prior to the **Human Rights Act 1998**, actions by the Government could only be challenged by way of judicial review if they were "irrational"—a decision "so outrageous in its defiance of logic or accepted moral standards that no sensible person who had applied his mind to the question to be decided could have arrived at it" (Lord Diplock). However, where there has been a prima facie violation of a right protected by the Convention, the European Court of Human Rights has adopted a more stringent standard in considering whether the State can justify the limitation of that right—the principle of proportionality. This means that even if a particular policy or action which interferes with a Convention right is pursuing a legitimate aim (for example, the prevention of crime), this will not justify the interference if the means used to achieve that aim are excessive in the circumstances. The English courts have adopted the principle of proportionality with enthusiasm. As Lord Woolf has noted, "the courts follow in the footsteps of Strasbourg, and in deciding whether or not the interference is justified will inquire whether the conduct which it is sought to justify was proportionate to the objective to be achieved. It is the Court which has the responsibility of determining questions of proportionality. Admittedly, this is a more intrusive approach than was possible prior to the HRA, but the decision which results is more likely to be just".

The margin of appreciation

In relation to some Convention rights (particularly those requiring a balance to be struck between competing considerations) the European Court of Human Rights may allow a "margin of appreciation" to the domestic authorities. This means that it may be reluctant to substitute its own views of the merits of the case for those of the national authorities in determining whether a limitation is necessary in a democratic society. In *Handyside v UK* [1976], the Court stated, "By reason of their direct and continuous contact with the vital forces of their countries, state authorities are in principle in a better position than the international judge to give an opinion on the exact content of those requirements as well as on the "necessity" of a "restriction" or "penalty" intended to meet them". Some commentators, such as *Liberty*, argued that since the margin of appreciation is, strictly speaking, a concept belonging to international law it should not prevent the UK courts examining the merits of a decision, policy or law and the reason for its adoption. Others, however, suggested that the UK courts may develop a principle similar to the margin of appreciation. It was not possible, in advance of the Act coming into force, to say precisely how this will work in practice. In some cases the court may conclude that there are insufficient reasons to support the decision, policy or law. However, in others it may be willing to accept the opinion of expert decision-

NOTES

makers, such as a government department, health authority or Parliament. In fact, experience has now shown that courts have adopted a similar principle to that of the margin of appreciation. As Lord Woolf has observed, "the British courts have developed a parallel doctrine to the margin of appreciation to deal with relations between the domestic courts and our Parliament and our executive . . . The parallel doctrine that has been developed is the doctrine of deference, or as I prefer to say the doctrine of respect. This requires the United Kingdom courts to recognize that there are situations where the national legislature or the executive are better placed to make the difficult choices between competing considerations than the national courts", and that "situations for deference are ones with high political, economic, social or security content." However, as Lord Irvine has noted, it is not sufficient for the State in such circumstances simply to assert the doctrine of deference: "we recognize that we cannot simply recite the need for 'deference' . . . Rather, we must, where appropriate, argue the case for it carefully and persuasively. This often involves 'policy advocacy'—the equivalent of 'Brandeis briefs' in the US Supreme Court—by which the Government gives the court a through analysis of the policy behind legislation", continuing "our judges have been receptive to this approach. Lord Bingham demonstrated that in the Scottish case of *Brown v Stott*. The case was about drink-driving and the rule . . . requiring a suspect to declare who had been driving a car at the material time. The defendant argued that the rule infringed her right to a fair trial, and in particular her privilege against self-incrimination . . . Lord Bingham accepted evidence of the social menace presented by drink-driving, and was persuaded that the Road Traffic Act was a fair way of countering and punishing that behaviour. The case ceased to be a legalistic debate about self-incrimination. Instead, It showed an astute awareness by our Judges of the needs of the community and the responsibilities of Government."

The position under UK law

We will now consider the current position under UK law in relation to four particular Convention rights, and what the effect of the **1998 Act** may be when in comes into force in October 2000.

Article 5—Right to liberty and security

This Article states:

"1. Everyone has the right to liberty and security of person. No one shall be deprived of his liberty save in the following cases and in accordance with a procedure prescribed by law:

(a) the lawful detention of a person after conviction by a competent court;

NOTES

(b) the lawful arrest or detention of a person for non-compliance with the lawful order of a court or in order to secure the fulfilment of any obligation prescribed by law;

(c) the lawful arrest or detention of a person effected for the purpose of bringing him/ her before the competent legal authority on reasonable suspicion of having committed an offence or when it is reasonably considered necessary to prevent his committing an offence or fleeing after having done so;

(d) the detention of a minor by lawful order for the purpose of educational supervision or his lawful detention for the purpose of bringing him/her before the competent legal authority;

(e) the lawful detention of persons for the prevention of the spreading of infectious diseases, of persons of unsound mind, alcoholics or drug addicts or vagrants;

(f) the lawful arrest or detention of a person to prevent his effecting an unauthorised entry into the country or of a person against whom action is being taken with a view to deportation or extradition.

2. Everyone who is arrested shall be informed promptly, in a language which s/he understands, of the reasons for his/her arrest and of any charge against him.

3. Everyone arrested or detained in accordance with the provisions of paragraph 1(c) of this Article shall be brought promptly before a judge or other officer authorised by law to exercise judicial power and shall be entitled to trial within a reasonable time or to release pending trial. Release may be conditioned by guarantees to appear for trial.

4. Everyone who is deprived of his/her liberty by arrest or detention shall be entitled to take proceedings by which the lawfulness of his/her detention shall be decided speedily by a court and his/her release ordered if the detention is not lawful.

5. Everyone who has been the victim of arrest or detention in contravention of the provisions of this Article shall have an enforceable right to compensation."

Under current English law, state powers in each of these areas are regulated by statute: the **Police and Criminal Evidence Act 1984, Bail Act 1976**, and **Criminal Justice Act 1991** (as amended). For a more detailed examination of police powers, see **Chapter 6.** The rights of people in their relations with the police are also protected by the ancient writ of *habeus corpus* (requiring detention to be justified to a court), the right to legal advice, the duty solicitor schemes, and the activities of the Police Complaints Authority. Furthermore, a number of civil actions may be used to remedy any unlawful infringement of personal freedom: assault; wrongful arrest; false imprisonment; and malicious prosecution. Regarding mental health, under the **Mental Health Act 1983**, a person suffering from a mental disorder can be detained against his/her will, provided two doctors certify that this is necessary to protect the individual him/herself or society at large. Specific protection is offered as the validity of any such detention (or its continuation) may be challenged before the Mental Health Review Tribunal.

NOTES

Article 8—Right to respect for private and family life

This Article states:

"1. Everyone has the right to respect for his/her private and family life, his/her home and his/her correspondence.

2. There shall be no interference by a public authority with the exercise of this right except such as is in accordance with the law and is necessary in a democratic society in the interests of national security, public safety or the economic well-being of the country, for the prevention of disorder or crime, for the protection of health or morals, or for the protection of the rights and freedoms of others."

This is the one right under the Convention that is not already recognised to some degree by statute or common law. It is likely to have important consequences regarding the interception of communications, whether written, telephonic or electronic (for example, emails). It may also require some revision to the rules relating to data protection. We should note that privacy is not limited to the home but extends, for example, to the workplace. However, the limitation of the duties under the Act to "public authorities" means that this does **not** create a general right to privacy (for example, privacy from media intrusion). However, recent cases such as that involving the film stars Michael Douglas and Catherine Zeta-Jones indicate that the issue of a general right to privacy will remain a live and contentious issue for some time to come.

Article 10—Freedom of expression

This Article states:

"1. Everyone has the right to freedom of expression. This right shall include freedom to hold opinions and to receive and impart information and ideas without interference by public authority and regardless of frontiers. This Article shall not prevent States from requiring the licensing of broadcasting, television or cinema enterprises.

2. The exercise of these freedoms, since it carries with it duties and responsibilities, may be subject to such formalities, conditions, restrictions or penalties as are prescribed by law and are necessary in a democratic society, in the interests of national security, territorial integrity or public safety, for the prevention of disorder or crime, for the protection of health or morals, for the protection of the reputation or rights of others, for preventing the disclosure of information received in confidence, or for maintaining the authority and impartiality of the judiciary."

Freedom of expression is an essential democratic right. However, it is also one that is subject to significant restrictions under existing English law. A general level of censorship is imposed

NOTES

by the **Obscene Publications Act 1959** and common law offences of corrupting public morals and outraging public decency. More specific powers to censor, regulate and certify exist under the **Cinemas Act 1985**, the **Video Recordings Act 1984**, and the **Indecent Displays (Control) Act 1991**. Television broadcasting is regulated by the **Broadcasting Act 1990** and the **Broadcasting Standards Commission**. Newspapers are, for the moment, subject to self-regulation by the **Press Complaints Commission**. This is an area that generates almost constant controversy. The possibility of Art.10 defences may well add to this.

The **Official Secrets Act 1939** protects information sensitive to national security. However, the Act has been criticised on many occasions for being too widely drawn, and a number of prosecutions (for example, that of Clive Ponting in 1985) have proved controversial. There have been repeated calls for greater openness and freedom of information in government. However, the law has a difficult task here in balancing legitimate national security concerns with the equally legitimate need for a democratic government to be subject to public scrutiny. The incorporation of the Convention rights may require reform in this area, particularly regarding the use of Public Interest Immunity Certificates (so-called "gagging" orders).

Less controversial restrictions are imposed by the law of **defamation**, designed to protect an individual's reputation from untrue and damaging allegations. The balance between the general interest in free speech and the individual's interest in protecting his good name is maintained through the availability of various defences (for example, fair comment on a matter of public interest). It is likely that Art.10 will strengthen the public interest defence. Furthermore, a duty not to disclose information (personal or commercial) may exist under a contract (for example, contracts of employment) or in tort—a **duty of confidentiality**.

Article 11—Freedom of assembly and association

This Article states:

"1. Everyone has the right to freedom of peaceful assembly and to freedom of association with others, including the right to form and to join trade unions for the protection of his/her interests.

2. No restrictions shall be placed on the exercise of these rights other than such as are prescribed by law and are necessary in a democratic society in the interests of national security or public safety, for the prevention of disorder or crime, for the protection of health or morals or for the protection of the rights and freedoms of others. This Article shall not prevent the imposition of lawful restrictions on the exercise of these rights by members of the armed forces, of the police or of the administration of the State."

The freedom for people to associate together (for example, in political parties, pressure groups or trade unions) and to assemble together (for example, to hold meetings, rallies or protest

Notes

marches) are, again, essential democratic rights. However, this needs to be balanced against the need to maintain public order and to enable others to pursue their own lawful and legitimate activities. Therefore, there are restrictions on freedom of association under the **Public Order Act 1936** (which outlaws quasi-military organisations and the wearing of uniforms or military insignia by political groups—originally introduced to counter the rise of the fascist "blackshirts" in the 1930s), and the prevention of terrorism legislation (which outlaws paramilitary groups). Regarding freedom of assembly, the **Public Order Act 1986** grants the police, together with local authorities, the power to regulate protest marches, and also incorporates three specific public order offences: riot; violent disorder; and affray. Further restrictions were introduced, despite considerable public opposition, by the **Criminal Justice and Public Order Act 1994** in relation to "raves", "travellers" and protests. It may well be the case that those facing criminal proceedings in this area will seek to raise both Article 11 and Article 10 defences.

Revision Notes

You should now write your revision notes for this topic. Here is an example for you and some suggested headings:

> ### R&L①—Restrictions under the Convention
>
> - not all Convention rights are absolute
> - absolute—inc. Arts 3,4,7
> - limited (specific limitations in Convention)—inc. Art.5
> - qualified (may be qualified by State where qualification has basis in law and is necessary in a democratic society [pressing social need/legitimate aim/ proportionate])—inc. Arts 8,9,10,11

R&L①—Restrictions under the Convention

R&L②—Rule of Law

R&L③—Proportionality

R&L④—Margin of Appreciation

R&L⑤—Art.5—Liberty

R&L⑥—Art.8—Privacy

NOTES

R&L⑦—Art.10—Expression

R&L⑧—Art.11—Assembly

Using your cards, you should now be able to write a short paragraph in response to each of the following questions:

1. Explain the basis of restrictions under the Convention.

2. Explain the principle of the rule of law under the Convention.

3. What is meant by the "principle of proportionality?

4. Explain the notions of the 'margin of appreciation" and the "doctrine of deference".

5. Discuss the position under English law in relation to the following convention rights, including the effects of the Human Rights Act 1998:

    (a) Art.5 (Liberty)
    (b) Art.8 (Privacy)
    (c) Art.10 (Expression)
    (d) Art.11 (Assembly)

Useful Websites

- Lord Woolf, "Human Rights: Have the Public Benefited?"— **www.britac.ac.uk/pubs/src/tob02/index.html**

- Lord Woolf, "The Impact of Human Rights"—**www.lcd.gov.uk/judicial/speeches/lcj060303.htm**

- Lord Irvine, "The Human Rights Act Two Years On: An Analysis"—**www.lcd.gov.uk/speeches/2002/lc011102.htm**

- See also those listed at the end of **Chapter 36**

NOTES

38 | Human Rights—Protection and Enforcement

Key Points

What you need to know:

- The main provisions of the Human Rights Act 1998.
- The duty on public authorities.
- The definition of a "victim" under the Act.
- Explain how laws found to be in breach of the Convention can be rectified.
- Explain the remedies available to the victim.

What you need to discuss:

- The role of the UK courts under the Act.
- The position of the European Court of Human Rights.
- Whether a Human Rights Commission is required.

The Human Rights Act 1998

The Convention rights are incorporated into English law by **s.1**. We must now consider the main provisions of the Act in relation to the duties it imposes, the powers it grants, and the remedies it provides.

The duty on public authorities

By **s.6**, it is unlawful for a "public authority" to act in a manner incompatible with the Convention. This covers all aspects of the public authority's activities including:

- drafting rules and regulations;

- internal staff and personnel issues;
- administrative procedures;
- decision-making;
- policy implementation;
- interaction with members of the public.

The term "public authority" covers three broad categories:

- obvious public authorities such as a Minister, a Government Department or agency, local authorities, health authorities and trusts, the Armed Forces and the police;
- courts and tribunals;
- any person or organisation that carries out functions of a public nature. Under the Act, however, they are only considered a public authority in relation to their public functions (*e.g. Railtrack* is a public authority in relation to its work as a safety regulator for the railways, but not when acting as a commercial property developer).

We should note that Parliament is expressly excluded from the scope of the Act. This means that Parliament remains fully sovereign and free to enact incompatible legislation should it so wish. By **s.19**, the minister promoting a Bill must, before second reading, make a written statement either that, in his view, the provisions of the Bill are compatible with the Convention, or that, although not compatible, the Government nevertheless wished to proceed with the Bill. As Lord Justice Laws has noted, "In its present state of evolution, the British system may be said to stand at an intermediate stage between parliamentary supremacy and constitutional supremacy . . . Parliament remains the sovereign legislature; there is no superior text to which it must defer. . .there is no statute which by law it cannot make. But at the same time, the common law has come to recognize and endorse the notion of constitutional, or fundamental, rights. These are broadly the rights given expression in the European Convention on Human Rights". However, we should note that the Act has political, as well as legal, consequences and effects. As Lord Irvine has acknowledged, the Act "retains Parliament's *legal* right to enact legislation which is incompatible with the Convention. But it dramatically reduces its political capacity to do so. It does this by introducing, through the Declaration of Incompatibility, a limited form of constitutional review, which serves as a political and perhaps moral disincentive to legislate incompatibly."

The victim

By **s.7**, a person is able to rely on his/her Convention rights by bringing proceedings (for example, judicial review) or in any proceedings brought against him/her (for example, by

---

NOTES

way of counterclaim or defence). However, s/he may only do so if he/she is (or would be) a victim of the unlawful act. A "victim" is someone who is directly affected by the act in question. Victims can include companies as well as individuals and may also be relatives of the victim where a complaint is made about his/her death. An organisation, interest group, or trade union cannot bring a case unless it is itself a victim, but there is nothing to stop it providing legal or other assistance to a victim.

The UK courts

By **s.3(1)**, the courts must, so far as it is possible to do so, interpret legislation in such as way as to make it compatible with the Convention. However, as noted above, the Act expressly preserves the full sovereignty of Parliament. Thus, while the courts may quash decisions or actions incompatible with Convention rights, or annul delegated legislation on grounds of incompatibility, they cannot disapply an Act of Parliament (**s.3(2)(b)**). The Government gave its reasons for this in the **'Rights Brought Home' White Paper**:

"The Government has reached the conclusion that courts should not have the power to set aside primary legislation, past or future, on the ground of incompatibility with the Convention. This conclusion arises from the importance which the Government attaches to Parliamentary sovereignty. In this context, Parliamentary sovereignty means that Parliament is competent to make any law on any matter of its choosing and no court may question the validity of any Act that it passes. In enacting legislation, Parliament is making decisions about important matters of public policy. The authority to make those decisions derives from a democratic mandate. Members of Parliament in the House of Commons possess such a mandate because they are elected, accountable and representative. To make provision in the Bill for the courts to set aside Acts of Parliament would confer on the judiciary a general power over the decisions of Parliament which under our present constitutional arrangements they do not possess, and would be likely on occasions to draw the judiciary into serious conflict with Parliament. There is no evidence to suggest that they desire this power, nor that the public wish them to have it. Certainly, this Government has no mandate for any such change."

This echoes the fears expressed by some that the Human Rights Act will politicise the judiciary in response to the many Convention-based arguments they are expected to receive when the Act comes into force. However, as Lord Irvine has observed, "Our Judges have always had to decide cases in areas of political controversy. The Human Rights Act has ushered in only a difference of degree, not of kind." Nevertheless, *Liberty* identified 70 areas of law, ranging from police powers to access to health care, where they believed urgent action was required to avoid violations of the new law. However, it is at least questionable whether the judges have been as open to Convention-based arguments as some anticipated. Wall J., in

Notes

re F (minors—care proceedings—contact) [2000], stated that he would be disappointed if the Convention were to be routinely paraded as a makeweight ground of appeal. In *A National Health Service Trust v D* [2000], Cazalet J. held that a medical decision to provide only palliative care, thus allowing a patient to "die with dignity" was not a violation of either Arts 2 or 3. Thus, it seems that common law common-sense may well prevail over any risk of a politicised judiciary. As Lord Irvine has stated, "Just as those who predicted catastrophe in the Courts have been proved wrong, so have those who said the Human Rights Act would add nothing. In examining what impact the Act has had on the Courts, and on our system of law, the overriding theme that emerges is balance: balance between scrutiny and deference; between the individual and the community; and between interpretation and declarations of incompatibility", and as Lord Woolf has observed, "the informed view is that making the European Convention part of our domestic law has proved to be a great success. Furthermore, that the process of implementation has gone extremely smoothly."

The European Court of Human Rights

It will still be possible for a person to petition the European Court of Human Rights, but only where all domestic remedies, including any action under the Act, have been exhausted. In this respect, we should also note that, by **s.2(1)(a)**, the English courts are required to have regard to the jurisprudence and case-law of the European Court when dealing with any case involving the Convention.

A Human Rights Commission?

Some commentators, such as the leading civil rights lawyer Lord Lester, see the decision not to establish a Human Rights Commission to oversee the working of the Act as a serious weakness. However, in the "Rights Brought Home" White Paper, the Government expressed concerns regarding an unnecessary overlap between any Human Rights Commission and the work of the Commission for Racial Equality, the Equal Opportunities Commission and the new Disability Rights Commission. Nevertheless, the White Paper also states that the Government has not closed its mind to the idea of a Commission at some future stage in light of practical experience of the working of the Act.

Remedies

To the law

As we noted earlier, the Act does not allow the courts to disapply primary legislation incompatible with the Convention. However, by **s.4**, the courts may, in such circumstances,

NOTES

issue a declaration of incompatibility. Following this, the relevant minister may amend the offending legislation by statutory instrument (**Sch.2, para.1(2)**). As this involves the exceptional power to use secondary legislation to amend primary legislation, any such statutory instrument is subject to the positive affirmation procedure in Parliament (**para.2**)—for more details on this procedure, see **Chapter 2**.

For the victim

By **s.8**, the court may, following a violation of the Convention by a public authority, grant such relief or remedy, or make such order as it considers just and appropriate. However, the court may only award damages where, taking into account all the circumstances of the case (including any other relief or remedy granted or order made), it is satisfied that damages are necessary to ensure just satisfaction for the victim.

Conclusion

The residual approach to freedoms resulted from a traditional view of England, and a peculiarly English view that liberty is best defined and protected by an informal consensus, emerging from the shared values of an essentially homogenous society. However, while this view may have had some validity in the distant past (and even this is questionable), it hardly corresponds to British society today. Societies and their political systems develop and evolve, and the law must itself develop to meet these new challenges. Indeed, the European Court of Human Rights regards the Convention as a "living instrument" that must be interpreted in the light of present day conditions. Britain today is an increasingly diverse and heterogenous culture. This has placed increasing strains on the present constitutional settlement. The Government has sought to address this in a number of ways: devolution in Scotland, Wales and Northern Ireland, reform of the House of Lords, and the introduction of the Human Rights Act 1998. Regarding the Act in particular, Lord Irvine has stated that "It has transformed our system of law into one of positive rights, responsibilities and freedoms, where before we had only the freedom to do what was not prohibited. It has corrected a 50–year anomaly, by which British people *had* rights but could only access them in Europe, not at home." Hopefully, this process will create a modern constitution to replace the informal guarantees of a social consensus that no longer exists—a new legal consensus that allows social diversity to flourish within a secure framework of judicially-protected fundamental rights and freedoms.

Revision Notes

You should now write your revision notes for this topic. Here is an example for you and some suggested headings:

NOTES

P&E④—ECHR

- can still petition
- only when domestic remedies (inc. under Act) exhausted
- UK cts must consider jurisprudence/case law of ECHR (s.2(1)(a))

P&E①—Duty on PAs

P&E②—Victims

P&E③—UK courts

P&E④—ECHR

P&E⑤—Human Rights Commission?

P&E⑥—Remedies (law)

P&E⑦—Remedies (victim)

P&E⑧—Conclusion

Using your cards, you should now be able to write a short paragraph in response to each of the following questions:

1. Explain the duty on public authorities under the Human Rights Act 1998.
2. Who may be a victim under the Act?
3. Explain the obligations on the UK courts under the Act.
4. What is the position of the European Court of Human Rights following the Act?
5. Discuss whether there should be a Human Rights Commission.
6. How can law found incompatible with the Convention be remedied?
7. What remedies are available to the victim of a Convention violation?
8. Consider what the overall consequences of the Act may be.

Useful Websites

⊙ See those listed at the end of **Chapters 36** and **37**.

NOTES

SECTION SEVEN: CONCEPTS OF LAW

39 Law and Morality

Key Points

What you need to know:

- The characteristic features of moral and legal codes.
- The reasons for the relationship between law and morality.

What you need to discuss:

- The moral influence on English law.
- The approaches the law may take to issues of moral controversy.

Introduction

Both law and morality are concerned with the regulation of social conduct. Therefore, they share many similar, though not synonymous, features:

Moral Codes	Legal Codes
General statements of principle.	Precise rules or norms of behaviour.
Voluntary subscription.	Compulsory subscription.
Informal enforcement (for example, through peer group pressure).	Formal enforcement (for example, through the police and the courts).
Concerned with how people **ought** to behave.	Concerned with how people **shall** behave.

It is this contrast between "ought" and "shall", highlighting concerns over whether the law should be used to enforce particular moral values, that has proved the most problematic aspect of the relationship between the two concepts.

The relationship between law and morality exists for both **historical** and **functional** reasons:

- **Historically**, legal codes tend to emerge from moral codes. In primitive societies, there is often little or no difference between the two. However, as a society grows larger and more sophisticated, this close relationship begins to fracture. As the society becomes more diverse (socially, culturally, economically and morally) the need for a distinct and universally applicable set of rules (a legal system) emerges. Thus, while links between the legal and moral codes remain, these tend to become increasingly insecure and sometimes controversial.

- **Functionally**, both law and morality are used to perform similar social tasks—to preserve order and maintain acceptable standards of behaviour through the promotion and enforcement of rules and principles.

Thus, it is not surprising that the relationship between law and morality is a complex one, and that moral influences pervade much of the law. However, this is not to suggest all that may be regarded as immoral is necessarily illegal (for example, adultery) or vice versa (for example, parking offences).

The Moral Influence in English law

It may be argued that moral notions form the background or context of many aspects of English law, with its concerns for the protection of the person, property, the family, etc. This reflects the influence of an essentially judaio-christian moral tradition. However, as noted above, the legal rules will tend to be more specific and precise than their moral counterparts— for example, while there may be a general moral precept against telling lies, this will only be illegal in certain specific circumstances (for example, perjury and fraud). In the vast majority of instances, this moral context or background to the law is uncontroversial. Indeed, we may see it as positively beneficial, as it tends to enhance the legitimacy of the law and encourage the observance of legal rules.

However, problems may well arise where moral issues become foregrounded, rather than merely providing a background context—*i.e.* where the law is used specifically to enforce particular moral positions. In the legislative sphere, we can see this in the **Abortion Act 1967**, the **Obscene Publications Act 1956** (with its problematic test of a tendency to deprave and corrupt), and more recently in the debate regarding the repeal of **s.28** of the **Local Government Act 1988** (banning the "promotion" of homosexuality). Similarly, in the judicial sphere, this is evident in the common law offences of conspiracy to corrupt public morals (*Shaw v DPP* [1962]; *Knuller (Publishing, Printing and Promotions) Ltd v DPP* [1973]) and conspiracy to outrage public decency (*R. v Gibson* [1991]). Moral values can also be seen to have exercised a clear, though indirect, influence in a range of other cases—for example, those

NOTES

relating to sexual conduct (*R v Brown and others* [1993]). The legal foregrounding of particular moral positions becomes problematic where the social consensus on that issue has broken down or fragmented—and, as indicated above, the more diverse a society becomes, the greater the potential for fragmentation.

In these circumstances, the law cannot simply withdraw unless and until consensus is restored—there can be no "no-go" areas. The law must, therefore, identify an acceptable approach to issues of moral controversy:

- **The libertarian approach**—some writers, such as **Schur** and **Hart**, have argued that the law should not interfere in private behaviour except in order to prevent harm to others. However, it is sometimes difficult to identify the boundaries between private and public conduct and the limits of harm—for example, drug use may be a "private" activity but can have "public" and "harmful" consequences, such as additional burdens on the public health system and criminal activity to feed the habit. Furthermore, it is arguable that the consent of the participants does not necessarily make an activity "victimless", and that there may be circumstances where it is justifiable to use the law to override individual consent.

- **The liberal approach**—this is typified by the **Wolfenden Committee on Homosexual Offences and Prostitution**, which reported in **1957**. The view of the Committee was that the law should not interfere in private behaviour except where necessary to preserve public order and decency, to protect against the offensive and injurious, and to safeguard individuals (particularly the most vulnerable) against corruption and exploitation. However, difficulties again arise with this approach due to the subjective nature of the criteria advanced—by whose standards is something to be judged "offensive" or "injurious"?

- **The duty/aspiration approach**—this arguably more satisfactory approach was advanced by the American legal philosopher **Lon Fuller**. He distinguished between what he termed the morality of duty and the morality of aspiration. The morality of duty, he argued, indicates the standard of behaviour that most people would be prepared to tolerate—*i.e.* the bare minimum level of acceptable conduct. By contrast, he argued that the morality of aspiration indicates the standard of behaviour to which most people should aspire. Thus, Fuller is seeking to come to terms with the problematic distinction between "ought" and "shall" indicated earlier. Fuller's solution was that while the law may be employed to enforce the morality of duty, it cannot and should not be used to enforce the morality of aspiration—*i.e.* it is legitimate to use the law to prevent people behaving badly, but not to use it in an attempt to force people to behave virtuously. This was echoed by **Lord Devlin**, when he argued that "the law is concerned with the minimum and not with the maximum". We can also see it in the famous "neighbour principle" advanced by **Lord Atkin** in *Donoghue v Stevenson* [1932]:

NOTES

"The liability for negligence . . . is no doubt based upon a general public sentiment of moral wrongdoing for which the offender must pay. But acts or omissions which any moral code would censure cannot in a practical world be treated so as to give a right to every person injured by them to demand relief. In this way rules of law arise which limit the range of complainants and the extent of their remedy. The rule that you are to love your neighbour becomes in law: you must not injure your neighbour, and the lawyer's question: who is my neighbour? receives a restricted reply".

Conclusion

As we have seen, the link between law and morality is a close and complex one. Furthermore, for both historical and functional reasons, such a relationship is inevitable—it is impossible to conceive of or to construct an amoral legal code. In many respects, this relationship is both uncontroversial and beneficial, as it often reflects a general moral consensus in society, thereby enhancing the legitimacy of the law and encouraging observance. However, difficulties do exist regarding the proper response of the law to issues where this consensus has fragmented or broken down. Given the benefits that may be gained from social development and diversity, the law must seek to establish a stable social framework within which such diversity can flourish safely.

Revision Notes

You should now write your revision notes for this topic. Here is an example for you and some suggested headings:

L&M④—Libertarian approach

- only intervene to prevent harm to others (**Schur, Hart**)
- boundary between public/private? (*e.g.* drug use)
- really "victimless"?
- paternalist intervention justified?

L&M①—Intro (nature of legal/moral codes)

L&M②—Historical/Functional links

NOTES

L&M③—Moral Influence in English law

L&M④—Libertarian approach

L&M⑤—Liberal approach

L&M⑥—Duty/Aspiration Approach

L&M⑦—Conclusion

Using your cards, you should now be able to write a short paragraph in response to each of the following questions:

1. Define and differentiate between legal and morals codes.

2. Why do legal codes tend to have a moral component?

3. What evidence is there for a moral element in the development of English law?

4. What approaches might the law take to issues of moral controversy?

NOTES

40 | Law and Justice

Key Points

What you need to know:

- The different definitions of abstract justice.
- The role of formal justice in the English legal system.
- The role of substantive justice in English law.

What you need to discuss:

- The extent to which the English Legal System both strives for and delivers justice.

Introduction

It may seem obvious to say the primary aim of any legal system is to deliver justice. However, it is far from obvious what this actually means, as the concept of "justice" is extremely difficult to define. Not only are there different definitions of justice, but the question "what is justice?" means different things in different contexts—is a particular law just? is the legal system just? does the combination of law and system produce a just result?

Definitions of Justice

- **Aristotlean justice**—one of the earliest attempts to formulate a theory of justice was that made by the Ancient Greek philosopher **Aristotle**. He argued that the basis of justice is fairness, and that this takes two forms:

> ➤ **distributive justice**—whereby the law is used to ensure social benefits and burdens are fairly distributed throughout society;
> ➤ **corrective justice**—whereby the legal system acts to correct attempts by individuals to disturb this fair distribution.

However, we can argue that such an approach simply replaces the question "what is just?" with "what is fair?"

- **Utilitarian theory**—the central principle of utilitarianism is that society should be organised to achieve the greatest happiness for the greatest number. Thus, according to a utilitarian approach, a law is just where it brings about a net gain in happiness for the majority, even if this is at the cost of increased distress or unhappiness to a minority. However, it is this willingness to trade the unhappiness of the minority against the happiness of the majority that liberal theory finds most objectionable in this approach.

- **Liberal (or natural rights) theory**—liberal theory, in contrast to utilitarianism, judges the justice of any form of social organisation by the extent it protects its minorities and most vulnerable groups. Therefore, liberal theories tend to incorporate notions of natural rights—that there are certain basic rights (God-given or otherwise) to which all people are entitled. However, this approach has its own problems, not least in establishing agreement over the content and extent of any list of "natural" rights—for example, the right to vote is now regarded as an essential and universal right. However, for many years this was subject to a property qualification, and was not one to which women were entitled until last century. A recent attempt to identify a universal set of rights and principles was undertaken by the American legal philosopher **John Rawls**. Rawls' theory is based upon a hypothesis of what a group of individuals, placed in what he termed the "original position", would agree upon. The original position exists behind a "veil of ignorance"—*i.e.* the individuals would not know of their individual talents and circumstances (whether they are rich or poor, young or old, male or female, able or disabled, etc). Therefore, Rawls argues, rational self-interest would lead them to agree a set of basic rights and principles that each would find acceptable if it turned out they were the least advantaged of the group. However, persuasive though this hypothesis may seem, it does not resolve the question of precisely what those rights and principles should be. In fact, it seems to lead back to Aristotle's question—what is fair?

- **Libertarian (or market-based) theory**—libertarian theory, such as that advanced by **Nozick**, argues intervention in the natural (or market) distribution of advantages (as required by the other theories) is an unjust interference with individual rights. Libertarian analysis only permits very limited intervention to prevent unjust distribution (for example through theft and fraud). However, such a narrow approach is open to many of the same objections as the utilitarian approach.

NOTES

Therefore, it may be argued that the question of abstract justice seems to be as much a political as philosophical one.

Justice and the English Legal System

Whether a particular law is just is, therefore, essentially a political question. However, as noted earlier, consideration must also be given to whether the system is just, and whether it produces a just outcome. This involves both **formal justice** (regarding the system) and **substantive justice** (regarding outcomes):

- **Formal justice** requires a system of independent tribunals for the administration of law and the resolution of disputes, as is recognised by **Art.6** of the **European Convention on Human Rights**, now incorporated into English law by the **Human Rights Act 1998**. The formal trial and appellate courts, together with the various forms of alternative dispute resolution, ensure the English legal system largely meets this requirement, though there remain doubts about the judicial role of the Lord Chancellor (see **Chapter 11**). Formal justice also requires these institutions follow known and fair rules and procedures. Again, this is met through the rules of due process and fair procedure, rules regarding the admissibility of evidence, limitation periods, etc, that apply in the English courts. An important contribution is also made by the rules of natural justice—for example, *audi alterem partem* (both sides must be heard). Finally, it is important that any citizen with a grievance has access to these institutions. Here we can argue that more needs to be done to ensure this, particularly for the poorest and least-advantaged sections of our society. As noted in **Chapter 13**, the reforms under the **Access to Justice Act 1999** will hopefully improve this situation.

- **Substantive justice**—the English legal system has a variety of mechanisms to ensure just outcomes. Regarding the common law, the principle of *stare decisis*, together with devices such as overruling and distinguishing, enable the courts to work towards both the just development of the common law itself and a just outcome in any given case. A good example of this in the civil law is negligence. First of all, liability will not be imposed on the defendant unless he was at fault in causing injury or loss to the claimant. Secondly, the defence of contributory negligence allows the court to apportion liability in a just and fair way where the claimant was partly responsible for his own damage. In the criminal law, the principles of sentencing seek to achieve a just balance between the interests of the victim in achieving retribution, of society through deterrence and rehabilitation, and the defendant in ensuring the punishment fits the crime and is not excessive. The courts may also turn to the principles of Equity where the strict application of common law rules would lead to injustice. Furthermore, where

NOTES

the courts are unable to resolve such issues, because they are dealing with statute or they have reached the limits of proper common law development, Parliament may act to remedy matters through legislation (for example, the **Law Reform (Frustrated Contracts) Act 1943**). Indeed, it is this capacity to be self-correcting that is one of the most important aspects of the English legal system's ability to ensure just outcomes.

Conclusion

Given the variety of essentially subjective, often vague, and sometimes contradictory notions of abstract justice, perhaps the best that any **system** of justice can hope to achieve is **justice according to law**. It seems this is a task the English legal system is well-equipped to perform, not least in its capacity for development and self-correction.

Revision Notes

You should now write your revision notes for this topic. Here is an example for you and some suggested headings:

L&J⑥ Formal Justice

- Formal justice requires:
    - ➤ Independent tribunals (ELS—trial and appeal courts, ADR, independent judiciary)
    - ➤ Fair procedures (ELS—due process, admissibility, limitation periods, rules of natural justice)
    - ➤ Equal access (ELS—less successful here—unmet need—reforms in AJA 1999)

L&J①—Intro

L&J②—Aristolean Justice

L&J③—Utilitarian Justice

L&J④—Natural Rights Theory

L&J⑤—Libertarian Theory

NOTES

L&J⑥—Formal Justice

L&J⑦—Substantive Justice

L&J⑧—Conclusion

Using your cards, you should now be able to write a short paragraph in response to each of the following questions:

1. Why is such an apparently simple idea as "justice" so problematic?

2. Describe and comment upon the major theories of justice.

3. To what extent does the English legal system achieve formal justice?

4. To what extent does the English legal system deliver substantive justice?

Notes

41 The Judge as Law-Maker

Key Points

What you need to know:

- How judges are involved in the law-making process.
- The different judicial styles of law-making.

What you need to discuss:

- The difference between issues of principle and issues of policy.
- The proper role of the judiciary in the law-making process.
- Potential improvements to the process of judicial law-making.

The Role of the Judge

Judges are involved in the law-making process in a number of ways—through:

- their participation in various advisory committees, commissions and inquiries;
- the participation of the Law Lords in the legislative business of the House of Lords—though this is limited by convention to law reform measures and issues of legal technicality;
- their role as the definitive interpreters of legislation;
- their responsibility for the development and evolution of the common law and Equity.

For many years the judiciary denied that they exercised any law-making role, arguing they merely declared the law as laid down by statute or fundamental principles of common law. However, the modern judiciary has increasingly abandoned the fiction of this declaratory approach and acknowledged they do indeed exercise a law-making role.

Lee argues there are three main factors that influence judicial law-making:

- the previous history of legislative development;

- the consequences of the present law and the likely consequences of any given change;

- the judiciary's own perception of the proper limits of their law-making role.

Principles and Policies

Given this variety of influences, it is not surprising that differences can be observed in judicial approaches to their law-making role. **Harris** contrasts two judicial "styles":

- **The Formal Style**, which is characterised by caution and a tendency to rely on formal devices such as distinguishing.

- **The Grand Style**, which is characterised by boldness and a willingness to recognise issues of policy as well as principle.

Paterson observed similar variations in judicial approaches to "hard" cases:

- **The positive response** (similar to the Grand Style).

- **The adaptive response** (similar to the Formal Style).

- **To withdraw** on the basis that the proposed change is properly one for Parliament rather than the judges to make.

The majority of judges would seem to adopt the Formal or adaptive position. However, a minority of judges, particularly in the higher courts, have always followed a more adventurous path (for example consider the different positions adopted by **Lords Wilberforce** and **Scarman** in *McLoughlin v O'Brian* [1982]). More recently, the House of Lords, dealing with an appeal regarding manslaughter by provocation, allowed *Liberty, Justice for Women* and *Southall Black Sisters* to make submissions on behalf of domestic violence victims (*R. v Smith* [2000]). These different styles or responses draw our attention to the distinction between law-making according to established principles and law-making according to policy considerations. It is generally felt judges should confine their attention to issues of principle, as these are seen as politically neutral. It is for Parliament to determine the political acceptability or otherwise of any legal development according to principle. However, it may be argued that this is something of a false distinction as the boundary between principle and policy is easily blurred. Furthermore, Parliament, as we have seen earlier, cannot be expected to legislate for everything. In a common law system, judges not only have scope for law-making but, as **Lord Lane** pointed out in *R. v R (rape: marital exemption)* [1991], are under a **duty** to do so, provided

---

Notes

this is done in the context of a proper regard for the superior role of Parliament. One of the few judges to have written on this relationship was **Lord Devlin**. He drew a distinction between:

- **activist** law-making—by which he meant changing and developing the law **in response to** changes in the social consensus;

- **dynamic** law-making—by which he meant changing and developing the law **in order to promote** change in the social consensus.

For Lord Devlin, while it was proper for judges to engage in activist law-making, dynamic law-making should be left to Parliament. He also pointed out judges had far less scope and authority for law-making when dealing with statute than with the common law.

Therefore, while allowing for variations in judicial approach, it seems clear there are three main constraints on judicial law-making:

- the judge is bound by the rules of precedent when dealing with the common law;

- the judge is bound by the rules of statutory interpretation when dealing with statutes;

- the judge is bound by his own perception of the proper limits of the judiciary's law-making role and of the superior role of Parliament in the law-making partnership with the courts

Improving the System

Defined and limited in this way, judicial law-making is an important and beneficial aspect of the law-making process in a common law system. The fact that much of the law of contract and negligence is still the product of common law development, with only limited statutory intervention, is clear proof of the judiciary's capacity to develop sound and just principles of law. There are, however, a number of reforms that could enhance the effectiveness of this role:

- **A formal procedure** by which the courts could refer issues to Parliament when it is felt that further development is beyond the scope of legitimate judicial law-making.

- The introduction of an **independent advisor** in the appellate courts to perform a similar role to the Advocate General in the Court of Justice of the European Union.

- The provision of **research attorneys** to the judiciary in the appellate courts. Following a pilot scheme in 1997, judges in the Court of Appeal are now provided with **Judicial**

NOTES

Assistants (appointed on a full or part-time basis for up to one year). In 2000, this was extended to the House of Lords with the appointment of **Legal Assistants** on one-year contracts to assist the Law Lords.

We should also note that if the judiciary is to continue with its law-making role, and give increasing consideration to issues of policy, at least in the higher courts, then it becomes even more urgent to take steps to ensure:

- the judiciary is trained effectively to discharge this role;
- the social, racial and gender composition of the judiciary becomes more representative of society at large.

Conclusion

Regarding the judge as law-maker, it is clear that judicial law-making must be an important element within any common law system. It is a role that the English judiciary currently performs both well and responsibly, though steps could be taken to improve this still further, most notably through enhancing the provision of research attorneys to the senior judiciary.

Revision Notes

You should now write your revision notes for this topic. Here is an example for you and some suggested headings:

JLM④ _Judges and Parliament_

- In CL system, judges under duty to develop law in partnership with Parl.
- Judges' approach must reflect superior role of Parl, and that judges' role is to follow consensus, not promote own policy.
- Devlin:
    - ✓ Activist—changing law in response to changes in social consensus.
    - ✗ Dynamic—changing law to promote change in social consensus.

JLM①—Intro (judicial involvement in law-making)

NOTES

JLM②—Judicial Styles

JLM③—Principle v Policy

JLM④—Judges and Parliament

JLM⑤—Improvements

JLM⑥—Conclusion

Using your cards, you should now be able to write a short paragraph in response to each of the following questions:

1. Describe the various ways judges are involved in law-making.

2. What different styles of judicial law-making have been observed by commentators?

3. Discuss the difference between considerations of policy and principle.

4. What is the proper role of the judges in developing the law in partnership with Parliament?

5. How could the system be improved to help judges in their law-making role?

Useful Websites
For websites relating to the judiciary, see those listed at the end of **Chapter 11**.

NOTES

42 Fault and Liability

Key Points

What you need to know and discuss:

- The role of fault in **criminal liability**.
- The role of fault in **tortious liability**.
- The role of fault in **contractual liability**.

Introduction

We have seen in our earlier examination of the criminal law, tort, and contract that liability is frequently bound up with notions of fault. However, we have also seen that different forms of liability employ different notions of fault, and indeed in some instances proof of fault is not required at all. We should now consider the extent to which fault both is and should be the basis of liability.

Crime and fault

The criminal law is perhaps the most obvious candidate for fault-based liability. A person should not be found guilty of a crime and, at least potentially, deprived of his/her liberty without proof of individual fault. This insistence upon fault can be seen in the general requirements of liability—the *actus reus* and *mens rea*. We can also argue the absence of fault is the underlying rationale for the various general defences. Finally, the degree of fault shown is a major determining factor in sentencing.

Regarding the *actus reus*, the general requirement of a positive, voluntary act and the limited liability for omissions are evidence of the need for fault, as is the requirement of causation in relation to result crimes—if the defendant did not cause the unlawful consequence, it is not his/her fault and hence s/he is not liable.

The different states of mind employed to construct the *mens rea* of different offences demonstrate the relationship between degree of fault and liability. Generally, a person can only be convicted of the most serious offences on proof of intention to commit that offence. Less serious offences may be committed recklessly, and minor offences, frequently of a regulatory nature, can be committed negligently.

Some defences, such as automatism, operate by showing lack of fault through the involuntary nature of the defendant's conduct. Others, such as insanity and intoxication, operate by establishing a lack of mental control or awareness on the part of the defendant. Still others, such as duress and self-defence, operate by establishing that the defendant's conduct was justified or should be excused. Finally, the partial defences to murder, such as provocation and diminished responsibility, demonstrate a lesser degree of fault, resulting in conviction for the lesser offence of manslaughter.

The degree of fault on the part of the defendant also plays a very significant role in sentencing. Both the type of sentence imposed (custodial, community or fine) and its severity is in large part determined by the degree of fault shown by the defendant. This can also be seen in the impact of both aggravating and mitigating factors. This is why some are opposed to the use of minimum and mandatory sentences, as they break the relationship between the degree of fault present in the offence committed and the sentence imposed.

However, we have also seen there is a limited role for strict liability in the criminal law. In relation to both regulatory offences and offences of social danger, we can argue the interests of society as a whole, determined by Parliament—the courts are extremely reluctant to create strict liability offences at common law, or even to recognise them in statute—can sometimes justify the imposition of liability without fault. Nevertheless, it should be noted that the degree of fault still plays an important role in determining the sentence following conviction.

Therefore, both fault and the degree of fault on the part of the defendant can rightly be said to play a central role in both establishing criminal liability and sentencing.

Tort and Fault

The aim of tort is to provide a remedy (usually in the form of financial compensation) for the victims of wrongs, and fault on the part of the defendant is the device most generally used to attach liability for this. Negligence liability is clearly dependent upon proof of fault—a failure to take reasonable care—on the part of the defendant. While nuisance liability, as we have seen, may sometimes take on the appearance of strict liability, it remains essentially fault-based—the defendant is liable for failing to meet the reasonable expectations of his/her

NOTES

neighbours. Furthermore, the general defences in tort can be said to have their basis in the absence or lesser degree of fault in the same way as those in criminal law.

However, it is true to say that strict liability plays a larger role in tort than criminal law. This is generally in areas where we can argue there are overriding social concerns in encouraging the greatest possible (rather than merely reasonable) care—for example, in ensuring products are safe, and that hazardous materials and activities are safely dealt with. Hence, strict liability in tort is to some extent deployed regarding defective products, the keeping of animals, and certain forms of industrial and environmental activity. Those engaged in such activities will frequently choose, and are sometimes obliged, to insure against liability.

Furthermore, while there are clear arguments in favour of a fault-based system of liability regarding torts such as negligence, the present insistence of fault in these areas can place significant obstacles in the path of the very people the system is intended to benefit. This has given rise to increasing concerns, particularly regarding personal injury cases.

The arguments in favour of fault-based liability in Tort

- It is a just approach to the apportioning of liability. Where fault indicates the person responsible for the damage, justice requires that person compensate the victim. However, it is at least questionable whether justice requires that in the absence of fault, the loss should be borne by the blameless victim.

- The requirement of fault acts as an incentive to take care, as if liability were to be imposed regardless of fault, people would take less care because no advantage would accrue to the careful. However, this rests on the rather dubious assumption that people take care to avoid injuring others solely or largely in order to avoid legal liability.

- The requirement of fault deters deliberate self-maiming. It is true that in jurisdictions with no-fault systems there have been instances of people injuring themselves in order to obtain compensation. However, the numbers currently denied access to compensation by the requirement of fault far exceed any likely number of self-maiming claims. Furthermore, it should be possible to build safeguards into a no-fault system to deal with such cases.

- To move to a no-fault system would involve a massive extension of liability and place an excessive burden on defendants. Whether this would in fact result depends upon how the system is funded, but even under the present arrangements the bulk of any additional costs would be spread throughout society at large, through a rise in insurance costs, rather than falling directly upon individuals.

NOTES

The arguments against fault-based liability in Tort

- The practical consequences of a fault-based system are unacceptable. The difficulties in establishing both fault and causation make the system a "forensic lottery". Furthermore, it is an extremely inefficient mechanism. The **Pearson Commission (1978)** found the administrative costs of the tort system were equivalent to 85 per cent of sums paid in compensation, amounting to 45 per cent of the total compensation and administration costs. By contrast, compensation via the social security system would involve administration costs amounting to only 11 per cent of the total, providing a substantially cheaper and quicker compensation mechanism.

- A fault-based system is wrong in principle as well as practice. While fault may provide a good reason for taking money from defendants, it is an inappropriate basis to decide which victims will receive compensation. Furthermore, except where there is joint liability or contributory negligence, the present system takes no account of the degree of fault. Thus, an act of momentary carelessness that results in serious damage will give rise to far greater liability than an act of gross negligence which results in only minor harm. Also, because the aim is to compensate the victim, the assessment of damages takes no account of the defendant's ability to pay (unlike the criminal law when assessing the level of fines). Finally, we can argue that the present system has itself recognised these failings by allowing (and even in some cases making compulsory) the use of loss-distribution devices such as insurance and developing notions such as vicarious liability.

The main alternative—a no-fault system

The main alternative is a no-fault compensation system (such as that in New Zealand), financed either through compulsory private insurance or public revenues. Critics of such schemes often point to the fact that levels of compensation are lower than those provided by damages at common law. However, the fact remains that a system that ensures adequate compensation for all would seem preferable to a system that provides full compensation for only a few.

Contract and fault

By contrast with both criminal law and much of the law of tort, contractual liability is essentially strict. The reasons for this are fundamentally pragmatic rather than based on any clear difference of principle. An example may be helpful here. A person buys a new washing machine from a high street retailer. The first time the machine is used, it breaks down. The "fault" may in fact lie with the manufacturer of a defective component who has supplied that

NOTES

component to the manufacturer of a larger component, who has in turn supplied that component to the manufacturer of the machine, who then supplies the machine to a wholesaler who in turn supplies it to the retailer. However, it would clearly be absurd to require the purchaser to undertake the trouble and expense of identifying where this fault ultimately lies. It makes far more practical sense to establish a chain of liability from retailer to wholesaler to manufacturer to component supplier and, as we have seen earlier, this is precisely what the law of contract does.

Having said this, there are circumstances where the fault principle does tweak the conscience of contract law. For example:

- the remedies available to a misrepresentee are, in part, determined by the degree of fault on the part of the misrepresentor;

- where a contract is void for illegality, the normal principles of restitution will not apply;

- where a contract is discharged by frustration, the law seeks to achieve a fair apportioning of loss between two innocent parties.

Conclusion

We can argue that all forms of liability at least commence from the basic proposition that a person should not be liable without fault. In the criminal law, where the liberty of the citizen or his reputation is at stake, we have seen that this principle can only, quite rightly, be displaced in exceptional circumstances, and usually only when sanctioned by Parliament. By contrast, in the law of contract, very sensible practical considerations result in a regime of essentially strict liability, with fault playing only a limited role in order to mitigate occasional harshness. It is one of the great virtues of a common law system that it is able to employ such a sensitive mix of principle and pragmatism. However, this is not to argue that English law always gets the balance right. There are some problematic areas resulting from the law's attachment to the fault principle, most notably regarding personal injury compensation.

Revision Notes

You should now write your revision notes for this topic. Here is an example for you and some suggested headings:

NOTES

Fault⑤—Tort & Strict Liability

- larger role than in Criminal law
- areas with overriding social reasons to encourage greatest care
- *e.g.* product safety, keeping animals, industrial/environmental protection
- people often choose (sometimes obliged) to insure against this liability

---

Fault①—Intro

Fault②—Crime & Fault

Fault③—Crime & Strict Liability

Fault④—Tort & Fault

Fault⑤—Tort & Strict Liability

Fault⑥—Fault/No-Fault debate

Fault⑦—Contract & Fault

Fault⑧—Conc

Using your cards, you should now be able to write a short paragraph in response to each of the following questions:

1. Discuss the role of fault in the criminal law.

2. Discuss the role of fault in the sentencing process.

3. What role does strict liability play in the criminal law?

4. Discuss the role of fault in tortious liability.

5. Discuss the role of strict liability in tort.

6. What difficulties may arise from fault-based tortious liability?

7. Discuss the role of fault in contractual liability.

NOTES

SECTION EIGHT: STUDY SKILLS

43 Study Skills—Essay Writing

Whether you are writing an essay, answering questions based on source material provided by the examining board, or answering a 'case study' or 'problem' style question, it is essential to bear in mind the assessment objectives of the course, as the marks available are awarded according to how well you meet these objectives:

Assessment Objective	What you are expected to do
AO1	Recall, select, deploy and develop knowledge and understanding of legal principles accurately and by means of example and citation
AO2	Analyse legal material, issues and situations, and evaluate and apply the appropriate legal rules and principles
AO3	Present a logical and coherent argument and communicate relevant material in a clear and effective manner using appropriate legal terminology

The most important thing to remember when answering an essay question is to ensure you answer the **specific** question set, and **not** merely recite a stock answer or write all you can remember about the particular topic concerned.

It is also essential to **PLAN** your answer carefully before you begin. This is true both of homework and timed or examination essays. A clear plan is vital to ensure relevance, accuracy, clarity and logical argument (AO3).

Generally, an essay should have three main parts:

Introduction

This should state what you understand the question to be asking. You should not do this by simply re-writing the question in your own words. Rather you should indicate the issues and ideas the question is raising, providing a context for the discussion that will follow.

Thus, the introduction provides a "gateway" to the main part of the essay. This can be helped by finishing the introduction with a **link statement**, indicating what is coming next. It may be useful to use the language of the question itself in constructing this statement. This will help to ensure relevance, to show you are in control of your knowledge, and that you are seeking to answer the particular question set.

Description and Evaluation

A Level questions generally require both description (AO1) and evaluation (AO2). AS level questions will tend to be more descriptive (AO1), but will still require simple evaluation (AO2). It is important that in this part of the essay you develop your arguments in a clear and logical manner (AO3). This again emphasises the need for a good plan. A fairly typical structure might be:

- the law at present:

    - describe (AO1);
    - evaluation (advantages and disadvantages) (AO2);
    - how satisfactory is this? (AO2).

- possible reforms:

    - describe (AO1);
    - evaluate (AO2);
    - which, if any, are desirable? (AO2).

Conclusion

This should draw together the various arguments you have developed in the main part of the essay into a **coherent overall response** to the question set. It should follow logically from the preceding discussion and not come as a surprise to the reader (again emphasising the need for a good plan).

Two more general points

- remember the **THREE Cs**:

NOTES

➤ be **CONCISE**;
➤ be **CLEAR**;
➤ be **CORRECT**.

You will only be able to score highly under the time constraints of the examination by ensuring you are able to communicate accurate knowledge and understanding in a clear and concise style.

- when citing authorities, try to give a brief description of the relevant facts—for example:

(*Olley v Marlborough Court Ltd* [1949]—exclusion notice in hotel bedroom not incorporated as contract made in reception)

Remember that the citing of authorities should be used to support arguments or propositions you have already clearly and concisely stated.

NOTES

44 Study Skills—Problem Answering

In answering "case study" or "problem" style questions, you should consider using the following approach:

1. Read the facts and all the questions carefully—use the questions to help you identify the relevant issues and facts.

2. List the important and relevant facts, in the order in which they happen, together with the issue(s) each raises in a **facts and issues table**.

3. Write mini-plans for each question, identifying the main issue(s) and relevant facts.

4. Answer each question in full, referring to the mini-plans and facts and issues table, using the **three-stage approach**:

   - **identify** and **define** the **issues** raised.
   - **state** and **explain** the relevant **rules** of law (with **authorities**).
   - **apply** the **rules** to the **facts** and **suggest** the likely outcome.

NOTES

45 Study Skills—Revision and Exams

Revision

Revision isn't something you should wait to do until the exams arrive. You should be revising the material you are studying as you work through the course. Each chapter in this book closes with some suggested revision headings and examples of revision cards. As part of reviewing the material in each chapter, possibly in preparation for a homework essay or problem question, you should complete your cards (I think the 6"x4" cards are best).

This means that when the exams begin to get close, you will already have a complete set of revision notes ready, and can concentrate on exam preparation. Your revision at this stage should be **active**, rather than passive. Of course you will have to read over your notes, homework, textbooks and so on, but by this stage you really need to be practising exam questions under timed conditions, writing outline plans to past exam questions and other active tasks that will consolidate your knowledge and prepare for the exam to come.

Keeping up-to-date

As you will have gathered from reading this book, the law is a living thing, always changing and evolving through both legislation and case law to meet new challenges. Therefore, it is important that you try to keep up-to-date with changes that take place during your studies. You should do this by:

- reading a quality newspaper, such as *The Times* or *Guardian*, each day or visiting their on-line editions daily (**www.the-times.co.uk**, **www.guardianunlimited.co.uk**). Both these papers also have weekly law sections (*The Times* on Mondays, *Guardian* on Tuesdays);

- reading a specialist law magazine, such as the *New Law Journal* (published weekly). Hopefully your school or college library will subscribe to this. Some of its contents are also available on the internet (**www.butterworths.co.uk/nlj/index.htm**);

- visiting the "what's new" section of the Home Office website (**www.home-office.gov.uk**) and Lord Chancellor's Department website (**www.open.gov.uk/lcd**) on a regular basis.

NOTES

Exams

To prepare for your examinations, it is important to find out as much as possible about what to expect. You should obtain copies of the specification for the Board you are studying. These can be found on the Boards' websites (**www.aqa.org.uk**, **www.ocr.org.uk**). You should also obtain copies of past papers, mark schemes, and chief examiner's reports, as these can help you understand the examiner's expectations, how best you can meet them, and the sorts of common mistakes to avoid.

As for the exam itself, make sure you know when it is, where it is, what time it starts and what time you have to be there. You should also know how long the exam lasts and how many questions you have to answer. This will enable you to have a time plan for the exam. It is essential that you stay in control of the exam—don't let it take control of you! You should also make a list of all the things you have to take with you—identification, statement of entry, pen, spare pen, etc. Make sure you follow the instructions on the exam paper and that you try to support the points you make in your answers by reference to relevant cases or statutes.

Once the exam is over, turn your attention to your next one—don't dwell on lengthy post-mortems of the one you've just done. Once all your exams are over, relax—if you've been studying properly, you will have earned a rest. Then try and forget about it all until the results are published. If you've been working hard and done your best, no-one can criticise you. Hopefully, you will have enjoyed your course and achieved the result you deserve—good luck!

NOTES

Index